Sunset
THE GREAT OUTDOORS
=COOKBOOK=

ADVENTURES IN COOKING
UNDER THE OPEN SKY

Edited by **ELAINE JOHNSON** and **MARGO TRUE**

Oxmoor
House®

CONTENTS

FOREWORD

If you ask an Italian whether he'd rather eat inside or outside, there's no contest. I'd rather cook and eat outside even in the dead of winter.

Outdoor cooking adds deep flavor to a meal—a dimension that goes beyond just the taste of it. That's what this book's editors understand too. These are people who love cooking outside as much as I do. Their recipes are guides to having a good time, and to making food seasoned with that flavor of the outdoors.

What I also love about cooking outside is the whole process of it: setting up your gear to cook, getting the wood ready, and arranging the tools you'll need. It's kind of like a beautiful speed bump—it slows you down and makes you more aware of where you are and what you're doing. My mother has a saying: "When your hands are busy, your mind is free." It's why I especially like the third chapter of this book, which has some unusual recipes that involve some setup. Each one is the center of a menu, and of your day. You don't rush those recipes—you enjoy them; it's food that has a beginning, middle, and end.

That's how I like to cook—and have ever since I was a kid. I grew up in California, in Mount Shasta country, and we cooked outside all the time, even on vacation. We'd go up to Coos Bay, in Oregon, during albacore tuna season, and we'd preserve the tuna we caught in olive oil, right on the beach. Some of us would be butchering, some digging clams; the kids would gather the wood. Pretty soon there'd be a big pot on the fire and we'd drop in the clams with some chopped onions, and eat them with bread we'd toast on the fire.

Every time you're building a fire outside, it's a community event. You gather around it, cook from it, and have conversations that are longer and deeper and more honest. The recipes in this book are good ways to get there.

—MICHAEL CHIARELLO
TV host, vintner, cookbook author, and
chef-owner of Bottega (Yountville, California)
and Coqueta (San Francisco)

Sunset's July 1917 issue. The cover story took us "auto vacationing in three states."

Cooking on an
Uruguayan-style
grill at Belcampo
Farms, near
Mount Shasta;
see page 204.

IN NATURE'S KITCHEN

The minute you start cooking outside, you've embarked on an adventure. You've left the confines of the house, and the scenery and the weather are now part of your cooking just as surely as your ingredients.

Whether you're 25 feet from your own back door or 250 miles from home in a campsite under the pine trees, it's not about turning a knob to 350° and patiently waiting for golden brown. No. Your fire is leaping and snapping, and you're closing the vents or moving the coals, taming the flames until they produce the crisp-edged, juicy steaks everyone's waiting for. There is no greater thrill in cooking than guiding the forces of nature to a delicious end.

This book is all about celebrating that thrill—first, by giving you recipes so reliable that you'll genuinely enjoy the experience of cooking them. Nothing is more disappointing than watching your hotly anticipated outdoor dinner go up in smoke, or turn into a greasy, half-raw lump. That's why each of the recipes in this book has been tested repeatedly, until it's rock solid. We've also included the key things you need to know about camp cooking and outdoor grilling, like how to set up a fire for direct or indirect heat, and if you follow our advice, your success is pretty much guaranteed.

When you trust a recipe, you start having fun. It's exciting to smoke a turkey when you know it will emerge burnished and crisp-

skinned. It's a pleasure to cook over wood when it delivers a delicious leg of lamb.

Using this book, you can make camp food that amazes your family and friends—from dutch oven cinnamon rolls to pizza in a skillet. In the backyard, you'll learn to use your gas or charcoal grill in unexpected (but easy) ways, like grill-roasting vegetables on a baking sheet or grilling strawberry short-cake kebabs. And please don't think that by "adventure" we mean "complicated and hair-raising"; many of our recipes are fast enough for a weeknight dinner.

But we couldn't resist the call of some larger adventures too. Our third chapter, "Inspired Fires," takes you beyond familiar outdoor cooking—and into the fullest spirit of the Great Outdoors. Here you will learn to improvise a firepit in 15 minutes (really! and use it to cook an entire menu if you like), roast a whole pig (or a mixed grill) in a box, pull off a seafood boil at the beach, and even build your own backyard pizza oven.

Call of the Wild

Inventive but doable outdoor cooking is in *Sunset's* DNA. From the magazine's earliest days more than a century ago, our writers

told readers how to get out there and cook in the majestic Western landscape.

In fact, the first recipes ever published in *Sunset* were cooked outdoors. "Practical Hints on Camp Cooking," a 1901 report from the High Sierra by Helen M. Gompertz, cheerily described how to make "delicious hash-balls" of dried flaked potatoes and canned corned beef fried in bacon grease, and a stew of just-shot grouse, onion, and bacon, so enticingly fragrant that "the whole camp hovers about the pot with hungry, anticipatory sniffs."

It must have been a hit with readers, because just a year later we went back to the Sierra with a story called "Housekeeping in the Summer Camp." Katherine A. Chandler politely scoffed at "opulent" camping in tents, and described the "most independent way… afoot with pack horses, or better still, with burros." Chandler, photographed on the slopes in a hat and full-length, flowing skirts, apparently camped this way for several summers, cooking on a simple iron frame set over burning logs. Her favorite dish: a layered concoction of macaroni, stewed tomatoes, and cheese, flavored with bacon grease. Chandler loved

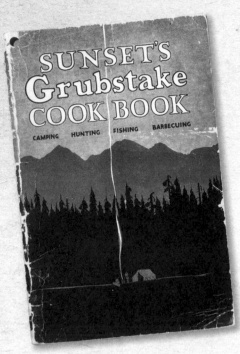

SKILLET REFLECTOR

INDIAN WAY OF
BROILING FISH
BASTE WITH WATER

FOR WOOD SEE "JERKY"

TRENCH FIREPLACE

BARBECUE TABLES
Carry around coolie-style

"long tramps" and sleeping under the stars on "soft aromatic boughs" of pine or fir covered with blankets, and concluded, "…it is little wonder that…even a fortnight's outing will reawaken in one the old enthusiasm for the beauty of life."

By 1916, "motor camping" had become the big thrill. Writer L. W. Peck described efficient new camping equipment like nesting pots and a folding "kitchenette" complete with gasoline stove and oven (this was several years before the invention of the Coleman camp stove). He also marveled at a "well balanced little two-wheeled carry-all called a 'trailer' which hitches on behind the gasoline steed."

Dozens of camping stories followed over the next few decades, filled with helpful suggestions—how to build a cooking fire in a trench; make a "snow refrigerator" by lining a pit with snow; and construct a "portable" oven out of pipes and flat pieces of galvanized iron (the author claimed you could fold it right up and slip it into a sack). The recipes grew more appetizing: 1930 featured baked corned beef and wild-berry shortcakes; 1931 brought us skillet trout with bacon, ash-roasted potatoes and maple sugar–filled apples, and beans with salt pork and molasses cooked in a hole overnight. "Good? My adjectives are too limited to describe them," said the cook, a Mrs. Dick Cole, in "We Eat—and How! When We Go Camping." By the '40s we were eating flame-toasted spiral-shaped biscuits (you wind the dough around a stick, hold it over the fire, slide it off, and fill the center with butter, jam, or apple butter).

The most entertaining guide to camp cooking in those early days, though, was our first camp cookbook, *Sunset's Grubstake Cook Book*, published in 1934. Charles M. Mugler (nickname: "Hot Rock") was a hunter, angler, trapper, and prospector, and you can practically hear him growl as you read his advice: "Every outfit should be equipped to fry, broil, stew, roast, and bake. Know how to cook and serve grub that is neither messy nor cold. Know how to use your utensils to their utmost advantage. Know how to set a kettle so its chances of spilling are slim. I say, know how—*and like it*."

His illustrated instructions show all kinds of cooking setups, from a pit lined with hot rocks to an ingenious "skillet reflector" technique in which the bread cooks off to one side of the fire. The recipes themselves are telegraphed in just a few sentences apiece: cornbread, sourdough bread, stews, fricassees, and snow ice cream— a mix of instant coffee, powdered milk, sugar, and snow scraped off the bank with a spoon. Mugler spells out how to catch and cook fish, harvest shellfish, dress and cook bear, deer, and small game like squirrel and birds—plus raccoon, beaver, and porcupine (no advice about how to get rid of the quills, though maybe the parboiling took care of that). He tells you how to smoke jerky, snare a wild rabbit, pack a horse, tie knots, get rid of ticks and chiggers, read a compass, and find constellations in the night sky. It's hard to imagine what else a camper might need.

Other forms of outdoor cooking showed up early too. We learned how to roast salmon on a wooden frame from an elder of the Skokomish tribe in 1936, and wood-framed and planked salmon would appear again and again in our pages. Pit barbecuing—another venerable cooking technique used by Native Americans and the vaqueros of 1850s California—first appeared in the magazine in 1911, in a report on a gargantuan party thrown by Adolphus Busch (founder of Anheuser-Busch) at his sunken gardens in Pasadena. He hosted an entire American Medical Association convention of 5,000 doctors and their wives to feast from multiple pits filled with steaming beef, pork, and lamb. Clearly we were fascinated by this, because we went on to publish several stories on how to do it ourselves, though mercifully on a smaller scale.

Outdoors at Home

The modern elevated barbecue, which revolutionized leisure time as we know it, materialized by the 1920s. A 1932 story called "How We Use Our Barbecue" proudly describes the writer's "unusual" barbecue pit, which features a

raised hearth, a surrounding brick wall to make it "a little easier on the back," and a "device for lowering or raising the grate"—all of which sound remarkably like the barbecues used today in and around Santa Maria, on California's Central Coast (see page 214).

In that time before mass-produced grills, if you wanted a barbecue, you had to build one, and *Sunset* showed you how. In 1938, *Sunset's Barbecue Book* covered grills for all construction abilities—from a simple raised trench, to a deluxe built-in model with cabinets, to a pit serving 600—and supplied the recipes to go with them. It was the first such book in America, and such a novelty that the Library of Congress catalogued it under "fireplaces."

It was a time when the new "barbecuisine" dominated our pages. We built tiny grills you could carry around on either end of a shoulder pole like a Chinese street vendor, and barbecues that looked like wheelbarrows (anticipating the Caja China hot box; see page 188). We reported on

FACING PAGE: The 1934 *Grubstake Cook Book* was filled with helpful illustrations. The barbecue tables are from a 1940 issue. THIS PAGE, FROM TOP: Our 1938 *Barbecue Book* was the nation's first. It had a redwood cover and gave readers detailed plans for dozens of backyard setups. Even as early as 1933, we were grilling our holiday turkeys outside.

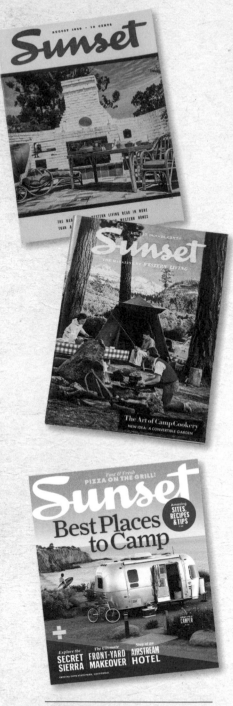

hundreds of beautiful backyard barbecues and outdoor fireplaces around the West—one memorable creation incorporated the base of a giant redwood tree—and entire outdoor kitchens complete with rotisseries, pothooks, cabinets, ovens, and sinks with running water. The *Sunset Barbecue Book,* in its original format, went through several editions. By the time the last one was published, the convenient, affordable, portable Weber kettle grill, invented in 1951, had become the choice for many backyard barbecuers.

Our appetite for ingenious outdoor cooking devices and recipes continued, though, on our pages and in several subsequent books. In the years since, we've shown readers how to build a columnar firepit especially for woks, and given tips for cooking in tiny galley kitchens on boats (hint: Layer all your food in a single pot). We've smoked seafood on the beach in newspaper packets and barbecued meat in converted steel drums. Backyard ovens were a repeat topic: We described how to build an "old Spanish-Mexican beehive oven" in 1940, built another in 1971 for a story that proved hugely popular, and did it again in 1998. Our updated version is at the end of this book (with complete instructions even a novice can follow).

We've come back to camping, and camp cooking, just about every year, often with big roundup stories on the finest sites for pitching a tent and the best gear, including camp stoves or backpacking stoves. In the last couple of decades, campsites have become glampsites and cooking is no longer "grub," with

influences from all over the world updating our outdoor pantry and our imaginations. When a group of *Sunset* staffers went camping with our families for a story in 2003, we made Vietnamese chicken satay and pad Thai, because both were fast-cooking and used hardly any fuel. With the redwoods towering above us, we gobbled down those recipes, savoring the fresh, spicy flavors. What's remained constant through all these years, no matter what we were cooking up, is great practical advice that makes familiar recipes seem new, and a knack for demystifying new recipes and food projects so that everyone can do them.

Wrangling Recipes

One day several months ago, when we were deep in creating the recipes for this book, associate editor Elaine Johnson strode triumphantly into the kitchen at *Sunset,* hauling a dutch oven filled with steaming Yucatecan-style pork swathed in banana leaves. A veteran camper, she'd created the recipe on a trip to California's Santa Cruz Mountains with her family, and now we were all getting a taste of this unbelievably delicious, cinnamon-scented stew. The next day, recipe editor Amy Machnak pulled a pot of *feijoada*— the bean-and-pork national dish of Brazil—from a solar oven in a courtyard outside the *Sunset* kitchen, and shortbread cookies the day after. We couldn't believe how sophisticated the food was, given all it had done was sit in the sun. And that same week, test kitchen manager Stephanie Spencer conquered the big black outdoor water smoker, and turned out fabulous brisket, turkey, trout, and sablefish. It was a week of pure exploration, of trying things we'd never done before and pulling them off. And that's what this book offers you: a chance to go on a few cooking adventures and have a great time along the way—and good food at the end.

You may be wondering, given our penchant for ambitious projects, how often we fail. Let's just say that there's usually a learning curve involved. In 1970, Jerry Anne Di Vecchio, *Sunset's* former longtime food editor, worked on a story about a Hawaiian-style pit-roasted pig. She and several others spent days digging a giant cavity in what is now our test garden. In the early morning, they filled it with wood and lit it up. "It was a big pit, hence a big fire, and as a result big smoke," she remembers. "The next thing you know, there were fire engines all over the place." As soon as the firefighters realized that the smoke was related to barbecue, with a pig prepped and ready to go, they not only relaxed but helped get the pork in the pit. That wasn't the last lesson of the day: The cooks poured too much water into the pit for steaming, and so instead of browning, the pig emerged ghastly pale and flabby. Suffice it to say that many further tests ensued until the pit produced delicious pork, and a recipe that could be replicated, catastrophe-free.

We still believe in figuring out all the problems so you won't have to, while preserving the excitement of cooking. Early this year, Elaine Johnson—my main collaborator on this book and a fearless

Sunset's DIY pizza oven team, June 2013 (left to right): Thomas Keller, Margo True, Elaine Johnson, Kiko Denzer. Not shown: Tina Keller, Scott Vanderlip, Molly Vanderlip.

culinary explorer—and I decided to update *Sunset's* 1998 backyard pizza oven plans, which were inspiring but inscrutable, at least to inexperienced builders like us. We decided that we would build a pizza oven for the construction-challenged, describing every detail to make it accessible to all, not just the Home Depot–handy. Well, we got in way over our heads. The project consumed us for months, and we ended up with an oven that molded, cracked, shed its adobe coat, and had to be knocked down.

It's amazing how good a teacher failure can be. Our second oven was a pleasure in every way (see page 232). It took us less than a day, with the help of a few friends, and was surprisingly affordable. But we couldn't have done it without failing first. In the tradition of this magazine and the long line of outdoor cooks who have preceded us, we figured it out and got it

right, so that it would be worthy of your time.

A couple of days after we finished the second oven, in Elaine's backyard, we made pizzas in it, followed by juicy steaks with roasted green beans and corn slathered with cilantro *queso fresco* butter. With her family, we drank good red wine and relaxed and laughed about our crazy adventure. Meanwhile, the oven baked our dessert—a raspberry rhubarb crisp. It was a sweet finish to an experience we will never forget.

Pick a recipe from these pages and let it lead you into the great outdoors, whether that's a campsite, your backyard, or another opportune place to build a fire. The journey will be its own reward, and dinner will be delicious.

—MARGO TRUE
October 2013

CAMPFIRES

PICTURE THIS. You've spent the day taking in the drama of the geysers at Yellowstone, or the grandeur of Yosemite Falls' triple tiers. Now the gang has gathered back in camp, hiking boots swapped for sneakers, ready to inhale some dinner. You impress everyone by whipping up a quick pizza in a skillet on the stove. The next night the extended family sits down to margaritas, warm tortillas, and Yucatecan pork roast for 12, simmered in a dutch oven.

Whether you're aiming for easy or extravagant, great meals make any camping trip more memorable. And you can count on a captive audience too. Maybe it's the fresh air sharpening appetites, maybe it's the simplicity of time spent without the distractions of home, but meals in the great outdoors become as much about entertainment as nourishment. Even if you're a first-time camper, the right recipes and a little know-how are all you need to pull them off.

CAMP KITCHEN BASICS

Organize Your Food

The real secret to eating well in camp is in the planning: thinking through meals, gathering gear, and prepping before you even pull out of the driveway.

Make a plan. Start by jotting down the meals you'll be cooking. Read through recipes and decide what you'll eat when and what equipment you'll need (see "Gather Your Gear" at right). You'll want to eat the most perishable foods—seafood, unfrozen meats, and delicate fresh produce such as berries—early in the trip. Foods you've packed frozen, as well as sturdy produce such as apples and, of course, packaged and canned food, last longer.

Prep ahead. Many recipes in this chapter have steps marked "At Home"—such as making your own cocoa

or pancake mix, or a marinade to freeze with meat—which streamline the cooking you do in camp. For the first night's dinner, you might want to cook a meal ahead of time that you reheat once you arrive, or plan an easy meal like the appetizer spread called *meze* (page 57), which is good at room temperature.

Bring a few "bailout" foods. If you get cold or wet, a near-instant meal like packaged miso soup hits the spot. After an extra-long hike, when all the cooks are tired, pasta topped with good pesto or marinara from a tub goes together in a hurry.

Gather Your Gear

Outdoor outfitters carry a slew of snazzy cooking gear, if you want to go that route, but you may already own most of what you need, or be able to borrow from friends what you don't have. For sources, see the Resource Guide on page 244.

Camp stove. You can cook over it just like your stove at home. The best ones have powerful burners (upward of 20,000 BTUs), an easy-clean design, and enough real estate to accommodate a cooking pot and a frying pan side by side. Most are powered by small propane canisters, sold separately.

Cooler. Some campers like to bring two—a big one for food and a medium one for drinks.

Cast-iron skillet. You'll need this for everything from cooking pancakes and bacon to browning trout. A 12-inch pan is the most versatile size.

Cooking pots. It's handy to have both a small saucepan and a pot big enough for cooking pasta or washing dishes.

Camp dutch oven. To expand your cooking repertoire (see page 28), you'll want a camp dutch oven—one with feet and a flanged lid. Both the 4-quart (10-inch) and 6-quart (12-inch) sizes are useful.

Fuel for the fire. Check your campground's rules before you go to see whether campfires are allowed, and whether you need to bring your own wood. Even if you can build a fire, you might also want charcoal briquets for dutch oven cooking, as they make it easier to control the temp. Don't forget newspaper and matches or a fire starter, plus a metal chimney for lighting charcoal, and a hatchet if you'll be cutting kindling.

Dishware. Unbreakable plates, bowls, and cups, plus flatware, should all go in your gear box.

A mixing bowl or two. Bowls are handy for everything from salad to pancake batter. The collapsible ones flatten for easy transport.

Tools. Add these to the list: a wooden spoon, wide spatula, can opener, wine opener, whisk, and long tongs, which double as a tool for lifting a dutch oven lid. Also pack up a chef's knife and paring knife or small serrated knife; if you don't have a travel-size knife case, you can wrap the knives in a couple of thick dish towels and secure them with rubber bands.

Cutting board. Depending on space, you can bring a traditional one or the plastic kind that rolls up.

Oven mitts. Thick ones are useful for handling tools around the fire.

Coffee-making gear. You can keep it simple, with a plastic drip cone and filters, or brew like a barista, starting with a hand grinder for the beans and a titanium French press or camp espresso maker for the coffee.

Headlamp. It leaves both hands free when you're cooking after dark.

Dishwashing equipment. Outdoors shops sell collapsible sinks, though a pot or big bowl works fine too. Toss in some biodegradable soap, a sponge, a plastic scrubber for cleaning cast iron, and a couple of kitchen towels.

Pantry staples. Don't leave home without salt, a pepper grinder, olive oil, and cooking oil.

Miscellaneous. A box of foil, paper towels, plastic containers for lunches and leftovers, resealable plastic bags, and a few trash bags all come in handy.

HOW TO PACK A COOLER

There's an art to stashing food so it stays cold, is space-efficient, and doesn't get squished.

MAKE A SANDWICH BOX. Slice tomatoes and cucumbers and stack lettuce leaves for grab-and-go lunches.

THINK LIKE A BAG BOY. Pack fragile stuff, like salad mixes and fresh herbs, toward the top.

PREWASH YOUR GREENS. Then wrap them in paper towels and seal in a plastic bag or container.

PREP FRUIT. Wash and cut bulky fruit like melons and pineapple so they take up less space.

PREMIX YOUR SAUCES. Seal make-aheads such as barbecue sauce in leak-proof containers.

MAKE ICE BLOCKS. A day or two before you leave home, freeze water in flat Nalgene containers. Not only will they keep things cold longer than ice cubes alone, you'll have a container of drinking water as they melt.

MULTIPURPOSE YOUR MEATS. Marinate meats and then freeze them; they'll act as ice blocks until they defrost.

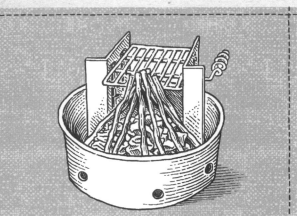

HOW TO BUILD A CAMPFIRE FOR COOKING

1. SET OUT FUEL. Check with your campground to find out whether you're allowed to gather fuel. Ideally, you want a mix of tinder (dry grasses, pine needles, and small pinecones), kindling (small sticks up to wrist-size logs), and medium-size logs. It's also helpful to bring some newspaper. If you can't collect materials, bring them from home or buy logs from the camp store and make some kindling: Set a log upright on a sturdy, larger piece of wood. Rest the sharp edge of a hatchet or ax on top of the log, parallel to the grain. Strike the wood, repeating as needed to break it into pieces.

2. MAKE A TIPI AND IGNITE. In a fire ring over a small pile of crumpled newspaper and tinder, arrange kindling into a tipi about 1 foot in diameter. Light tinder. When the pile starts smoking, resist the urge to pile on wood; instead, blow on it gently a few times until flames emerge.

3. ADD TWIGS AND LOGS. Once flames are lively, gradually add twigs. Graduate to wrist-size logs, then 5 or 6 medium-size logs.

4. LET IT BURN, THEN COOK. Once you have ashy chunks with low flames (1½ to 2 hours), you're ready to cook on the grill in the fire ring or, for certain recipes, right in the embers. Keep another log burning at the back of the fire ring in case you need more fuel.

5. PUT IT OUT RIGHT. Stop adding fuel at least an hour before you plan to leave camp. Spread out the coals, then douse them with plenty of water. Leave your campsite only when the coals are cool enough to touch with your hand.

Using a Camp Grill

Most campsites come with a metal fire ring that has a built-in grill for use over a wood fire, or a box-shaped grill for use over charcoal. Both work well for cooking; just know that grill grates sometimes need a wipe-down with paper towels and a little vegetable oil to get rid of any rust. Also, the grilling surface is likely smaller than you're used to at home, so for large groups you'll be cooking food in batches.

Caring for Cast Iron

Given the right care, a cast-iron skillet or dutch oven will develop a beautiful seasoned surface that's naturally nonstick. A lot of new cast ironware gives you a jump-start on this process, as it's sold preseasoned (meaning it's been baked at a high temperature with a coating of oil), so all you have to do is maintain it. Here's how.

Each time after you use a pan, hand-wash it with hot water—no soap—and a sponge or plastic mesh scrubber (not metal, which can scrape off the seasoning). Dry the pan by setting it over the heat to drive off any moisture. Then rub the warm pan with a paper towel and enough vegetable oil to coat lightly. This maintains the seasoning and keeps moisture out so the pan won't rust.

Outwitting the Bears

Bears are so smart, and have become so good at getting into coolers, cars, and campsites, that many parks in bear country now make it mandatory to stash all food and coolers in a bear box (a sturdy storage locker at each campsite) except when you're actually cooking. Since this means transferring supplies from bear box to picnic table several times a day, it's helpful to arrange food and gear in easy-to-carry containers that are organized by mealtime (all the coffee and cocoa-making supplies for breakfast, say, in the same bin).

In the backcountry, bear-proofing means sealing up food in a plastic bear canister that you carry with your backpack. Many parks have the canisters available for rent.

quality of baked goods. Leavening gases (air, carbon dioxide, water vapor) expand faster. Also, flour tends to absorb more liquid in the low humidity of high altitudes. If you're camping at 3,000 feet or below, first try a recipe as is. Sometimes few, if any, changes are needed. But the higher you go, the more you'll have to adjust your recipe.

For quick breads such as biscuits, cornbread, cakes, and pancakes, try decreasing baking powder or soda by ⅛ to ¼ teaspoon per teaspoon called for. If that's not working, cut back on flour by about 2 tablespoons per cup called for.

For yeast breads, you may need less flour, so mix in about two-thirds of what's called for in the recipe, then check the dough to see whether it looks and feels the way it does at sea level before adding more. Keep an eye on the dough's rise; yeast doughs rise more quickly—sometimes twice as fast—in the reduced pressure of higher altitudes. Instead of letting dough rise until doubled in volume, let it rise only by about a third. That will compensate for its tendency to overexpand as it bakes in the dutch oven.

High-altitude Baking Tips

On any given mountain, you're likely to find a frustrated baker. That's because most baking recipes, including ours for camp, are developed and tested for use from sea level to about 3,000 feet. With the help of high-altitude baking authorities Pat Kendall, formerly of the Colorado State University Cooperative Extension, and Nancy Feldman, formerly at the University of California Cooperative Extension; and also by consulting the invaluable book *Pie in the Sky* by Susan G. Purdy (William Morrow, 2005), we've assembled some guidelines that should help you bake successfully above 3,000 feet.

At high altitudes, liquids boil at lower temperatures (below 212°) and moisture evaporates more quickly—both of which significantly impact the

DEL'S GRAND CANYON GRANOLA

MAKES 8 CUPS ★ 45 MINUTES AT HOME

Sunset reader Elaine Bohlmeyer of Payson, Arizona, gave us a recipe her husband created when they were planning a hiking trip to the bottom of the Grand Canyon. "The object was to get the most energy for the least amount of weight," says Bohlmeyer. "The added bonus is that it's delicious." The granola is on the sweeter side; feel free to cut back on the sugar.

2 cups rolled oats (regular or quick-cooking)
¼ cup nonfat dried milk
½ cup wheat germ
½ cup shredded unsweetened coconut
½ cup slivered almonds
½ cup sunflower seeds
½ cup roasted soy nuts (optional; or use peanuts
    or pumpkin seeds)
1 cup pecans or walnuts
¼ cup sesame seeds (optional)
½ cup honey
¼ cup maple syrup
1 tsp. vanilla extract
¼ cup firmly packed light brown sugar
¼ cup vegetable oil
½ cup raisins
Milk (optional)

AT HOME

1. Preheat oven to 300°. In a large bowl, mix together oats, dried milk, wheat germ, coconut, nuts, and seeds.
2. In a small saucepan, combine honey, maple syrup, vanilla, brown sugar, and oil and bring to a boil. Pour over dry mixture and mix together with a wooden spoon. Oil a rimmed baking sheet and pour mixture onto sheet. Bake 15 minutes. Stir granola and bake another 10 minutes. Sprinkle in raisins and bake 5 minutes more. (Granola will look sticky but will dry out as it cools.)

3. Let granola cool completely on baking sheet, then transfer to an airtight container.

IN CAMP

4. Serve granola with milk if you like.

Make ahead: Up to 2 weeks, stored airtight.

PER CUP 535 CAL., 31% (261 CAL.) FROM FAT; 11 G PROTEIN; 29 G FAT (5.1 G SAT.); 63 G CARBO (5 G FIBER); 21 MG SODIUM; 0.4 MG CHOL. LS/V

HEARTY WHOLE-GRAIN PANCAKES WITH BLUEBERRIES

MAKES MIX FOR 4 BATCHES (EACH 8 TO 10 PANCAKES) ★ 15 MINUTES AT HOME; 15 IN CAMP

Take a few minutes at home to whip up your own pancake mix, and you'll have fresh pancakes in camp that are just as fast as instant and a whole lot tastier.

PANCAKE MIX
2½ cups all-purpose flour
3 cups whole-wheat flour
¼ cup *each* wheat bran, wheat germ, and packed
    light brown sugar
1 tbsp. *each* baking powder and kosher salt
1½ tsp. baking soda
1½ cups buttermilk powder*

PANCAKES WITH BLUEBERRIES
(1 batch)
2 cups Pancake Mix (above)
2 large eggs
About 4 tbsp. vegetable oil, divided
1 cup blueberries
Butter and maple syrup

AT HOME
1. Make pancake mix: Whisk together ingredients in a large bowl and transfer to an airtight container.

IN CAMP
2. Make pancakes: Whisk together 2 cups mix with 1¼ cups water, the eggs, and 2 tbsp. oil in a large bowl until mostly smooth. Heat a large cast-iron skillet over medium heat on a camp stove and grease skillet with ½ tbsp. oil. Ladle ⅓-cup portions of batter into skillet. Cook, turning once, until pancakes are golden brown on each side and cooked through, about 5 minutes. Add 1 tsp. oil to skillet and repeat with more batter to cook remaining pancakes. Serve with blueberries, butter, and syrup.

*Find buttermilk powder at well-stocked grocery stores.

Make ahead: Mix, up to 2 weeks, stored airtight.

PER 2-PANCAKE SERVING WITH BERRIES 390 CAL., 41% (160 CAL.) FROM FAT; 13 G PROTEIN; 18 G FAT (3.1 G SAT.); 42 G CARBO (4.5 G FIBER); 307 MG SODIUM; 101 MG CHOL. LC/LS/V

HEARTY WHOLE-GRAIN
PANCAKES with BLUEBERRIES

MASCARPONE
FRENCH TOAST with
WARM BLACKBERRY
SYRUP

MASCARPONE FRENCH TOAST WITH WARM BLACKBERRY SYRUP

SERVES 4 ★ 35 MINUTES IN CAMP

For guests of Sealegs Kayaking Adventures of Vancouver Island, B.C., the morning often starts with this decadent twist on French toast.

1 large egg
½ cup milk
¼ cup sugar
2 tsp. cinnamon
1½ tsp. vanilla extract, divided
1½ cups cold mascarpone cheese
2 tbsp. blackberry liqueur
8 thick (¾ in.) slices of day-old wide French bread, such as bâtard
¼ cup maple syrup
2½ cups blackberries
2 tbsp. butter
Cooked bacon

1. Heat a grill to medium-high (450°; you can hold your hand 5 in. above cooking grate only 4 to 5 seconds) or use a camp stove at medium-high heat.

2. Whisk together egg, milk, sugar, cinnamon, and ½ tsp. vanilla in a large bowl.

3. In another bowl, stir together mascarpone, remaining 1 tsp. vanilla, and the liqueur. Spread mascarpone mixture over 4 bread slices; top with remaining slices.

4. Cook maple syrup and berries in a small covered saucepan until berries start to break down, 5 to 10 minutes. Remove from heat.

5. Heat a large heavy frying pan or 2 smaller ones over grill or camp stove; swirl butter in pan(s). Dip sandwiches in egg mixture, then cook, turning once, until crisp and browned, 4 to 8 minutes. Serve French toast with syrup and bacon.

PER SERVING WITHOUT BACON 1,215 CAL., 65% (792 CAL.) FROM FAT; 26 G PROTEIN; 88 G FAT (47 G SAT.); 86 G CARBO (7.5 G FIBER); 705 MG SODIUM; 281 MG CHOL.

GRILLED FRENCH TOAST KEBABS

SERVES 4 ★ 30 MINUTES IN CAMP, PLUS OVERNIGHT FOR BREAD TO SIT

Slightly stale bread is not only okay here, it's one of the secrets to making these French toast bites come out perfectly (if the bread is too fresh, it falls off the skewers). You'll need 12 wooden skewers.

1 loaf (1 lb.) day-old unsliced *pain au levain* or sourdough
¾ cup whole milk
4 large eggs
1 tsp. vanilla extract
Vegetable oil
Melted butter
Maple or berry syrup
Powdered sugar (optional)

1. Soak 12 wooden skewers (10 to 12 in.) in water to cover for 20 minutes; drain. Meanwhile, heat a grill to medium (350°; you can hold your hand 5 in. above cooking grate only 7 seconds).

2. Cut enough of the day-old bread into 1-in. chunks, including some crust on each, to make 2 qts. (save extra for other uses).

3. Whisk milk, eggs, and vanilla in a large bowl to blend. Add bread and stir to coat, then thread onto skewers.

4. Oil cooking grate, using tongs and an oiled wad of paper towels. Grill skewers until browned, turning once, 3 to 5 minutes.

5. Serve with a drizzle of butter and syrup and dust with powdered sugar if you like.

PER SERVING 322 CAL., 22% (71 CAL.) FROM FAT; 17 G PROTEIN; 7.9 G FAT (2.8 G SAT.); 46 G CARBO (1.8 G FIBER); 584 MG SODIUM; 216 MG CHOL. V

> **TIP** MAKE MONTE CRISTO SANDWICHES WITH SLICED BREAD SOAKED IN EGG AND MILK, FILLED WITH HAM AND CHEESE, AND TOASTED IN A PAN.

cooking grate only 4 to 5 seconds). Add eggs and milk; scramble in skillet. Cook until barely set, then stir in salt, pepper, chives, jalapeños, tomato, and salmon.

2. Spread 2 tbsp. cream cheese onto center of each tortilla. Spoon egg mixture over cheese. Roll up burritos, tucking in ends of tortillas. Serve with salsa.

*To warm tortillas, roll them up, then wrap in foil and heat directly over camp stove or grill, turning often.

PER SERVING 840 CAL., 41% (347 CAL.) FROM FAT; 59 G PROTEIN; 39 G FAT (13 G SAT.); 63 G CARBO (4.5 G FIBER); 1,205 MG SODIUM; 493 MG CHOL.

EGGS IN JAIL

SERVES 4 ★ 30 MINUTES IN CAMP

We borrowed this fancy take on eggs-in-a-frame from San Francisco's Outerlands restaurant. You'll need a bread knife and a 1½-in. round cutter.

8 slices thick-cut applewood-smoked bacon (10 oz. total)
1 loaf (12 oz.) unsliced brioche*
About 4 tbsp. softened butter, divided
4 large eggs
About ⅛ tsp. *each* kosher salt and pepper

1. Set a 12-in. cast-iron skillet over medium-high heat on a camp stove. Brown bacon in skillet, 8 to 10 minutes. Transfer bacon to paper towels and drape with foil. Discard fat from pan and wipe pan somewhat clean with a paper towel.

2. Meanwhile, cut 4 brioche slices, each 1¼ in. thick (you'll have bread left over). Spread both sides with 3 tbsp. butter. Cut a hole in each slice; set centers aside.

3. Put bread in pan, pressing down slightly to flatten, and set over medium-low heat. Put about ½ tsp. butter in each hole, then crack an egg into each. Sprinkle eggs with a little salt and pepper. Cook until bottom of bread is golden, 3 minutes.

4. Flip toast and eggs carefully with a wide spatula. Sprinkle eggs with salt and pepper. Cook until underside of toast is golden and eggs are done the way you like, 3 minutes for softly set. Transfer to plates. Quickly toast bread centers, then set on servings. Serve with bacon.

*Find brioche bread at well-stocked grocery stores.

PER SERVING 587 CAL., 66% (386 CAL.) FROM FAT; 24 G PROTEIN; 43 G FAT (22 G SAT.); 26 G CARBO (1.7 G FIBER); 1,214 MG SODIUM; 453 MG CHOL.

SMOKED SALMON BURRITOS

SERVES 4 ★ 20 MINUTES IN CAMP

The cream cheese, salmon, and jalapeño in these wraps from *Sunset* reader Jane Belanger of San Diego give the scrambled eggs a big flavor boost.

About 1 tbsp. vegetable oil
8 large eggs
2 tbsp. milk
½ tsp. kosher salt
1 tsp. pepper
2 tbsp. chopped chives
2 jalapeño chiles, halved, seeded, and sliced
1 cup diced tomato
8 oz. smoked salmon, cut into bite-size pieces
½ cup cream cheese, softened
4 large flour tortillas (10 to 12 in.), warmed*
Salsa

1. Heat oil in a cast-iron skillet over high heat on a camp stove, or over a charcoal or wood-fired grill heated to medium-high (450°; you can hold your hand 5 in. above

EGGS in JAIL

PINNACLES
SCRAMBLE

PINNACLES SCRAMBLE

SERVES 4 ★ 40 MINUTES AT HOME; 15 IN CAMP

Annie Somerville, legendary chef of Greens Restaurant in San Francisco, created this dish years ago on a camping trip to Pinnacles National Park in California with her husband, and it's been a brunch favorite at the restaurant ever since.

CHIPOTLE POTATOES

1 can (7 oz.) chipotle chiles in *adobo* sauce
1 tbsp. olive oil
¼ tsp. *each* kosher salt and pepper
1 lb. large Yukon Gold potatoes, quartered lengthwise
    and sliced crosswise ½ in. thick
1 large poblano chile
4 green onions, sliced diagonally

THE SCRAMBLE AND SERVING

8 large eggs
2 tbsp. milk
About ¼ tsp. *each* kosher salt and pepper
2 tbsp. unsalted butter
¾ cup shredded sharp cheddar cheese
2 tbsp. chopped cilantro
2 cups fire-roasted tomato salsa
Crème fraîche
Warm corn tortillas*

AT HOME

1. Make potatoes: Preheat oven to 475°. Purée chipotles and adobo sauce in a blender. Spoon 2 tbsp. into a bowl (save the rest for other uses). Stir in oil, salt, and pepper, then potatoes. Spread potatoes on a rimmed baking sheet lined with parchment paper, leaving a corner empty; put poblano in corner. Bake, turning chile and potatoes occasionally, until chile is blackened and potatoes are well browned, 20 to 25 minutes. Let cool. Peel, stem, seed, and coarsely chop chile. In a plastic container, combine potatoes, chile, and onions; chill.

IN CAMP

2. Make scramble: Whisk eggs and milk in a bowl to blend with ¼ tsp. *each* salt and pepper; set aside. Heat a large cast-iron skillet over medium-high heat on a camp stove, or over a charcoal or wood-fired grill heated to medium-high (450°; you can hold your hand 5 in. above cooking grate only 4 to 5 seconds). Melt butter, then add potato mixture and stir occasionally with a wide spatula until hot, 2 to 3 minutes.

3. Add egg mixture, reduce heat to medium, and cook, scrambling gently, until set, 2 to 4 minutes; add cheese

and cilantro during last minute. Serve with salsa, crème fraîche, and tortillas, plus more salt and pepper to taste.

*To warm tortillas, wrap in foil and heat directly over camp stove or grill, turning often.

Make ahead: Through step 1, up to 2 days, chilled.

PER SERVING 461 CAL., 51% (236 CAL.) FROM FAT; 21 G PROTEIN; 26 G FAT (12 G SAT.); 36 G CARBO (2.4 G FIBER); 1,045 MG SODIUM; 461 MG CHOL. LC/V

HUEVOS RANCHEROS CON BACON

SERVES 4 ★ 30 MINUTES IN CAMP

Gilbert Flores, a *Sunset* reader from Visalia, California, shared this recipe. The sauce is easy to make, and in summer, you could double the fresh tomato and skip the canned sauce. No matter what time of year you make it, don't skip the bacon.

8 oz. thick-cut bacon
½ white onion, chopped
½ green bell pepper, cut into ½-in. dice
1 jalapeño chile, halved and thinly sliced
1 medium tomato, chopped
1 can (8 oz.) tomato sauce
8 large eggs
Warm corn tortillas* and refried beans

1. Set a large frying pan over medium-high heat on a camp stove, or over a charcoal or wood-fired grill heated to medium-high (450°; you can hold your hand 5 in. above cooking grate only 4 to 5 seconds). Cook bacon until almost crisp, about 10 minutes. Transfer to paper towels.

2. Drain most of fat from pan and reserve. Add onion, pepper, and chile to pan and cook until starting to soften, about 2 minutes. Stir in tomato, tomato sauce, and ½ cup water. Bring to a simmer.

3. Meanwhile, working in batches, heat a little reserved fat and fry the eggs in a large nonstick frying pan (discard the rest of fat). Set tortillas on each plate and top with 2 eggs. Spoon sauce over eggs and crumble bacon on top. Serve with refried beans.

*To warm tortillas, wrap in foil and heat directly over camp stove or grill, turning often.

PER SERVING 256 CAL., 57% (144 CAL.) FROM FAT; 20 G PROTEIN; 16 G FAT (5.3 G SAT.); 7.4 G CARBO (1.8 G FIBER); 826 MG SODIUM; 390 MG CHOL. GF/LC

How to Cook in a DUTCH OVEN

Lewis and Clark used one. So did the early pioneers in Utah (today it's the state's official cooking pot). And you should too, because you'll get to simmer stews and bake and eat warm treats like cinnamon rolls right in camp.

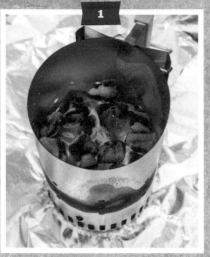

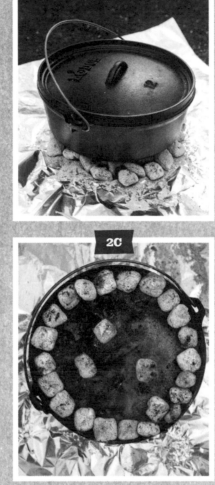

A camp dutch oven, with feet and a flanged lid, is one of a camp cook's most versatile tools. Both the 4-quart (10-inch) and 6-quart (12-inch) sizes are useful. You also need long tongs; thick gloves; charcoal briquets (regular, not competition-style) and newspaper, a fire starter, and a charcoal chimney starter for lighting them; or a campfire with hot embers. (It's easier to control the heat with charcoal than with embers.) Then you need a cleared, fireproof area—a fire ring, if your campsite has one—or bricks, concrete, or sand with a double layer of heavy-duty foil set on top.

1 PREP THE FIRE

If using charcoal, light 50 regular briquets in a chimney starter and burn until spotted gray, 15 minutes. If using a campfire, mound hot embers (2 to 3 qts.' worth) to the side in the fire ring, clearing a level space the size of the dutch oven.

2 ARRANGE THE COALS

BOTTOM HEAT COOKING (2A). For recipes in which you want concentrated heat from underneath, to sauté meats or vegtables, say, or simmer a quick soup, just use tongs to spread the coals into an even layer the size of the dutch oven and set the pot on top.

TOP AND BOTTOM HEAT COOKING (2B). For recipes like long-cooking stews, you need heat coming from top and bottom. Use tongs to arrange some of the coals in a circle a little smaller than the circumference of the dutch oven. Set the oven on top, then arrange the rest of the coals evenly over the lid.

BAKING (2C). Here you need heat coming from top and bottom, arranged carefully for even browning. Use tongs to arrange some of the coals in a circle a little smaller than the circumference of the dutch oven. Set the oven on top, then arrange a single ring of coals on top of the lid, around the lip. Space a few more across the lid.

3 CHECK THE FOOD

To check food and temp, lift the lid occasionally by sliding tongs through the pot lid's center handle and bracing them against the edge of the lid closest to you.

4 TWEAK THE TEMP

To decrease heat, scrape away some fuel. To increase heat, or to cook longer than 45 minutes, add 5 to 6 new briquets to both the top and the bottom of the dutch oven (touching lit ones, so they'll ignite) about every 30 minutes, or add wood embers. If briquets don't light, be ready to ignite them in the chimney.

SPICED OATMEAL

MAKES ABOUT 9 CUPS MIX; 12 SERVINGS ★ 20 MINUTES AT HOME; 10 IN CAMP

To avoid the excess packaging of single-serving instant oatmeal, *Sunset* reader Lynn Lloyd of Mt. Shasta, California, came up with her own mix.

3 cups regular rolled oats
3 cups 4- or 7-grain cereal flakes; or use more oats
1 cup *each* chopped dried dates, dried apples, walnuts
½ cup packed light brown sugar
4 tsp. cinnamon
1 tbsp. ground ginger
½ tsp. ground cloves
¾ tsp. salt (optional)

AT HOME

1. Combine all ingredients in a large container (at least 2½ qt.) with a lid.

IN CAMP

2. Bring water (1 cup per serving) to a boil in a saucepan on a camp stove and stir in oatmeal mix (¾ cup per serving). Remove from heat, cover, and let stand until most of water has been absorbed, 5 to 10 minutes.

Make ahead: The mix, up to 1 month, stored airtight.

PER SERVING 283 CAL., 26% (73 CAL.) FROM FAT; 6 G PROTEIN; 8.2 G FAT (0.9 G SAT.); 51 G CARBO (6.5 G FIBER); 91 MG SODIUM; 0 MG CHOL. LC/LS/VG

OATMEAL with THE WORKS

SERVES 10 ★ 10 MINUTES AT HOME; 10 IN CAMP

Add-ons, including zingy pomegranate molasses and a topping bar, elevate oatmeal (see photo, page 32).

6 cups regular or quick-cooking rolled oats
1 cup chopped dried apricots (preferably Blenheim)
1 cup tart dried cherries
½ cup packed light brown sugar
¾ tsp. salt (optional)
1 cup *each* chocolate chips, toasted unsweetened coconut flakes, and roasted hazelnuts
Pomegranate molasses* or brown sugar

AT HOME

1. Combine oats, fruit, sugar, and salt in a large bowl with hands until fruit isn't sticking together. Store in a container with a lid. Package toppings separately.

IN CAMP

2. Bring water (¾ cup per serving) to a boil in a saucepan on a camp stove and stir in oatmeal mix (¾ cup per serving). Remove from heat, cover, and let stand until most of water has been absorbed, 5 minutes. Set out with toppings.

*Find pomegranate molasses at well-stocked grocery stores.

Make ahead: The mix, up to 1 month, stored airtight.

PER 1-CUP SERVING 501 CAL., 38% (188 CAL.) FROM FAT; 9.7 G PROTEIN; 21 G FAT (8.7 G SAT.); 76 G CARBO (12 G FIBER); 9.2 MG SODIUM; 0 MG CHOL. LS/VG

CAMPFIRE RASPBERRY DOUBLE DUTCH BABY

SERVES 4 TO 6 ★ 1 HOUR IN CAMP

Over the years, we've published many versions of the golden, custardy pancake called Dutch baby, but this is the first one we've done in a dutch oven in camp. (It's easy.) The Dutch baby puffs way up as it cooks, then sinks down when you cut into it.

6 large eggs
1 cup flour
1 cup milk
1 tsp. kosher salt
2 tbsp. sugar
¼ cup butter
2 cups raspberries, divided
Raspberry or maple pancake syrup

1. Prepare a fire (see "How to Cook in a Dutch Oven" on page 28) and arrange the coals for baking.

2. Meanwhile, in a large bowl, whisk eggs and flour until smooth. Then whisk in milk, salt, and sugar until blended.

3. Set a 6-qt. (12-in.) camp dutch oven over the ring of coals and add butter to pot. When butter melts, stir to coat pot and pour in batter. Scatter 1½ cups berries on top. Cover with lid and more coals as directed on page 29. Cook until Dutch baby is puffed and deep golden all over with no liquid in the center, 20 to 25 minutes.

4. Scatter remaining ½ cup berries over Dutch baby. Cut into wedges and serve with syrup.

PER SERVING 278 CAL., 46% (129 CAL.) FROM FAT; 10 G PROTEIN; 14 G FAT (7.2 G SAT.); 27 G CARBO (3.2 G FIBER); 396 MG SODIUM; 236 MG CHOL. LC/LS/V

CAMPFIRE RASPBERRY
DOUBLE DUTCH BABY

OATMEAL with THE WORKS
(see recipe on page 30)

DUTCH OVEN
CINNAMON
ROLLS

DUTCH OVEN CINNAMON ROLLS

MAKES 12 ★ 1½ HOURS AT HOME; 3½ IN CAMP

If anything could get a reluctant camper into the woods, it would be the promise of these oversize sticky rolls. Carolyn Beth Weil, author of Williams-Sonoma *Pie & Tart* (Simon & Schuster, 2003), shared the recipe from her days as a Girl Scout leader. Shape the dough into logs at home and freeze, then thaw in your cooler to bake in camp. You'll need a 2-gal. resealable plastic bag (for freezing) and some wooden skewers to test doneness.

DOUGH
1 pkg. (2¼ tsp.) active dry yeast
2 tbsp. honey or 1 tbsp. granulated sugar
1¼ cups warm milk (100° to 110°)
4 tbsp. butter, melted and cooled
2 large eggs
1½ tsp. salt
About 5⅓ cups flour

FILLING
6 tbsp. butter, softened
1½ cups packed light brown sugar
1 tbsp. cinnamon
1 cup raisins
1 cup walnut or pecan pieces (optional)

FINISHING
1 tbsp. butter (for greasing dutch oven)
3 tbsp. honey
1 cup powdered sugar

AT HOME
1. Make dough: In the bowl of a stand mixer, combine yeast with ¼ cup warm (100° to 110°) water and the honey. Let stand until bubbly, about 5 minutes. Add milk, butter, eggs, and salt. Using a dough hook, gradually mix in 5 cups flour, then mix on medium-low speed until dough is smooth and elastic, about 10 minutes; if dough is still sticky, add another tbsp. or so of flour. (You can also mix and knead the dough by hand.)

2. Put dough into an oiled mixing bowl, turning so it's oiled on all sides, and cover with a damp towel or plastic wrap. Let rise at room temperature until double, about 1 hour.

3. Punch down dough; knead a few times on a lightly floured work surface. Roll into a 12- by 24-in. rectangle.

4. Make filling: Spread butter on dough. Combine brown sugar, cinnamon, raisins, and walnuts; sprinkle evenly over dough, leaving a 1½-in. strip clear along the top long edge.

5. Roll up, starting at other long edge, and pinch seam closed. Cut log in half crosswise. Using paper towels, oil inside of a 2-gal. resealable freezer bag. Put half-logs inside, leaving some space between them, and seal bag. Freeze until solid, at least 6 hours.

IN CAMP
6. Transport frozen dough in a cooler up to 1 day before baking. Remove logs from bag, ideally while still somewhat firm, and cut each crosswise into 6 slices.

7. Finish rolls: Butter a 6-qt. (12-in.) camp dutch oven. Arrange slices cut side up in pot. Cover with lid and let rise in the sun until dough is puffy and holds a small impression when pressed, 1½ to 3 hours.

8. Meanwhile, prepare a fire (see "How to Cook in a Dutch Oven" on page 28) and arrange the coals for baking.

9. Cover rolls with lid and coals as directed on page 29. Bake rolls until they're browned and a skewer inserted into bread comes out clean, 30 to 45 minutes.

10. Remove pot from fire, uncover, and let cool about 15 minutes. Meanwhile, mix honey and powdered sugar with 2 to 3 tsp. water. Loosen rolls with a table knife and spread honey mixture on top.

Make ahead: Through step 5, up to 1 month, frozen.

PER ROLL 533 CAL., 21% (114 CAL.) FROM FAT; 8.4 G PROTEIN; 13 G FAT (7.5 G SAT.); 98 G CARBO (2.5 G FIBER); 399 MG SODIUM; 66 MG CHOL. V

WHAT'S DUTCH ABOUT DUTCH OVENS?

Although not actually Dutch—similar pots have been used for centuries in many countries around the world—sturdy cast-iron pots were sold by Dutch traders during American colonial times, which may be how they got their name. Another explanation is that some pots sold then were made using Dutch metal-casting techniques. The ovens traveled West with the pioneers and explorers, and were indispensable to cowboys on the range.

FOOD for the PACK and the POCKET

Just because you're in the middle of nowhere doesn't mean you have to compromise on food. From full meals for backpackers to superior hiking snacks, here are recipes to make—or take—on the trail.

Lightweight freeze-dried meals for backpacking have been around for decades now, but recently they've gotten much better—some are actually excellent—and more varied. Creating your own is possible, but they often cost more to make than to buy. Instead, we opted for putting a fresh twist on these quick meals with ingredients that can be packed easily.

You'll need a backpacking stove, and we recommend two. The Whisperlite, a wee burner with a fuel pump, weighs less than 12 ounces. All you need to go with it are a small pot (pack your clothes in it) and a tiny skillet (use it as a pot lid and a plate). The JetBoil Flash (15.25 ounces) is a cooking cup with a burner, lit by clicking a button; it boils water fast, and you can detach the burner to use with a skillet. For buying information, see Resource Guide, page 244.

BACKPACKER'S CHICKEN AND RICE BURRITOS

SERVES 2 ★ 15 MINUTES IN CAMP

Pack flour tortillas to turn a Mexican-inspired freeze-dried meal into burritos. You could also use a bean enchilada mix or a beef and bean chili instead of the rice and chicken.

1 pkg. (about 5 oz.) freeze-dried Mexican-style rice and chicken*, such as Mountain House
4 large flour tortillas (10 to 12 in.)
About ⅔ cup shredded cheddar cheese
Handful of fresh cilantro leaves*, or 2 tsp. dried cilantro

1. Cook rice and chicken in pouch according to package directions. Fold tortillas and warm in a pan on a backpacking stove.

2. Sprinkle cheese down center of a tortilla. Fill with about one-quarter of the rice mixture. Top with a few cilantro leaves and roll tortilla around filling to create a burrito. Repeat with remaining tortillas and fillings.

*Find freeze-dried mixes at outdoor-recreation gear stores (see Resource Guide, page 244). Pack fresh cilantro wrapped in paper towels and sealed in a plastic bag, and use as soon as possible.

PER 2-BURRITO SERVING 813 CAL., 22% (179 CAL.) FROM FAT; 41 G PROTEIN; 20 G FAT (6.8 G SAT.); 118 G CARBO (14 G FIBER); 2,053 MG SODIUM; 34 MG CHOL.

BACKPACKER'S INDIAN-SPICED CHICKPEAS WITH SPINACH

SERVES 2 ★ 20 MINUTES IN CAMP

We chose a vegetarian option here, but freeze-dried chicken korma (a creamy curry) would also be good.

1 pkg. (about 7 oz.) freeze-dried *chana masala** (Indian-spiced chickpeas), such as Backpacker's Pantry
2 handfuls baby spinach leaves*
About 1 cup toasted almonds
2 naan breads (each about 3½ in. by 8 in.; 18 oz. total)*

1. Cook chana masala in pouch according to package directions. In last 2 minutes, open pouch and add spinach, stirring to combine and submerge spinach. Let sit another 4 to 5 minutes.

2. Meanwhile, warm naan over a low flame on a backpacking stove. Top chana masala mixture with almonds and serve with naan.

*Find freeze-dried mixes at outdoor-recreation gear stores (see Resource Guide, page 244). Pack a small bag of fresh spinach, and use it the first night out. Or pack a wedge of cabbage and shred right before using. Find naan, an Indian flatbread, in well-stocked grocery stores.

PER 2-CUP SERVING 1,103 CAL., 36% (398 CAL.) FROM FAT; 44 G PROTEIN; 44 G FAT (4 G SAT.); 149 G CARBO (28 G FIBER); 1,886 MG SODIUM; 0 MG CHOL. V

EASY BEEF JERKY

MAKES 18 OZ. ★ 15 MINUTES, PLUS ABOUT 8 HOURS TO MARINATE AND DRY, AT HOME

This lightweight protein dates back centuries in the West; Native Americans have been drying strips of meat since at least the time of the Spanish conquistadors. Homemade jerky is free of preservatives and is also incredibly delicious.

We like using an Excalibur dehydrator (see Resource Guide, page 244), because it heats the meat to 160°—a temperature that, combined with moisture loss from drying, kills microbes. It has easy-to-load shelves and a fan, so food dries quickly and evenly. If you don't have a dehydrator, you can use an oven set to 175°.

¾ cup soy sauce
1½ tsp. garlic powder
2 tbsp. *each* Asian chili paste and sugar
2 lbs. lean beef, such as London broil, cut into long strips ¼ to ½ in. thick*

1. Mix soy sauce, garlic powder, chili paste, and sugar in a large bowl. Add meat, turning to coat well. Chill meat 4 to 5 hours, stirring occasionally.

2. Drain meat; discard liquid. Lay strips of meat on racks of dehydrator (or, if you're using an oven, on metal racks set on rimmed baking sheets), making sure pieces don't overlap.

3. Dehydrate jerky according to manufacturer's instructions (at about 155°, the meat will hit 160°) or in an oven at about 175°, until dry but still pliable when bent, about 4 hours.

4. Let cool completely before packing into an airtight container.

*Freezing the meat briefly before slicing firms it up so you can slice it thinner; a very sharp knife helps too.

PER 3-OZ. SERVING 319 CAL., 37% (117 CAL.) FROM FAT; 44 G PROTEIN; 13 G FAT (5.1 G SAT.); 4.8 G CARBO (0 G FIBER); 1,440 MG SODIUM; 69 MG CHOL.

continued

SOY AND SESAME KALE CHIPS

MAKES 6 CUPS; 18 SERVINGS
★ 35 MINUTES AT HOME

Though commercial kale chips are widely available, it's still fun to bake your own. The key to getting them crisp is to avoid crowding the leaves on the baking sheets. Keep an eye on them as they cook, as they can scorch quickly.

7 to 8 oz. (1 small bunch*) Lacinato kale (often sold as "dinosaur kale" or "Tuscan kale")
1½ tbsp. olive oil
1 tbsp. soy sauce
1 tbsp. sesame seeds

1. Preheat oven to 300°. Rinse kale and thoroughly blot dry with a kitchen towel. Tear leaves from ribs; discard ribs. Tear leaves into 4-in. pieces. Pour oil and soy sauce into a large bowl, add kale, and toss to coat evenly.

2. Arrange leaves in a single layer on 2 rimmed baking sheets. Bake, switching pan positions after 13 minutes. Sprinkle with sesame seeds and bake until leaves are crisp but not browned, 5 to 7 minutes more.

*You can use larger bunches, but you'll need more oil and seasonings and maybe a third baking sheet.

Make ahead: Up to 1 week, stored airtight.

PER ⅓-CUP SERVING 18 CAL., 72% (13 CAL.) FROM FAT; 0.2 G PROTEIN; 1.4 G FAT (0.2 G SAT.); 1 G CARBO (0.2 G FIBER); 54 MG SODIUM; 0 MG CHOL. LC/LS/VG

EAST INDIAN SNACK MIX

MAKES 5½ CUPS; ABOUT 10 SERVINGS
★ 15 MINUTES AT HOME

Imagine Chex Mix, but made with rice cereal and Indian seasonings. The flavors are an addictive combination of spicy, tart, and salty.

1 qt. crisp puffed rice cereal, such as Rice Krispies
1 cup salted cashews
1 cup dried banana chips, broken into pieces
1½ tbsp. canola oil
2 tsp. brown mustard seeds
1 tsp. ground turmeric
½ tsp. *each* **salt and cayenne**
½ tsp. citric acid powder, such as Ball Fruit-Fresh*

1. Combine cereal, cashews, and banana chips in a large bowl.

2. Cook oil and mustard seeds in a small covered frying pan over medium heat until seeds pop, 1 to 2 minutes. Remove from heat and stir in remaining ingredients. Scrape from pan over cereal and mix to coat.

*Find citric acid powder in your store's baking aisle.

Make ahead: Up to 1 week, stored airtight.

PER ½ CUP 171 CAL., 53% (90 CAL.) FROM FAT; 2.8 G PROTEIN; 10 G FAT (3.2 G SAT.); 18 G CARBO (0.9 G FIBER); 229 MG SODIUM; 0 MG CHOL. GF/LC/LS/VG

SPICY–SWEET NUT MIX

MAKES ABOUT 3⅓ CUPS; 12 OR 13 SERVINGS
★ 40 MINUTES AT HOME

These are just the thing for a burst of energy along the hiking trail, or for an exciting snack with a pre-dinner cocktail back in camp.

1½ cups pecan halves
¾ cup pine nuts
¾ cup hulled raw or roasted pumpkin seeds *(pepitas)***

⅓ cup shelled roasted or raw pistachios
3 tbsp. vegetable oil
3 tbsp. sugar
¾ to 1¼ tsp. ground dried chipotle chile or cayenne
About ½ tsp. salt

1. Preheat oven to 325°. Combine pecans, pine nuts, pumpkin seeds, pistachios, and oil in a large bowl. Add sugar, ¾ tsp. chile, and ½ tsp. salt; mix to coat nuts evenly. Add more chile and salt to taste.

2. Oil a 10- by 15-in. baking pan. Spread nuts in pan. Bake, stirring occasionally, until nuts are browned, 15 to 20 minutes. Cool.

*Find at well-stocked grocery stores and Latino markets.

Make ahead: Up to 1 week, stored airtight.

PER ¼ CUP 219 CAL., 78% (171 CAL.) FROM FAT; 4.6 G PROTEIN; 19 G FAT (2.2 G SAT.); 9.9 G CARBO (1.9 G FIBER); 98 MG SODIUM; 0 MG CHOL. GF/LC/LS/VG

PEANUT BUTTER CRANBERRY GO-BARS

MAKES 16 ★ 1 HOUR, PLUS 30 MINUTES TO CHILL, AT HOME

Loaded with good-for-you ingredients, these not-too-sweet bars still taste like a treat, and they'll withstand cold, heat, and being stuffed in a backpack or pocket. Natural peanut butters vary from brand to brand in terms of spreadability; we prefer Laura Scudder's Old Fashioned Nutty Peanut Butter, because it makes a moister, chewier bar.

Cooking-oil spray
1 cup regular rolled oats
⅓ cup oat bran
3 tbsp. flax seeds
1 cup whole-wheat flour
½ tsp. *each* **baking powder and salt**
½ cup *each* **chopped roasted salted peanuts, dried cranberries, and finely chopped dried Mission figs**

¾ cup old fashioned–style chunky
   peanut butter
¼ cup low-fat milk
1 large egg
½ cup honey
Zest of 1 lemon
1 tbsp. lemon juice

1. Line a 9- by 13-in. pan with plastic wrap, leaving an overhang on the 9-in. sides, and coat with cooking-oil spray. In a large bowl, stir together oats, oat bran, flax seeds, flour, baking powder, salt, peanuts, cranberries, and figs until well blended.

2. In the bowl of a stand mixer, beat together peanut butter, milk, egg, honey, lemon zest, and lemon juice until well blended.

3. Add flour mixture to peanut butter mixture and beat until completely blended. Scrape dough into pan and, with wet fingers or a rubber spatula, pat to fill pan completely and evenly (dough is sticky, so you may need to wet your hands a few times). Chill dough until firm, about 30 minutes.

4. Meanwhile, preheat oven to 300°. Invert pan onto a work surface, lift off pan, and peel off plastic. Using a bench scraper or knife, cut straight down lengthwise through middle, then crosswise to make 16 bars, each 1½ in. wide. Place bars about 1 in. apart on a baking sheet lined with parchment paper.

5. Bake bars until lightly browned and somewhat firm to touch, about 20 minutes. Remove from oven and let cool completely.

Make ahead: Up to 2 weeks, stored airtight, or 2 months, frozen.

PER BAR 227 CAL., 40% (90 CAL.) FROM FAT; 7.4 G PROTEIN; 10 G FAT (1.5 G SAT.); 29 G CARBO (4.1 G FIBER); 160 MG SODIUM; 13 MG CHOL. LC/LS/V

PEANUT BUTTER CRANBERRY GO-BARS

CASHEW BARS

An energy bar with a little bit of sophistication. Follow directions for Peanut Butter Cranberry Go-Bars (recipe at left), but substitute ½ cup chopped **roasted salted cashews** for the peanuts, an additional ½ cup chopped **dried Mission figs** for the cranberries, and ¾ cup **cashew butter** for the peanut butter. Makes 16.

PER BAR 216 CAL., 40% (87 CAL.) FROM FAT; 6.1 G PROTEIN; 9.7 G FAT (1.8 G SAT.); 30 G CARBO (3.6 G FIBER); 183 MG SODIUM; 13 MG CHOL. LC/LS/V

SESAME DATE BARS

This bar is rich with the flavors of the Middle East. Follow directions for Peanut Butter Cranberry Go-Bars (recipe at left), but increase **oat bran** to 1 cup. Substitute ½ cup **toasted sesame seeds** for the peanuts, 1 cup chopped **pitted dates** for the figs and cranberries, and ¾ cup **tahini** (sesame paste) for the peanut butter; then add 2 tbsp. more **honey**. Makes 16.

PER BAR 235 CAL., 38% (90 CAL.) FROM FAT; 6.7 G PROTEIN; 10 G FAT (1.5 G SAT.); 35 G CARBO (5.2 G FIBER); 109 MG SODIUM; 13 MG CHOL. LC/LS/V

BBQ CHICKEN SALAD SUBS

SERVES 4 ★ 30 MINUTES IN CAMP

You can find most of the ingredients for these quick and delicious sandwiches already prepped at the grocery store. *Sunset* reader Beverly Wise of Fairfax, Virginia, shared the recipe with us.

3 cups shredded rotisserie chicken
¾ cup barbecue sauce
4 sub rolls (each about 3 oz.)
2 cups spinach leaves
1 cup fresh corn, cut from the cob
½ cup shredded sharp cheddar cheese
¼ cup sliced onion
¼ cup store-bought or homemade vinaigrette

1. Set a saucepan over medium to medium-low heat on a camp stove, or over a charcoal or wood-fired grill heated to medium (300° to 350°; you can hold your hand 5 in. above cooking grate only 7 seconds). Combine chicken and barbecue sauce in saucepan and heat, stirring often, until hot. Meanwhile, split rolls, keeping one side attached. Warm 2 at a time, cut side down, in a cast-iron skillet or on grill grate. Transfer to a plate and tent with foil.

2. In a medium bowl, combine spinach, corn, cheddar cheese, onion, and vinaigrette. Fill rolls with chicken mixture, then with spinach salad.

PER SANDWICH 562 CAL., 32% (180 CAL.) FROM FAT; 35 G PROTEIN; 20 G FAT (6.7 G SAT.); 61 G CARBO (4.5 G FIBER); 1,847 MG SODIUM; 109 MG CHOL.

COWBOY HOT DOGS

SERVES 4 ★ 30 MINUTES IN CAMP

The aroma of caramelizing onions builds anticipation for these over-the-top bison dogs, loaded with the onions—plus bacon and barbecue sauce.

1 tbsp. olive oil
1 large yellow onion, cut into half-moons
4 bison* or other hot dogs
4 potato hot dog buns
About 6 tbsp. mayonnaise
About 2 tbsp. spicy brown mustard, such as Gulden's
About 4 tbsp. barbecue sauce
½ cup shredded white cheddar cheese
6 slices cooked bacon, crumbled

1. Heat oil in a large frying pan over medium heat on a camp stove, or over a charcoal or wood-fired grill heated to medium (350°; you can hold your hand 5 in. above cooking grate only 7 seconds). Add onion and cook until deep golden and very tender, stirring frequently, about 20 minutes.

2. Meanwhile, if you don't already have it going, heat a charcoal or wood-fired grill to medium (see step 1). Grill hot dogs until slightly charred all over, about 6 minutes, turning occasionally. Add buns and grill, turning frequently, until warmed and lightly charred, about 3 minutes.

3. Spread buns with mayonnaise and drizzle with mustard and barbecue sauce. Set hot dogs in buns.

4. Sprinkle cheese on top, followed by caramelized onions and bacon.

*Find bison hot dogs at well-stocked grocery stores or see Resource Guide (page 244) for online ordering.

PER SERVING 633 CAL., 63% (399 CAL.) FROM FAT; 17 G PROTEIN; 44 G FAT (13 G SAT.); 9.5 G CARBO (1.7 G FIBER); 1,111 MG SODIUM; 69 MG CHOL.

COWBOY HOT DOGS

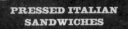
PRESSED ITALIAN
SANDWICHES

PRESSED ITALIAN SANDWICHES

SERVES 8 ★ 20 MINUTES, PLUS 30 MINUTES TO PRESS, IN CAMP

These hearty sandwiches from *Sunset* reader Catherine High of Bothell, Washington, pack beautifully in a knapsack if you want to tote them on a hike. Just wrap the filled and cut ciabatta loaf in foil, then in a large resealable plastic bag.

1 ciabatta loaf (about 8 by 14 by 2 in.)
½ cup store-bought black or green olive tapenade
2 tbsp. balsamic vinegar
2 tbsp. extra-virgin olive oil
¼ lb. *each* thinly sliced Genoa salami and spicy Italian cold cuts, such as coppa, capocollo, or hot salami
3 oz. thinly sliced prosciutto
8 oz. fresh mozzarella, sliced
1 roasted red bell pepper, chopped
6 leaves fresh basil, torn into bite-size pieces
Pepper

1. Cut ciabatta in half lengthwise. Spread bottom half with tapenade. Drizzle cut side of top half with vinegar and oil.

2. Arrange salami on top of tapenade, followed by the cold cuts, prosciutto, mozzarella, red pepper, and basil. Sprinkle with pepper to taste and place top half of loaf on filling.

3. Wrap sandwich thoroughly with plastic wrap or foil. Place a heavy cutting board or other flat object on top of sandwich and weight it down with a 2- to 4-lb. weight (such as a large pot or six-pack of soda). Let sit 30 minutes to 2 hours. Unwrap, cut into eighths, and serve.

PER SANDWICH 398 CAL., 66% (261 CAL.) FROM FAT; 20 G PROTEIN; 29 G FAT (8.5 G SAT.); 22 G CARBO (1.2 G FIBER); 1,449 MG SODIUM; 64 MG CHOL. LC

> **TIP** IN CASE YOUR ROLLS HAVE GOTTEN A BIT DRY IN CAMP: MAKE SANDWICHES AND WRAP THEM UP FOR A COUPLE OF HOURS. THE MOISTURE FROM THE FILLINGS WILL SOFTEN THE BREAD.

BRIE SANDWICHES WITH CARAMELIZED ONION MARMALADE

SERVES 4 TO 6 ★ 30 MINUTES AT HOME; 10 IN CAMP

Thin apple slices and your own sweet-tart, homemade onion spread transform simple cheese sandwiches into something pretty grand. Golden Delicious apples are a good choice if you're packing for lunch because they don't brown.

ONION MARMALADE
2 large onions, halved and thinly sliced
2 tbsp. butter
¾ tsp. pepper
⅓ cup packed dark brown sugar
½ cup apple cider vinegar
½ cup apple juice
Pinch of salt

SANDWICHES
4 to 6 soft or crusty sandwich rolls (each 3 oz.), split
½ lb. brie cheese, sliced
1 Golden Delicious apple, thinly sliced
1 to 1½ cups loosely packed baby arugula

AT HOME
1. Make marmalade: In a large frying pan over medium heat, cook onions in butter, stirring occasionally, until starting to brown, 6 to 8 minutes. Add pepper, sugar, vinegar, apple juice, and salt. Cook until most of liquid is absorbed, 8 to 10 minutes, then reduce heat and simmer gently until remaining liquid is absorbed and onion is soft and sticky, another 8 to 10 minutes. Let cool, then transfer to an airtight container.

IN CAMP
2. Make sandwiches: Spread rolls on one side with a thick layer of marmalade. Add brie, apple, and arugula.

Make ahead: Marmalade, up to 1 week, chilled.

PER SANDWICH 600 CAL., 21% (126 CAL.) FROM FAT; 21 G PROTEIN; 14 G FAT (9.0 G SAT.); 69 G CARBO (4.9 G FIBER); 1,056 MG SODIUM; 48 MG CHOL. V

6 Foods to
FORAGE

There's mystery and the thrill of discovery in foraging for wild foods. When you're out in forest or desert, or along the seashore, foraging makes a great excuse to explore, and it will open your eyes to the beauty of the natural world around you.

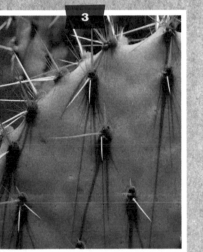

Though the following plants grow in many areas and are easy to identify, the number-one rule for foraging is to be positive of what you are picking. Take a guidebook with you if you're unsure; see the Resource Guide for our favorites. Additional tips: Avoid roadside areas near traffic, places where pets romp, and any area that might have been treated with agricultural sprays. Harvest responsibly, leaving some plants behind to regenerate and to feed wildlife. And when you try a new food, start by eating just a little.

SPRING

1 MINER'S LETTUCE. This mild, succulent green, which is full of vitamin C, helped keep miners healthy during California's Gold Rush. In forests and near streams, look for plants up to a foot tall. Try leaves, stems, and small flowers in salad with a simple vinaigrette.

2 NETTLES. Herbaceous nettles are excellent sautéed with garlic and chile flakes. Look for the fine-toothed, tapered leaves along streams. To harvest, grab your long gloves, clippers, and a big bag—you'll need them to avoid the formic acid "sting" in the hairs on nettles' leaves and chest-high stalks. Once you've deposited them in a pan, you can relax: Heat deactivates the sting.

3 NOPALES. The pads of the slightly tart, green bean–tasting nopal—aka prickly pear cactus—come armed with spines and barbed, fuzzy dots (glochids), so be ready with thick gloves.

Look for the cactus in deserts to more temperate areas. Cut tender young pads above the joint, leaving a stub to regrow. Remove everything prickly with a vegetable peeler or small knife. Slash pads in a couple of places and grill, or slice and sauté until sticky juices evaporate. Try nopales with scrambled eggs and salsa.

4 DOUGLAS FIR OR SPRUCE TIPS. The chartreuse tender new growth of these forest trees offers exciting tastes of citrus or resin. Pull the tips from trees and try them infused in vodka or syrup, chopped in salads, or minced and patted onto meats.

SUMMER

5 HUCKLEBERRIES. Intensely colored and flavored huckleberries come in many varieties and colors, from pink to blue to black. They thrive in high country meadows and forests and even grow at sea level. Shrubs may grow ankle-high to more than 10 feet. If any last past a trailside snack, they make the world's best cobbler.

6 SEA BEANS. In salt marshes and on sandy beaches at the high tide mark, mats of crunchy, salty succulents called sea beans (aka samphire or pickleweed) grow. Being careful not to stomp on their brittle stems, cut off the top few tender inches. Sea beans are good raw as a snack or in salad, soaked first in water for a half-hour if you like, to lessen their saltiness.

SPICY PEANUT, CARROT, and SNAP PEA WRAPS

SPICY PEANUT, CARROT, AND SNAP PEA WRAPS

SERVES 2 ★ 15 MINUTES IN CAMP

Instead of a PB&J, try this crunchy raw-vegetable wrap, with rich, spicy Asian peanut sauce added in.

¼ cup old-fashioned creamy or chunky peanut butter
1 tsp. Asian chili paste
1 tbsp. reduced-sodium soy sauce
2 whole-wheat tortillas (9 in.)
1 cup coarsely shredded carrots
1 cup snap peas, sliced diagonally

In a small bowl, whisk peanut butter, chili paste, soy sauce, and 2 tbsp. water to blend. Evenly divide mixture between tortillas and spread in a rectangle down the middle of each, leaving a small border. Evenly top rectangles with carrots and snap peas, then roll up burrito-style.

Make ahead: Peanut butter sauce, up to 3 days, chilled. Wraps, up to 4 hours, sealed in plastic or foil.

PER WRAP 396 CAL., 45% (178 CAL.) FROM FAT; 14 G PROTEIN; 20 G FAT (2 G SAT.); 39 G CARBO (6.8 G FIBER); 547 MG SODIUM; 0.8 MG CHOL. LC/VG

GRILLED MEDITERRANEAN VEGETABLE SANDWICHES

SERVES 4 ★ 30 MINUTES IN CAMP

Sunset reader Rebecca Jansen of Snohomish, Washington, won us over with this Mediterranean-inspired vegetable sandwich that cooks entirely on the grill. It's great for lunch or dinner.

¼ cup mayonnaise
2 garlic cloves, minced
½ tsp. lemon juice
2 small zucchini, thinly sliced lengthwise
2 portabella mushrooms, sliced ¼ in. thick
1 eggplant (14 oz.), sliced ¼ in. thick
2 tbsp. olive oil
½ tsp. kosher salt
¾ of a 1-lb. ciabatta loaf, split horizontally
2 oz. feta cheese, crumbled (½ cup)
2 medium tomatoes, sliced
2 cups baby arugula

1. Heat a charcoal or wood-fired grill to high (450° to 550°; you can hold your hand 5 in. above cooking grate only 2 to 4 seconds). Meanwhile, mix together mayonnaise, garlic, and lemon juice; set aside.

2. Brush zucchini, mushrooms, and eggplant with oil and sprinkle with salt. Grill, turning once, until softened and grill marks appear, about 3 minutes. Grill bread cut side down just until grill marks start to appear, 2 minutes.

3. Cut each half of loaf into 4 pieces. Spread bottoms with mayo mixture and smear tops with cheese. Make sandwiches with vegetables, tomatoes, and arugula.

PER SANDWICH 421 CAL., 65% (273 CAL.) FROM FAT; 10 G PROTEIN; 30 G FAT (6.5 G SAT.); 31 G CARBO (6 G FIBER); 711 MG SODIUM; 18 MG CHOL. LC/V

5 EASY CAMP SANDWICHES

Elevate lunch (or dinner) with these sandwich ideas based on proteins that keep well in your cooler or camp box.

ITALIAN HOAGIES. Brown chopped **onion**, sliced **red pepper**, and sliced **cooked Italian sausage** in a skillet. Stir in bottled **marinara sauce**. Simmer to blend flavors, then spoon into split, pan-toasted **hoagie rolls** and sprinkle with **parmesan.**

SALMON-CUCUMBER BAGELS. Spread one side of split **bagels** with **chive cream cheese**. Layer thinly sliced **cucumber, smoked salmon, red onion**, and **capers** on top. Then close up bagels.

EGG-AVOCADO PITAS. Tuck sliced ripe **avocado** and hard-cooked **eggs** into split **pita breads**. Sprinkle generously with **salt** and **extra-virgin olive oil**. Add crisp **bacon** slices and **arugula.**

TUNA-GREEN OLIVE CIABATTA. Combine **extra-virgin olive oil** and a little **lemon** juice with **salt, pepper**, and **smoked paprika**. Stir in drained **canned tuna**, lots of chopped **parsley**, and sliced **green olives**. Pile into a split **ciabatta loaf** and slice.

BLACK BEAN WRAPS. Heat drained **canned black beans** with some **chunky salsa**, and a little **dried Mexican oregano**, mashing a bit with a fork. Generously smear over **large flour tortillas**. Down the center, add chopped **romaine** and **tomato** and shredded **cotija** or jack **cheese**. Roll up.

CHIPOTLE CHICKEN QUESADILLAS

SERVES 4 ★ 10 MINUTES AT HOME; 35 IN CAMP

The chipotle adds a little smoky heat to these substantial quesadillas, which are a delicious choice for either lunch or dinner in camp. For an even more substantial meal, serve them with canned black or pinto beans (rinsed and heated in a little water); grilled corn and peppers; sliced green onions; and guacamole and sour cream.

1 canned chipotle chile, minced
¼ cup *each* sour cream and mayonnaise
1 tbsp. lime juice
1 tbsp. chopped cilantro
1½ lbs. boned, skinned chicken breast halves
3 tbsp. olive oil, divided
Salt and pepper
8 flour tortillas (8 to 10 in.)
2 cups (about 8 oz.) shredded jack cheese
Pico de gallo or other salsa

AT HOME

1. Whisk together chipotle chile, sour cream, mayonnaise, lime juice, and cilantro in a small bowl. Transfer sauce to a small container and chill.

IN CAMP

2. Brush chicken with 1 tbsp. oil and sprinkle with salt and pepper. Set a large frying pan over medium heat on a camp stove, or over a charcoal or wood-fired grill heated to medium (350°; you can hold your hand 5 in. above cooking grate only 7 seconds). Add chicken and cook, turning once, until cooked through, 10 to 12 minutes total. Transfer to a cutting board and cut into ¼-in.-thick slices.

3. Spread 1 tbsp. chipotle-lime sauce on each of the 8 tortillas. Top sauce on 4 of them with ½ cup cheese and a quarter of the chicken (they will be very full), then cover with remaining tortillas, sauce side down. Put each quesadilla on a plate.

4. Heat pan over medium heat and swirl 1 tbsp. oil in it. Slide 1 quesadilla off its plate into pan. Cook, turning once with a wide spatula, until cheese melts and both sides are golden, about 3 minutes total. Transfer quesadilla to a cutting board. Cook remaining quesadillas the same way, adding the remaining 1 tbsp. oil before the third quesadilla.

5. Cut quesadillas into wedges and serve as they're cooked, with salsa on the side.

Make ahead: Sauce, up to 3 days, chilled.

PER SERVING 873 CAL., 47% (414 CAL.) FROM FAT; 58 G PROTEIN; 46 G FAT (17 G SAT.); 52 G CARBO (3.4 G FIBER); 1,300 MG SODIUM; 169 MG CHOL.

BEER AND CHEESE FONDUE

SERVES 6 AS A MAIN DISH ★ 35 MINUTES IN CAMP

When you're having a hang-out-in-camp day, whip up this easy fondue, served with fresh vegetables, fruit, and sausage for dunking in the warm cheese. You don't need a special pot (the fondue cooks in a regular saucepan on a camp stove), but you'll need fondue forks or regular forks for dipping.

½ lb. *each* Swiss and jack cheeses, shredded
1 tbsp. cornstarch
1 tsp. dry mustard
½ tsp. cumin seeds
½ lb. *pain au levain* or other artisanal-style bread, cut into chunks
1 fennel bulb, trimmed and cut into slim wedges
2 Granny Smith apples, sliced
1 Belgian endive, separated into leaves
2 cups broccoli florets
12 oz. kielbasa, cut into chunks
1 garlic clove, peeled and cut in half
1 cup lager beer (don't use ale; it's too bitter)

1. Toss cheese in a medium bowl with cornstarch, mustard, and cumin. Put bread in a bowl and set fennel, apples, endive, and broccoli on a large plate or board.

2. Brown kielbasa in a large frying pan over medium-high heat on a camp stove, about 5 minutes. Remove from heat; tent with foil.

3. Meanwhile, rub a 1- to 2-qt. saucepan with garlic and leave garlic in pan. Heat beer in pan over medium heat until bubbles start to rise, about 3 minutes. Add cheese mixture a handful at a time, stirring until mostly melted before adding more. When completely melted, reduce heat so fondue barely bubbles.

4. Add sausage to plate with fennel and other ingredients and serve fondue with them and with bread for dunking on fondue forks. As you eat, stir fondue occasionally with a fork to keep it emulsified.

PER SERVING 586 CAL., 38% (224 CAL.) FROM FAT; 33 G PROTEIN; 25 G FAT (14 G SAT.); 56 G CARBO (5.6 G FIBER); 1,265 MG SODIUM; 94 MG CHOL.

CHICKEN ENCHILADA NACHO BOWLS

TOFU and EGGPLANT HOBO BUNDLES

TOFU AND EGGPLANT HOBO BUNDLES

SERVES 4 ★ 45 MINUTES, PLUS 1 HOUR TO CHILL, AT HOME/IN CAMP

An all-in-one meal wrapped in foil, cooked over a fire: That's the idea of hobo bundles, which lots of us first tried on childhood camping trips with Scouts. Here, instead of the usual meat and potato combo, we went for a fresh, vegetarian version. Tofu and eggplant cook in foil with a flavorful marinade. You open up the fragrant bundles and top them with a spicy salad.

TOFU AND EGGPLANT

20 oz. firm tofu, cut into 16 chunks
12 oz. Asian eggplant, quartered lengthwise and cut into chunks
2 tbsp. *each* minced ginger and garlic
¼ cup reduced-sodium soy sauce
5 tbsp. vegetable oil
2 green onions, chopped

SALAD AND SERVING

1 English cucumber, halved lengthwise and cut into chunks
1 cup *each* cilantro leaves and whole dill sprigs
1 red jalapeño chile, halved lengthwise and sliced
2 tbsp. *each* lime juice and vegetable oil
½ tsp. kosher salt
Cooked rice and soy sauce

AT HOME OR IN CAMP

1. Make tofu and eggplant: Seal ingredients in a resealable plastic bag, turn, and chill at least 1 hour.

IN CAMP

2. Heat a charcoal or wood-fired grill to high (450° to 550°; you can hold your hand 5 in. above cooking grate only 2 to 4 seconds). Divide tofu mixture among 4 large squares of foil and seal securely. Grill bundles, turning once, until eggplant is tender when pierced, about 10 minutes.

3. Make salad: Mix all ingredients except rice and soy sauce. Unwrap bundles and top with salad. Serve with rice and soy sauce.

PER SERVING 356 CAL., 76% (271 CAL.) FROM FAT; 14 G PROTEIN; 30 G FAT (4.4 G SAT.); 13 G CARBO (5.1 G FIBER); 166 MG SODIUM; 0 MG CHOL. LC/LS/VG

CHICKEN ENCHILADA NACHO BOWLS

SERVES 4 ★ 20 MINUTES AT HOME; 20 IN CAMP

This Mexican spin on the campground classic Frito pie is a guaranteed crowd-pleaser.

CHICKEN AND SAUCE

1 medium onion, cut into half-moons
1 tbsp. olive oil
1 can (10 oz.) enchilada sauce
1 cup canned crushed tomatoes
1 can (15 oz.) reduced-sodium black beans, drained and rinsed
1 tsp. dried Mexican oregano
1 canned chipotle chile, minced
1 tbsp. packed light brown sugar
2 cups shredded rotisserie chicken

NACHOS

8 oz. tortilla chips, coarsely crushed
1¼ cups shredded cheddar cheese
2 cups shredded lettuce
½ cup cilantro sprigs
Lime wedges and hot sauce

AT HOME

1. Make sauce: Sauté onion in oil in a large frying pan over medium-high heat until softened, about 7 minutes. Add enchilada sauce, tomatoes, beans, oregano, chile, and sugar and cook, stirring occasionally, until hot and slightly reduced, 4 minutes. Stir in chicken. Let cool, then transfer to a resealable plastic bag and chill.

IN CAMP

2. Assemble nachos: Reheat chicken mixture in a pan on a camp stove. Divide chips among bowls and top with chicken mixture, cheese, lettuce, and cilantro. Serve with lime wedges and hot sauce.

Make ahead: Chicken and sauce, up to 1 month, frozen. Thaw in cooler.

PER SERVING 772 CAL., 43% (332 CAL.) FROM FAT; 45 G PROTEIN; 36 G FAT (8.4 G SAT.); 70 G CARBO (13 G FIBER); 1,559 MG SODIUM; 38 MG CHOL.

GRILLED CHICKEN WITH WHISKEY BARBECUE SAUCE AND SPICY SLAW

SERVES 6 ★ 1 HOUR AT HOME; 45 MINUTES IN CAMP

Kelly Liken—chef of Restaurant Kelly Liken in Vail, Colorado, and an avid camper—simmers her special barbecue sauce and preps her slaw at home. All she has to do in camp is grill the chicken and toss the salad. You'll need to pack a heatproof brush for basting.

SAUCE
1¼ cups ketchup
1 to 1½ tsp. hot sauce, such as Tabasco
2 tbsp. *each* dark molasses; Dijon mustard; whiskey, such as Jack Daniel's; and Worcestershire sauce
1 tbsp. cider vinegar
1 large garlic clove, minced

SLAW
1 lb. cabbage, cut into shreds
¼ red onion, cut into long slivers
½ red bell pepper, cut into thin strips
2 tbsp. chopped cilantro
¼ cup extra-virgin olive oil
2 tbsp. *each* sugar and Champagne vinegar
1 tbsp. lime juice
½ tsp. *each* red chile flakes and kosher salt
¼ tsp. pepper

CHICKEN
6 chicken legs with thighs attached or small bone-in breast halves (3¾ lbs. total)
1 tbsp. olive oil

AT HOME
1. Make sauce: Combine ingredients in a medium sauce-pan. Cover and simmer 45 minutes to blend flavors, stirring occasionally with a long spoon (sauce spatters). Add a little water if sauce gets too thick to pour. Let cool, then transfer to a plastic container and chill.

2. Make slaw: Toss vegetables in a large bowl to blend. Transfer to a resealable plastic bag. Put remaining ingredients in a small container with a tight-fitting lid. Chill slaw and dressing.

3. Prepare chicken: In a large bowl, coat chicken in oil; pack in a resealable plastic bag and chill.

IN CAMP
4. Heat a charcoal or wood-fired grill to medium (350° to 450°; you can hold your hand 5 in. above cooking grate only 5 to 7 seconds). Bring salad dressing and barbecue sauce to room temperature. Set aside ½ cup sauce.

5. Grill chicken until browned all over, about 15 minutes, turning occasionally. Turn again, generously brush tops with some of remaining sauce, and cook a few minutes; repeat turning and brushing 2 more times, until the chicken is well-browned and cooked through, 10 to 15 minutes total.

6. Toss slaw and dressing in a large bowl and serve with chicken and reserved sauce.

Make ahead: Sauce, up to 1 week, and slaw, up to 2 days, chilled. Chicken, up to 2 days, chilled, or up to 1 month, frozen; thaw in cooler.

PER SERVING 463 CAL., 41% (190 CAL.) FROM FAT; 36 G PROTEIN; 22 G FAT (4.5 G SAT.); 30 G CARBO (2.3 G FIBER); 999 MG SODIUM; 119 MG CHOL. LC

TAKING YOUR CAMP GRILL'S TEMPERATURE

Grilling in camp means cooking in the open air over charcoal or wood (see page 18). While there's no thermometer, you can get a surprisingly accurate take on the fire's heat with the following hand test—the same test you use with a grill at home if you don't have a temperature gauge.

VERY HIGH. 550° to 650°; you can hold your hand 5 in. above the cooking grate only 1 to 2 seconds.

HIGH. 450° to 550°; you can hold your hand 5 in. above the cooking grate only 2 to 4 seconds.

MEDIUM. 350° to 450°; you can hold your hand 5 in. above the cooking grate only 5 to 7 seconds.

LOW. 250° to 350°; you can hold your hand 5 in. above the cooking grate only 8 to 10 seconds.

GRILLED CHICKEN with WHISKEY BARBECUE SAUCE and SPICY SLAW

THAI CHICKEN and NOODLE CURRY

THAI CHICKEN AND NOODLE CURRY

SERVES 4 TO 6 ★ 45 MINUTES IN CAMP

A Thai version of chicken and noodles might seem exotic for camp, but it's actually easy to pull off. The secret ingredient is the curry paste.

10 oz. wide rice noodles
2 tsp. vegetable oil
2 tbsp. minced garlic
¼ cup minced shallots
12 oz. boned, skinned chicken breast, thinly sliced crosswise
1½ tbsp. *panang* curry paste, such as Mae Ploy*
1 can (14 oz.) coconut milk, divided
1 tbsp. *each* sugar, lime juice, reduced-sodium soy sauce, and Thai or Vietnamese fish sauce
½ cup *each* sliced green onions, cilantro leaves and small sprigs, and fresh Thai* or small regular basil leaves and small sprigs
1 lime, cut into wedges

1. Bring a medium pot of water to a boil on a camp stove. Add noodles and cook until softened, about 4 minutes. Drain and rinse with cold water. Set aside.

2. Heat oil in a large cast-iron skillet over high heat. Add garlic and shallots and cook until fragrant, about 30 seconds. Add chicken, curry paste, and half the coconut milk. Stir well to dissolve paste and boil until liquid is slightly reduced, about 5 minutes. Stir in remaining coconut milk, the sugar, lime juice, soy sauce, and fish sauce, then bring to a boil. Reduce heat and simmer until liquid is slightly thicker, 2 to 3 minutes more.

3. Add noodles, toss to coat, and cook a few minutes until hot, stirring often. Pour mixture into bowls. Sprinkle with green onions, cilantro, and basil. Serve with lime wedges.

*Find panang curry paste at Asian markets or in the international aisle at well-stocked grocery stores, or see Resource Guide (page 244); find Thai basil at Asian markets.

PER SERVING 414 CAL., 38% (162 CAL.) FROM FAT; 14 G PROTEIN; 18 G FAT (13 G SAT.); 50 G CARBO (0.6 G FIBER); 526 MG SODIUM; 36 MG CHOL. LC

CHICKEN SATAY

SERVES 6 TO 8 ★ 20 MINUTES, PLUS 1 HOUR TO MARINATE, AT HOME; 25 MINUTES IN CAMP

The salty-sweet flavors of satay taste best cooked over a grill outdoors—just as it is all over Southeast Asia. Make the sauce and marinate the chicken at home, and at camp, you'll have a meal that goes together quickly and doesn't require much cleanup. Be sure to tuck in metal or bamboo skewers with your kitchen gear.

1 cup chunky peanut butter
2 tbsp. *each* sugar, hoisin sauce, and soy sauce
2 tsp. Asian chili garlic sauce
¼ cup lime juice
2 tbsp. toasted sesame oil
3 lbs. boned, skinned chicken breasts or thighs, sliced lengthwise into ½-in.-thick, 1-in.-wide strips
Vegetable oil
¼ cup roasted peanuts
2 tbsp. chopped cilantro leaves
1 lime, cut into wedges

AT HOME

1. Put peanut butter, sugar, hoisin, soy sauce, chili garlic sauce, lime juice, sesame oil, and ¾ cup water in a food processor and blend until just combined.

2. Pour half the peanut sauce into a medium bowl. Add chicken, tossing to coat evenly. Transfer to a resealable plastic bag or plastic container. Put remaining sauce in a small container. Chill at least 1 hour.

IN CAMP

3. Heat a charcoal or wood-fired grill to high (450 to 550°; you can hold your hand 5 in. above cooking grate only 2 to 4 seconds). Weave strips of chicken lengthwise onto 20 metal or soaked wooden skewers (10-in. long). Bring peanut sauce to room temperature.

4. Oil grill grate, using tongs and a wad of oiled paper towels. Lay skewers on grill and cook, turning once halfway through, until chicken is opaque and grill marks appear, 8 to 10 minutes total.

5. Arrange skewers on a board. Sprinkle with peanuts and cilantro and serve with lime wedges and reserved peanut sauce.

Make ahead: Through step 2, up to 1 day, chilled.

PER SERVING 467 CAL., 50% (233 CAL.) FROM FAT; 45 G PROTEIN; 26 G FAT (4.4 G SAT.); 15 G CARBO (3.3 G FIBER); 654 MG SODIUM; 109 MG CHOL. LC

PENNE ALL'AMATRICIANA

SERVES 4 ★ 30 MINUTES IN CAMP

Sunset reader Jane Ingraham of San Marcos, California, suggests using freshly grated parmesan and freshly ground pepper to take this simple but very satisfying dish to the next level.

8 oz. penne pasta
4 oz. pancetta or good-quality bacon, cubed
1 cup chopped onion
1 tbsp. minced garlic
1 large can (28 oz.) diced tomatoes
1 tsp. *each* kosher salt, pepper, and red chile flakes
¼ cup grated parmesan cheese

1. Cook pasta according to package directions on a camp stove; drain and set aside.

2. Meanwhile, cook pancetta in a large frying pan over medium-high heat until partly translucent. Spoon off most of drippings. Add onion and garlic; cook, stirring often, until browned, 5 minutes. Add remaining ingredients except parmesan and cook over high heat until juices have reduced by half, about 10 minutes. Add pasta, stir to coat, and transfer to plates. Sprinkle with parmesan.

PER SERVING 362 CAL., 23% (85 CAL.) FROM FAT; 14 G PROTEIN; 9.4 G FAT (3.3 G SAT.); 56 G CARBO (3.7 G FIBER); 856 MG SODIUM; 13 MG CHOL. LC

CAMP PIZZA WITH SAUSAGE AND FONTINA

SERVES 4 TO 6 ★ 45 MINUTES IN CAMP

Alan Rousseau, a guide with Seattle-based Mountain Madness mountaineering company, came up with this ingenious way to make pizza in a frying pan. Bring the olive oil in a small container such as a spice jar, and pack the other ingredients in sealed containers, grouped according to their use. You'll also need a large cutting board.

About 3 tbsp. olive oil, divided
1 baked 10- to 11-in. pizza crust, such as Boboli
2 onions, halved lengthwise, then thinly sliced
8 oz. bulk Italian sausage
¼ tsp. *each* salt and pepper
1 tbsp. fresh thyme leaves or 2 tsp. dried
About ½ cup store-bought or homemade pizza sauce

1½ cups (6 oz.) coarsely shredded fontina cheese
2 tbsp. grated parmesan cheese
1 tbsp. fresh oregano leaves

1. Heat a charcoal or wood-fired grill to medium (about 350°; you can hold your hand 5 in. above cooking grate only 7 seconds) or use a camp stove and medium heat. Warm a large heavy frying pan until hot, then oil all over inside of pan. Toast pizza crust (cheesy side down, if there is one), pressing down on edges, until it's crunchy and golden on bottom, 4 to 5 minutes. Transfer to a cutting board.

2. Stoke fire with 12 to 15 more briquets if using charcoal. Add 2 tbsp. oil to pan, then onions, sausage, salt and pepper, and thyme. Cook, stirring often, until onions are soft and medium golden brown, 8 to 12 minutes. Remove pan from heat. Scoop onion mixture into a bowl and wipe out pan.

3. Brush pan with remaining oil. Fit pizza crust into pan with toasted side up. Spoon on pizza sauce and two-thirds of onion mixture, followed by cheeses, remaining onion mixture, and oregano. Return pan to heat. Cook, covered with lid or foil, until cheese begins to melt (check underside to be sure it doesn't burn), 3 to 5 minutes.

4. Transfer pizza to cutting board. Tent with foil to melt cheese completely, then slice.

PER SERVING 482 CAL., 49% (237 CAL.) FROM FAT; 21 G PROTEIN; 26 G FAT (9.2 G SAT.); 40 G CARBO (2.7 G FIBER); 1,023 MG SODIUM; 62 MG CHOL. LC

CUSTOMIZE YOUR PIZZA

It's easy to adapt the Camp Pizza at left with any number of other toppings. Here are a few more of our favorites to try.

★ Pepperoni, sautéed green pepper, and onion

★ Caramelized onion with anchovies, Niçoise olives, and parmesan

Sautéed summer squash and mushrooms with mozzarella and dried basil

Barbecue sauce, rotisserie chicken, mozzarella, bacon, and red onion

CAMP PIZZA with SAUSAGE and FONTINA

TURKEY BLACK
BEAN CHILI

TURKEY BLACK BEAN CHILI

MAKES 3 QTS.; 8 SERVINGS ★ 1¼ HOURS AT HOME/IN CAMP

Kevin Nelson, executive chef at Terra Bistro at Vail Mountain Lodge in Colorado, refuels guests after skiing and other workouts with this flavorful lower-fat chili.

2 tbsp. safflower oil or olive oil
1 medium onion, chopped
1 yellow or orange bell pepper, chopped
1 large poblano chile, chopped
2 garlic cloves, minced
1 lb. ground turkey
2 cans (each 28 oz.) diced tomatoes
2 cans (each 15 oz.) black beans, preferably
    reduced-sodium, rinsed and drained
3 tbsp. tomato paste
3 tbsp. chili powder
2 tsp. ground cumin
1½ tsp. agave nectar, or 2 tsp. sugar
Juice of 1 lime
Kosher salt (optional)
Shredded cheddar cheese and chopped cilantro (optional)

AT HOME OR IN CAMP

1. Heat oil in a large pot over medium-high heat, on a camp stove if in camp. Sauté onion, bell pepper, chile, and garlic, stirring often, 5 to 6 minutes. Add turkey, increase heat to high, and cook, stirring often and breaking meat into chunks, until it's no longer pink, 4 to 5 minutes.

2. Stir in tomatoes, beans, tomato paste, chili powder, cumin, and agave. Cover and bring chili to a boil, stirring often. Reduce heat and simmer, stirring occasionally, until flavors are blended, 45 minutes to 1 hour. Stir in lime juice. If you like, add salt to taste and serve with cheese and cilantro.

Make ahead: Up to 3 days, chilled; reheat to serve.

PER 1½-CUP SERVING 251 CAL., 31% (79 CAL.) FROM FAT; 16 G PROTEIN; 8.8 G FAT (1.6 G SAT.); 27 G CARBO (6.4 G FIBER); 538 MG SODIUM; 45 MG CHOL. GF/LC

BUY-AND-SERVE *MEZE*

SERVES 8 TO 10 AS A MAIN DISH ★ 35 MINUTES AT HOME; 10 IN CAMP

When you make the quantities generous, the Mediterranean spread of appetizers called *meze* works beautifully as a full dinner, and it requires just a few minutes to set out, since you do the small amount of prep work at home. This is our go-to meal for the first night in camp, when everyone's busy with setup, but it's also perfect for nibbling over several hours on a more leisurely evening. Pack a big board or extra plates for serving.

4 Persian cucumbers or 2 English cucumbers
6 medium carrots
3 cups cherry tomatoes
1½ qts. tips of baby romaine lettuce leaves
1¼ lbs. feta cheese (preferably made from sheep's milk
    and brine-packed), in 3 or 4 chunks
½ cup extra-virgin olive oil
3 cups (1¼ lbs.) *tzatziki** (cucumber-yogurt dip),
    homemade (page 71) or storebought
3 cups (about 24 oz.) hummus
16 *dolmades* (stuffed grape leaves)*
12 pita breads (white or whole wheat; 24 oz. total)
3 cups (1 lb.) mixed Greek olives
2 tsp. *zaatar** (optional)

AT HOME

1. Cut cucumbers and carrots into sticks. Pack them, tomatoes, and romaine in containers with a lid.

2. Drain feta. Put in another container with a lid and drizzle oil on top. Chill containers and tzatziki, hummus, and dolmades.

3. Cut pitas into wedges and return to their plastic bags.

IN CAMP

4. Set out dishes of feta, tzatziki, hummus, dolmades, and olives on a board with vegetables and bread. Sprinkle feta and hummus with zaatar if you like.

*Find tzatziki at well-stocked grocery stores or make your own. Buy stuffed grape leaves in the deli or canned. Look for zaatar, a blend of thyme, sumac, and sesame seeds, with spices, or see Resource Guide (page 244) for online ordering.

Make ahead: Through step 2, up to 2 days, chilled.

PER SERVING 739 CAL., 54% (396 CAL.) FROM FAT; 23 G PROTEIN; 44 G FAT (14 G SAT.); 67 G CARBO (9.6 G FIBER); 2,351 MG SODIUM; 61 MG CHOL. V

DUTCH OVEN–BRAISED BEEF AND SUMMER VEGETABLES

SERVES 6 ★ 30 MINUTES AT HOME; ABOUT 2½ HOURS IN CAMP

After a day of hiking or swimming while camping, chef Adam Sappington of The Country Cat in Portland likes the simplicity of cooking a one-pot meal like this for his wife and their two young sons. He always brings along "Gramma" (a meat fork from his grandmother) for checking the beef's tenderness.

BEEF
6 garlic cloves, minced
2 tbsp. roughly chopped fresh rosemary leaves
2 tbsp. olive oil
About 1 tsp. kosher salt
About ½ tsp. pepper
1 boneless beef chuck roast (about 2 lbs.)

VEGETABLES
1 pt. cherry tomatoes
2 ears corn, shucked and cut into thirds
1 onion, cut into 6 wedges
½ lb. green beans, ends trimmed, cut in half
6 baby zucchini (½ lb. total), ends trimmed, or regular zucchini cut into chunks
¾ lb. thin-skinned potatoes (about 1 in. wide)

2 tbsp. butter
About 3 cups chicken broth, divided

AT HOME
1. Prepare beef: In a bowl, combine garlic, rosemary, oil, 1 tsp. salt, and ½ tsp. pepper. Rub all over beef and pack in a resealable plastic bag. Chill or freeze.

2. Prepare vegetables: Put tomatoes, corn, and onion in a resealable plastic bag and green beans and zucchini in another; chill. Don't chill potatoes.

IN CAMP
3. Prepare a fire (see "How to Cook in a Dutch Oven" on page 28) and arrange the coals for top and bottom heat cooking. Put a 4- or 6-qt. (10- or 12-in.) camp dutch oven in place, add butter, and melt. Add beef; cook until browned on underside, 10 minutes. Turn meat over, add 2 cups broth, cover, and arrange coals on top of pot. Add fuel now and every 30 minutes and cook 1 hour.

4. Turn meat over, add 1 cup broth, the tomatoes, onion, and potatoes; cook, covered, 1 hour. Turn meat and corn; add beans and zucchini, and more broth if pot is getting dry. Cook, covered, until meat is very tender, 15 to 30 minutes. Season with more salt and pepper to taste.

Make ahead: Through step 2, chilled (except for potatoes), for 2 days or frozen for 1 month; if frozen, thaw in your cooler.

PER SERVING 442 CAL., 42% (187 CAL.) FROM FAT; 38 G PROTEIN; 21 G FAT (6.9 G SAT.); 26 G CARBO (5.7 G FIBER); 582 MG SODIUM; 102 MG CHOL. GF/LC

SAUSAGE AND BEAN DUTCH OVEN STEW

SERVES 6 ★ 1 HOUR IN CAMP

Quick to throw together, this hearty dish uses cooked sausages. If you want to make it with uncooked sausages, cook them separately for a few minutes before adding the other ingredients.

1 can (15.5 oz.) cannellini beans, drained and rinsed
1 can (15.5 oz.) chickpeas (garbanzos), drained and rinsed
⅓ cup olive oil
1 tbsp. chopped fresh rosemary leaves
½ *each* red and yellow bell peppers, sliced
1 poblano chile, sliced
4 medium garlic cloves, chopped
1½ lbs. cooked Italian sausages, such as Saag's or Aidells, cut into 1-in. chunks
¼ cup fresh oregano leaves

1. Prepare a fire (see "How to Cook in a Dutch Oven" on page 28). Combine ingredients except for oregano with ¾ cup water in a 4- or 6-qt. (10- or 12-in.) camp dutch oven. Cover.

2. Arrange the coals for bottom heat cooking and cook, checking pot and stirring every 10 to 15 minutes, and adding more water if stew gets dry, until peppers soften and sausages swell, 30 to 45 minutes. Serve with oregano sprinkled on top.

PER SERVING 490 CAL., 44% (215 CAL.) FROM FAT; 32 G PROTEIN; 24 G FAT (4.5 G SAT.); 37 G CARBO (12 G FIBER); 804 MG SODIUM; 87 MG CHOL. GF/LC

DUTCH OVEN–BRAISED BEEF
and SUMMER VEGETABLES

YUCATECAN PORK

YUCATECAN PORK (COCHINITA PIBIL)

SERVES 12 ★ 40 MINUTES, PLUS 12 HOURS TO MARINATE,
AT HOME; 3½ HOURS IN CAMP

If you're looking for a special, splashy meal to serve a crowd, look no further than this succulent Mexican pork roast, bright with citrus. We adapted for the dutch oven a recipe from Rick Bayless's *Mexico: One Plate at a Time* (Scribner, 2000).

MARINADE AND MEAT

7 oz. (⅔ cup) red achiote paste*
2 tsp. dried Mexican oregano, crumbled
1½ tsp. pepper
1 tsp. *each* ground cumin and cinnamon
¼ tsp. ground cloves
2 tbsp. chopped garlic
½ cup lime juice
¼ cup orange juice
6 lbs. boned pork shoulder (butt), with some fat

PICKLED ONION

1 large red onion, cut into thin rings
⅔ cup lime juice
⅓ cup orange juice
¼ tsp. kosher salt

COOKING AND SERVING

4 frozen banana leaves* (each about 2½ ft. long), thawed
2 dozen corn tortillas (6 in.)
3 cups (5 oz.) cabbage cut into fine shreds
Sprigs from 1 bunch cilantro
Habanero hot sauce
4 limes, cut into wedges
Salt

AT HOME

1. Make marinade: Combine all ingredients except pork in a large bowl. Remove any ties from meat. With a sharp knife, slash crosshatching into meat on both sides, making parallel cuts about 1 in. deep and 2 in. apart. Put meat in bowl with marinade and rub all over, working marinade into the slashes. Transfer meat and any remaining marinade to a 1-gal. resealable plastic bag; press closed. Seal within a second bag. Chill at least 12 hours, turning occasionally.

2. Prepare onion: Combine ingredients in a small container with a lid. Chill at least 4 hours.

IN CAMP

3. Prepare a fire (see "How to Cook in a Dutch Oven" on page 28). Meanwhile, bring bag of meat to room temperature. Lay 2 banana leaves parallel to each other in a 6-qt.(12-in.) camp dutch oven, letting them hang over the sides, and lay the other 2 leaves across them. Set pork in leaves and pour any marinade on top. Fold leaves over meat. Pour 1 cup water into pot and cover with lid.

4. Arrange the coals for top and bottom cooking (see page 29). Add fuel now and every 30 minutes (liquid in pot should be simmering), adding water if needed so there's about ½ in. liquid in pot, until meat is very tender when pierced, 2½ to 3 hours total. During last half-hour, divide tortillas in half, wrap in foil, and warm on top of dutch oven, turning occasionally.

5. Open dutch oven and fold back banana leaves. Tip pot and scoop out juices into a bowl. Skim and discard fat; return juices to pot. Cut meat into chunks. Serve pork with tortillas, pickled onion, cabbage, and cilantro. Set out hot sauce, limes, and salt to add to taste.

*Find achiote paste with Latino foods, and frozen banana leaves in the freezer aisle at well-stocked grocery stores.

Make ahead: Meat and marinade, up to 2 days, chilled airtight. Onion, up to 1 day, chilled.

PER SERVING 583 CAL., 40% (234 CAL.) FROM FAT; 46 G PROTEIN; 26 G FAT (7.7 G SAT.); 41 G CARBO (3.7 G FIBER); 342 MG SODIUM; 159 MG CHOL. LS

> **TIP** CREATE DELICIOUS SANDWICHES WITH LEFTOVER YUCATECAN PORK: PILE SANDWICH ROLLS WITH PICKLED ONIONS, SHREDDED CABBAGE, GUACAMOLE, AND WARMED CHUNKS OF THE PORK.

GAUCHO STEAK WITH FOUR-HERB CHIMICHURRI

SERVES 6 ★ 30 MINUTES, PLUS 1 HOUR TO MARINATE, AT HOME/IN CAMP

The sharp, slightly herby marinade in this dish—from restaurateur and television personality Guy Fieri—tenderizes and flavors the meat and makes a great bridge to the chimichurri. If you want to cook the steak on the second day of your trip, freeze it in the marinade at home and let it defrost in the cooler.

1 garlic clove, minced
¼ cup cilantro leaves
2 tbsp. olive oil
3 tbsp. tequila
1 tbsp. *each* lemon and lime juice
½ tsp. salt
1 tsp. pepper
1½ lbs. skirt steak
Four-Herb Chimichurri (recipe follows)

AT HOME OR IN CAMP
1. Whirl garlic, cilantro, oil, tequila, lemon and lime juices, salt, and pepper in a blender or food processor. Transfer to a large resealable plastic bag. When ready to marinate steak (at least 1 hour before cooking), add steak to bag, shake to coat with marinade, reseal, and chill. Make chimichurri and chill.

IN CAMP
2. Heat a charcoal or wood-fired grill to high (450° to 550°; you can hold your hand 5 in. above cooking grate only 2 to 4 seconds). Grill steak, turning once, about 8 minutes total for medium-rare. Let sit 10 minutes, then cut across the grain into ½-in.-thick slices. Serve with chimichurri.

Make ahead: Through step 1, up to 24 hours, chilled.

PER SERVING (STEAK ONLY) 171 CAL., 53% (90 CAL.) FROM FAT; 18 G PROTEIN; 10 G FAT (3.5 G SAT.); 0.4 G CARBO (0.1 G FIBER); 147 MG SODIUM; 41 MG CHOL. GF/LC/LS

FOUR-HERB CHIMICHURRI

MAKES ABOUT ½ CUP ★ 15 MINUTES AT HOME

Guy Fieri likes a super-spicy chimichurri; if you'd like yours milder, go for the lower amount of chile powder.

4 chopped garlic cloves
½ cup cilantro leaves
½ cup flat-leaf parsley leaves
6 large fresh basil leaves
1 tbsp. fresh oregano leaves
2 tbsp. minced white onion
2 tbsp. minced red bell pepper
1 tsp. salt
2 tsp. pepper
½ tsp. ground cumin
1½ tsp. to 1 tbsp. ancho chile powder
2 tbsp. olive oil
2 tbsp. red wine vinegar

AT HOME
In a food processor, pulse all ingredients except for oil and vinegar until coarsely chopped. Pour in oil and vinegar and whirl to combine.

Make ahead: Up to 1 day, chilled.

PER 1½ TBSP. 53 CAL., 79% (42 CAL.) FROM FAT; 0.5 G PROTEIN; 4.7 G FAT (0.6 G SAT.); 2.7 G CARBO (0.9 G FIBER); 398 MG SODIUM; 0 MG CHOL. GF/LC/LS/VG

 TIP **TRY A SPOONFUL OF CHIMICHURRI OVER GRILLED CHICKEN OR FISH, EMBER-ROASTED POTATOES, GRILLED BREAD, OR SAUSAGE SANDWICHES.**

CHILI LIME CORN on the COB
(see recipe on page 75)

JICAMA SLAW
(see recipe on page 72)

GAUCHO STEAK
with FOUR-HERB
CHIMICHURRI

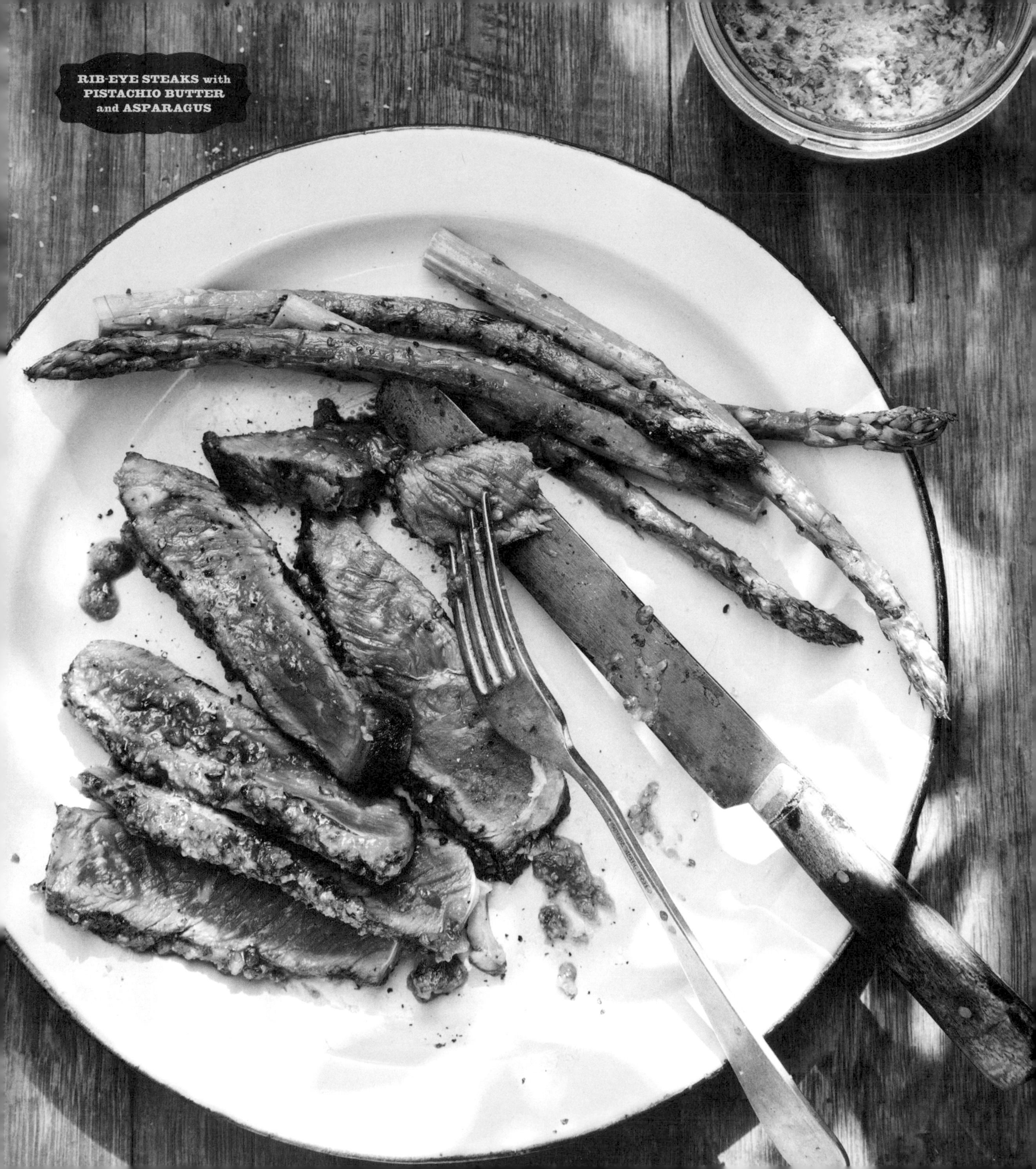

RIB-EYE STEAKS with PISTACHIO BUTTER and ASPARAGUS

RIB-EYE STEAKS WITH PISTACHIO BUTTER AND ASPARAGUS

SERVES 4 ★ 10 MINUTES AT HOME; 30 IN CAMP

Flavorful and generously marbled, rib-eye makes a great splurge for a special meal, particularly when topped with a distinctively flavored butter. If you can't find unsalted pistachios, use unsalted butter to balance the salty nuts. The amount of pistachio butter is generous; if you like, turn the asparagus in some right after it comes off the grill and top the steaks with the rest.

¼ cup shelled, roasted unsalted pistachios
1 cup arugula
¼ cup butter, softened
2 boneless rib-eye steaks (each about 12 oz.)
1 lb. asparagus, trimmed
2 tbsp. olive oil
1½ tsp. *each* kosher salt and pepper

AT HOME
1. Whirl pistachios and arugula in a food processor until minced. Add butter and whirl until smooth, scraping down inside of bowl as needed. Transfer to a small container and chill.

IN CAMP
2. Heat a charcoal or wood-fired grill to high (450° to 550°; you can hold your hand 5 in. above cooking grate only 2 to 4 seconds). Coat steaks and asparagus with oil and season with salt and pepper. Grill steaks, turning once, until done the way you like, 6 to 15 minutes for medium-rare. Grill asparagus in last few minutes, turning once, until tender-crisp.

3. Transfer everything to a cutting board, dollop steaks with butter, and tent with foil. Let rest 5 minutes. Slice steaks and serve with asparagus.

Make ahead: Pistachio butter, up to 1 week, chilled.

PER SERVING 506 CAL., 66% (334 CAL.) FROM FAT; 38 G PROTEIN; 37 G FAT (16 G SAT.); 5.2 G CARBO (2.3 G FIBER); 727 MG SODIUM; 172 MG CHOL. GF

SOY AND GINGER FLANK STEAK

SERVES 6 ★ 20 MINUTES, PLUS 24 HOURS TO FREEZE, AT HOME; 35 MINUTES IN CAMP

Freezing this steak right in the marinade has two advantages: The salty-sweet teriyaki-style ingredients flavor the meat, and the frozen bag helps chill other foods in your cooler. For a small group, you can put 1 steak in each of 2 smaller bags with half the marinade. *Sunset* reader Stephanie Stephens of San Leandro, California, shared the recipe.

2 flank steaks (each 1¼ lbs.), fat trimmed
2 tbsp. *each* minced fresh ginger and garlic
¼ cup *each* reduced-sodium soy sauce and regular
    soy sauce
½ cup dry red wine
¼ cup honey
2 tbsp. vegetable oil

AT HOME
1. Put steaks in a 1-gal. resealable plastic bag. Add remaining ingredients. Seal bag, turn to coat meat, and freeze (at least 24 hours).

IN CAMP
2. Let steak thaw in cooler (takes 1 to 2 days). Heat a charcoal or wood-fired grill to high (450° to 550°; you can hold your hand 5 in. above cooking grate only 2 to 4 seconds). Lift steaks from bags and lay meat on grill. Cook, turning once, until done the way you like it, 6 to 15 minutes for medium-rare.

3. Transfer steak to a cutting board and cut crosswise into thin slices.

Make ahead: Through step 1, up to 3 months, frozen; thaw in your cooler.

PER SERVING 242 CAL., 36% (88 CAL.) FROM FAT; 29 G PROTEIN; 9.9 G FAT (3.4 G SAT.); 7.8 G CARBO (0.2 G FIBER); 557 MG SODIUM; 50 MG CHOL. LC

TUNA, GREEN OLIVE, AND EGG SALAD ON TOAST

SERVES 4 ★ 30 MINUTES AT HOME/IN CAMP

The lunch standby gets a gourmet, supper-worthy makeover with a little smoky paprika, briny olives, and fresh vinaigrette instead of the expected mayo. It's part salad, part sandwich, and wholly delicious.

4 large eggs
¼ cup extra-virgin olive oil
1 tsp. lemon juice
½ tsp. *each* kosher salt, pepper, and smoked paprika
½ cup sliced green olives
1 can (5 oz.) tuna*, drained
About ¼ cup thinly slivered white onion
½ cup flat-leaf parsley leaves
1 ripe tomato, cut into 8 thin slices
4 kaiser rolls, split

AT HOME OR IN CAMP

1. Put eggs in a small saucepan. Cover with hot water and bring to a boil. Remove from heat, cover, and let sit 12 minutes. Drain and rinse eggs with cold water until they're cool.

IN CAMP

2. Peel and quarter eggs. In a bowl, whisk together oil, lemon juice, salt, pepper, and paprika. Add olives, tuna, onion, and parsley, and stir just to combine, leaving tuna in large chunks. Gently stir in eggs.

3. Arrange 2 tomato pieces on bottom of each roll. Add tuna mixture, dividing evenly, and tops of rolls.

*For the most sustainable choice, look for pole- or troll-caught tuna.

Make ahead: Through step 1, up to 3 days, chilled in an airtight container.

PER SANDWICH 444 CAL., 50% (223 CAL.) FROM FAT; 21 G PROTEIN; 25 G FAT (4.7 G SAT.); 34 G CARBO (2.6 G FIBER); 848 MG SODIUM; 227 MG CHOL. LC

TROUT WITH BROWN BUTTER AND CAPERS

SERVES 2 ★ 20 MINUTES IN CAMP

If you're lucky enough to catch your own trout, you want to be ready to show off its flavors simply, without too much fuss. Nutty browned butter and bright capers fit the bill, and the ingredients for the recipe are ones you can keep on hand.

2 tbsp. *each* flour and cornmeal
About ½ tsp. salt
About ¼ tsp. pepper
1 whole trout (8 to 10 oz.), cleaned and boned*
¼ cup butter
1 tbsp. drained capers
Lemon wedges and flat-leaf parsley sprigs

1. Combine flour, cornmeal, ½ tsp. salt, and ¼ tsp. pepper in a large, shallow dish. Rinse trout and pat dry, then set fish in flour mixture and turn to coat.

2. Bring butter to a simmer in a small pan over medium heat on a camp stove; remove from heat. Skim off and discard foam with a spoon.

3. Pour 1 tbsp. of butter into a large cast-iron skillet over high heat; set aside remaining butter. Place trout, skin side down, in skillet and cook until browned on the bottom, 2 to 3 minutes. Turn with a wide spatula, reduce heat to medium, and cook until fish is barely opaque but still moist-looking in center of thickest part (cut to test), 2 to 4 minutes more.

4. Meanwhile, add capers to remaining butter in pan and shake pan often over medium heat until capers pop open, 1 to 2 minutes.

5. Transfer trout, skin down, to a plate. Spoon caper butter over fish and garnish with lemon wedges and parsley. Add salt and pepper to taste.

*See "Hook and Cook" on page 69.

PER SERVING 363 CAL., 65% (235 CAL.) FROM FAT; 17 G PROTEIN; 27 G FAT (16 G SAT.); 14 G CARBO (0.8 G FIBER); 925 MG SODIUM; 135 MG CHOL. LC

HOOK AND COOK

From the lake to the frying pan, here's how to catch and clean a trout.

GET A LICENSE. Before you leave home, check online with your state's fish and game department for details.

BUY THE GEAR. Swing by a tackle shop for a pole and bait. Ask about any fishing restrictions for the area you're going to.

DISPATCH THE FISH. You caught one! Now apply a quick, sharp blow to the top of its head with a hatchet handle or heavy stick to kill it instantly (the most humane way, according to the Washington Department of Fish and Wildlife).

CLEAN IT. Make a shallow slit down the length of the belly. Pull out the guts with your fingers, then rinse well. Scale it by scraping from tail to head with a table knife. Rinse again. If the fish is too big for your pan, cut off the head and tail.

COOK IT. See Trout with Brown Butter and Capers on page 66.

NEGRONIS
(see recipe on
page 82)

ZUCCHINI and HARISSA
BRUSCHETTA

ZUCCHINI AND *HARISSA* BRUSCHETTA

MAKES 10; SERVES 5 ★ 30 MINUTES IN CAMP

The chile-and-spice paste *harissa* gives these simple but exciting appetizers their kick. For a bigger group, feel free to increase quantities, set out toppings and toasts, and let campers build their own.

1 medium zucchini
3 tbsp. crumbled feta cheese
2 tbsp. extra-virgin olive oil
Salt and pepper
About 2 tbsp. *harissa**
10 baguette slices, brushed with olive oil and grilled

1. Heat a charcoal or wood-fired grill to high (450° to 550°; you can hold your hand 5 in. above cooking grate only 2 to 4 seconds). Slice zucchini lengthwise and grill, turning once, until grill marks appear, about 4 minutes. Let cool, then chop. In a bowl, combine zucchini with feta and oil. Season to taste with salt and pepper.

2. Spread about ½ tsp. harissa on each baguette toast and top each with about 1 tbsp. zucchini mixture.

*Find harissa in the international foods aisle.

PER 2-TOAST SERVING 162 CAL., 36% (59 CAL.) FROM FAT; 4.9 G PROTEIN; 6.9 G FAT (1.6 G SAT.); 20 G CARBO (1 G FIBER); 276 MG SODIUM; 5 MG CHOL. LS/V

TZATZIKI

MAKES 2⅔ CUPS ★ 50 MINUTES AT HOME

Try this creamy, garlicky Greek dip with vegetables and pita bread, or with the *meze* on page 57.

2½ cups (20 oz.) whole-milk Greek yogurt
4 or 5 Persian cucumbers
3 garlic cloves, minced
About 1 tsp. kosher salt

Line a fine strainer with cheesecloth, set over a bowl, and drain yogurt until thick and creamy, about 30 minutes. Shred cucumbers and squeeze very dry; you should have 2 cups. Combine all the ingredients with salt to taste.

Make ahead: Up to 3 days, chilled.

PER ¼-CUP SERVING 97 CAL., 55% (53 CAL.) FROM FAT; 4.7 G PROTEIN; 5.9 G FAT (4.6 G SAT.); 7 G CARBO (0.7 G FIBER); 171 MG SODIUM; 10 MG CHOL. GF/LC/LS/V

DATES WITH BACON

MAKES 18 PIECES; SERVES 6 TO 8 ★ 25 MINUTES IN CAMP

The combination of warm, caramel-sweet Medjool dates and crisp, salty bacon is irresistible.

6 slices thin-cut bacon
18 pitted Medjool dates

1. Cut bacon crosswise into about 4-in. lengths. Wrap a length snugly around each date, overlapping ends.

2. Set dates, seam sides down, in a large cast-iron skillet over medium heat on a camp stove (you may have to fry dates in batches). Turn dates occasionally until bacon is browned and crisp on all sides, 6 to 8 minutes total. Transfer dates to paper towels to drain; blot dry. Serve warm or cool.

Make ahead: Up to 2 hours, at room temperature.

PER PIECE 122 CAL., 7% (8.5 CAL.) FROM FAT; 1.5 G PROTEIN; 0.9 G FAT (0.3 G SAT.); 30 G CARBO (2.7 G FIBER); 49 MG SODIUM; 2.3 MG CHOL. GF/LS

SMOKY CLAM DIP

MAKES 2 CUPS; SERVES 10 ★ 10 MINUTES AT HOME/IN CAMP

With the addition of good paprika, classic clam dip just gets better. You can make the dip at home and pack it in your cooler, or whip it up in camp.

1 pkg. (8 oz.) cream cheese, at room temperature
⅓ cup sour cream
1 garlic clove, minced
1 green onion, minced
1 tbsp. minced flat-leaf parsley
1 tsp. sweet smoked Spanish paprika
1 to 1½ cans (each 6.5 oz.) minced clams, drained
    and liquid reserved
Potato chips

AT HOME OR IN CAMP

Whisk together cream cheese, sour cream, garlic, onion, parsley, and paprika in a medium bowl. Add clams to taste and enough clam liquid for a good dipping texture. Serve with potato chips.

Make ahead: Dip, up to 3 days, chilled airtight.

PER SERVING 118 CAL., 71% (84 CAL.) FROM FAT; 6.2 G PROTEIN; 9.4 G FAT (5.1 G SAT.); 2.3 G CARBO (0.1 G FIBER); 99 MG SODIUM; 41 MG CHOL. LC/LS

1. Put cut vegetables in a large resealable plastic bag and chill.

2. Combine oil, vinegar, lime juice, 1 tbsp. cilantro, salt, pepper, sugar, chili powder, and chile flakes in a small sealed container. Chill dressing.

IN CAMP

3. Toss vegetables with dressing in a bowl and let sit 15 minutes, stirring 2 or 3 times. Garnish with more cilantro, if you like.

Make ahead: Cut vegetables and dressing, stored separately and chilled, up to 2 days.

PER SERVING 142 CAL., 63% (90 CAL.) FROM FAT; 1.3 G PROTEIN; 10 G FAT (1.4 G SAT.); 12 G CARBO (4.8 G FIBER); 306 MG SODIUM; 0 MG CHOL. GF/LC/VG

SPINACH AND ORZO SALAD

SERVES 4 ★ 20 MINUTES IN CAMP

Tossed with a homemade herb dressing and several colorful add-ons, this recipe is a step above other pasta salads.

1 cup orzo pasta
3 tbsp. *each* extra-virgin olive oil and red wine vinegar
½ tsp. *each* dried oregano and basil
About ½ tsp. kosher salt
¼ tsp. pepper
1 qt. lightly packed baby spinach leaves, roughly chopped
¼ cup slivered dried tomatoes packed in oil
12 pitted kalamata olives, sliced

1. Cook orzo according to package directions on a camp stove. Meanwhile, in a large bowl, whisk together oil, vinegar, oregano, basil, ½ tsp. salt, and the pepper and reserve.

2. Drain pasta, rinse with water until cool, and drain again. Add to bowl with dressing and gently mix in spinach, tomatoes, and olives to combine. Add more salt if you like.

Make ahead: Up to 2 hours, at room temperature.

PER 1-CUP SERVING 315 CAL., 44% (140 CAL.) FROM FAT; 6.9 G PROTEIN; 16 G FAT (1.7 G SAT.); 39 G CARBO (4.4 G FIBER); 550 MG SODIUM; 0 MG CHOL. VG

JICAMA SLAW

SERVES 6 TO 8 ★ 40 MINUTES AT HOME; 20 IN CAMP

This crisp, exciting slaw from TV personality Guy Fieri has a dressing with loads of flavor from black pepper, chile flakes, and cilantro. Cut the vegetables at home, make the dressing, then toss everything together when you're ready to eat. Use a handheld slicer (like a mandoline or a Benriner) to make cutting the vegetables easier.

2 carrots, peeled and julienned
1 small jicama (about 1¼ lbs.), peeled and julienned
1 large red bell pepper, cored and very thinly sliced
¼ head red cabbage, cored and very thinly sliced
½ red onion, halved lengthwise and very thinly sliced
  lengthwise, rinsed, and patted dry
6 tbsp. *each* extra-virgin olive oil and unseasoned
  rice vinegar
3 tbsp. lime juice
About 1 tbsp. minced cilantro
1 tsp. *each* salt, pepper, and sugar
½ tsp. *each* chili powder and red chile flakes

SPINACH and
ORZO SALAD

FIRE-ROASTED
VEGETABLE SALAD

FIRE-ROASTED VEGETABLE SALAD

MAKES 10 CUPS; SERVES 6 ★ 2 HOURS IN CAMP

Russell Moore of Camino restaurant in Oakland, California, cooks the onions and peppers for this dish right in the fire, infusing the salad with smokiness. It's great with fried eggs or any type of grilled meat or fish. Moore brings his own portable grill grate (see photo on page 15 and Resource Guide) for cooking the other vegetables, but you could also use your campsite's firepit grill. He cooks in and over wood; you can also cook all the vegetables over a medium (350° to 450°) charcoal fire, adding 8 briquets every 30 minutes.

1 garlic clove
2 tbsp. high-quality red wine vinegar
4 medium zucchini, sliced lengthwise ½ in. thick
3 ears corn, shucked
2 ripe tomatoes, cored
½ cup extra-virgin olive oil, divided
About ¾ tsp. kosher salt, divided
About ½ tsp. pepper, divided
2 whole onions, unpeeled
2 *each* red and yellow bell peppers
1 cup lightly packed fresh mint leaves, torn into pieces

1. Build a wood fire in a fire ring (see "How to Build a Campfire for Cooking," page 18), using about 4 logs and some kindling, but instead of letting fire burn to ashy chunks, let burn to medium (350°; you can hold your hand 5 in. above cooking grate only 5 to 7 seconds), about 1 hour. Adjust fire so there's a thick area of embers and smaller logs in the middle and larger logs to the sides.

2. Smash garlic, put in a small bowl with vinegar, and set aside. In a large bowl, combine zucchini, corn, and tomatoes with 2 tbsp. oil, ½ tsp. salt, and ¼ tsp. pepper.

3. Place onions in embers between some smaller logs and cook, turning every 10 minutes or so, until completely black and soft when squeezed with tongs, 25 to 40 minutes. Meanwhile, set peppers on embers and cook, turning every few minutes, until well charred, 20 minutes. Transfer vegetables to a cutting board and let cool.

4. Set cooking grate in place, if using a portable one. Grill zucchini, corn, and tomatoes (in batches, if needed), turning occasionally, until grill marks appear, 5 to 35 minutes, depending on distance from fire.

5. Pull off blackened skins from onions and peppers. Cut corn kernels from cobs into large bowl. Cut remaining vegetables into strips, discarding seeds; add to bowl.

6. Stir remaining 6 tbsp. oil into vinegar with remaining ¼ tsp. *each* salt and pepper. Toss gently with vegetables; add mint and more salt and pepper if you like.

PER 1½-CUP SERVING 269 CAL., 64% (171 CAL.) FROM FAT; 4.5 G PROTEIN; 20 G FAT (2.9 G SAT.); 23 G CARBO (5.2 G FIBER); 212 MG SODIUM; 0 MG CHOL. GF/LS/VG

CHILI LIME CORN ON THE COB

SERVES 6 ★ 35 MINUTES AT HOME/IN CAMP

Cooking corn on the cob in its de-silked husk keeps the kernels moist and adds a nice grassy flavor (see photo on page 63). You can also fully husk the corn and wrap it in foil. This recipe is from restaurateur and television personality Guy Fieri.

¼ cup butter, softened
1 tsp. *each* lime zest and chili powder
About ½ tsp. salt
½ tsp. pepper
¼ tsp. granulated garlic
6 ears corn in husks

AT HOME OR IN CAMP

1. Combine butter, lime zest, chili powder, ½ tsp. salt, the pepper, and garlic in a small resealable plastic bag. Mush around to combine thoroughly. If making at home, chill until ready to use, then bring to room temperature.

2. Pull back husk from each ear of corn without detaching from bottom of cob. Remove as much silk as possible. Spread evenly with butter mixture. Fold husks back over ears and tie in place with kitchen string or strips torn from outer husks.

IN CAMP

3. Heat a charcoal or wood-fired grill to medium (about 350°; you can hold your hand 5 in. above cooking grate only 7 seconds). Grill corn until tender and charred, turning often, 10 to 15 minutes. Serve with salt for sprinkling.

Make ahead: Through step 2, up to 24 hours, chilled.

PER SERVING 112 CAL., 39% (44 CAL.) FROM FAT; 3 G PROTEIN; 4.9 G FAT (2.5 G SAT.); 17 G CARBO (2.5 G FIBER); 150 MG SODIUM; 10 MG CHOL. GF/LC/LS/V

CAMP CORNBREAD

SERVES 9 ★ 50 MINUTES IN CAMP

Warm, buttery cornbread is practically a necessity with a batch of chili or stew, and this dutch oven recipe lets you enjoy it freshly baked. Medium-grind cornmeal gives the bread a rustic texture; if you prefer, you can use a finer grind.

1 cup flour
1 cup yellow cornmeal (preferably stone-ground medium coarse*)
¼ cup sugar
2½ tsp. baking powder
¾ tsp. salt
2 large eggs
1 cup buttermilk (or use dried buttermilk* mixed with water according to package directions)
About ¼ cup (⅛ lb.) butter, melted and cooled

1. Prepare a fire (see "How to Cook in a Dutch Oven" on page 28) and arrange the coals for baking.

2. Combine flour, cornmeal, sugar, baking powder, and salt in a bowl. In another bowl, beat eggs to blend with buttermilk and ¼ cup butter. Pour liquids into flour mixture and stir just until evenly moistened.

3. Scrape batter into a buttered 4-qt. (10-in.) camp dutch oven and spread smooth. Cover with lid and coals as directed on page 29.

4. Bake cornbread until it's golden and pulls from sides of pot, about 25 minutes. Loosen bread with a knife and cut into wedges.

*Find stone-ground cornmeal, such as Bob's Red Mill, and dried buttermilk in the baking aisle.

PER SERVING 204 CAL., 35% (71 CAL.) FROM FAT; 4.9 G PROTEIN; 8 G FAT (4.3 G SAT.); 28 G CARBO (1.3 G FIBER); 414 MG SODIUM; 64 MG CHOL. LC/V

MARK KLEVER'S DUTCH OVEN BISCUITS

MAKES 15 ★ 1 HOUR IN CAMP

Mark Klever, the general manager at Belcampo Farms near Mt. Shasta, California, learned to make these biscuits from his grandmother. He renders his own lard from Belcampo's free-range pigs, and bakes up a batch for his family nearly every week, just like his grandmother used to do. You'll need to pack a 2½-in. biscuit cutter; or use a small glass and cut around it with a knife. For more on Belcampo, see "Grill Like a Gaucho," page 204.

4 cups flour
2 tbsp. baking powder
2 tsp. salt
About ¾ cup cold lard or unsalted butter
1½ cups milk or buttermilk
Butter and honey (optional)

1. Prepare a fire (see "How to Cook in a Dutch Oven" on page 28) and arrange the coals for baking.

2. Mix dry ingredients together in a large bowl. Cut in ¾ cup lard with a pastry blender or 2 knives until lard is in pea- to walnut-size pieces. Stir in milk until dough looks shaggy. Transfer to a floured work surface and knead just slightly until it comes together. Pat dough out ¾ in. thick.

3. Cut biscuits using a 2½-in. round cutter, patting out scraps until all the dough is used.

4. Arrange biscuits in a greased 4- or 6-qt. (10- or 12-in.) camp dutch oven so they're touching but not scrunched. Cover with lid and coals as directed on page 29.

5. Cook biscuits until they're browned and puffed, 10 to 12 minutes.

6. Remove pot from fire and uncover. Serve biscuits with butter and honey, if you like.

PER BISCUIT 232 CAL., 45% (105 CAL.) FROM FAT; 4.2 G PROTEIN; 12 G FAT (4.6 G SAT.); 27 G CARBO (0.9 G FIBER); 516 MG SODIUM; 12 MG CHOL. LC

MARK KLEVER'S
DUTCH OVEN BISCUITS

COCONUT and PINEAPPLE
UPSIDE-DOWN CAKE

COCONUT AND PINEAPPLE UPSIDE-DOWN CAKE

SERVES 8 ★ 1¼ HOURS IN CAMP

No maraschino cherries here. Made with two kinds of coconut as well as fresh fruit, this dutch oven dessert tastes decadent without being overly sweet. It cooks more evenly if you use charcoal rather than wood for fuel.

CAKE
1⅓ cups flour
¼ cup sugar
1¼ tsp. baking powder
¼ tsp. salt
½ cup sweetened flaked coconut
⅓ cup vegetable oil
½ cup cream of coconut*
2 large eggs

TOPPING
⅓ cup butter
¼ cup sugar
2 cups fresh pineapple chunks (½ in.)

1. Make cake batter: Whisk together dry ingredients in a medium bowl. Then whisk in remaining ingredients until blended.

2. Prepare a fire (see "How to Cook in a Dutch Oven" on page 28) and arrange the coals for baking. Line a 4-qt. (10-in.) camp dutch oven with foil so it comes up the sides to the top.

3. Make topping. Melt butter in dutch oven, rotating to coat sides. Sprinkle sugar on bottom of pot, then scatter pineapple on top. Gently spread batter over pineapple. Cover with lid and coals as directed on page 29.

4. Cook cake until a toothpick inserted in several places comes out with no white dough sticking to it, and underside of cake is well browned (lift foil and check with a spatula), about 35 minutes. Let cool 10 minutes. Lift cake from pot using foil. Invert onto a plate and gently peel off foil, replacing any pineapple that sticks to it.

*Find cream of coconut with cocktail supplies at well-stocked grocery stores.

Make ahead: Whisk together dry ingredients for batter and store up to 1 week, airtight.

PER SERVING 401 CAL., 51% (204 CAL.) FROM FAT; 4.4 G PROTEIN; 23 G FAT (11 G SAT.); 47 G CARBO (1.7 G FIBER); 231 MG SODIUM; 66 MG CHOL. LS/V

CAMP-STOVE MOLTEN BROWNIES

SERVES 8 ★ 5 MINUTES AT HOME; 2 HOURS IN CAMP

Few desserts rival warm brownies, and with this steaming technique, you can pull them off in camp. You'll need a large pot, vegetable steamer, 8-in. cake pan, foil, and a few wooden skewers.

¾ cup flour
⅓ cup unsweetened cocoa powder, sifted
½ tsp. *each* baking powder and kosher salt
About ¾ cup unsalted butter, chopped
8 oz. bittersweet chocolate, finely chopped, divided
¾ cup sugar
1½ tsp. vanilla extract
2 large eggs
½ cup chopped toasted pecans

AT HOME
1. Mix flour, cocoa, baking powder, and salt; seal in a bag.

IN CAMP
2. Set an 8-in. round cake pan over low heat on a camp stove. Melt ¾ cup butter and 1 cup chocolate in pan, stirring, 3 to 5 minutes. Remove from heat and set aside. Set a vegetable steamer inside a 6- to 8-qt. pot. Add water until level with steamer, cover, and bring to a boil.

3. Whisk together sugar, vanilla, and eggs. Blend in chocolate mixture, then fold in flour mixture. Mix in remaining chocolate and pecans. Spread batter level in (unwashed) cake pan. Butter a sheet of heavy-duty foil a bit larger than pan, set buttered side over pan, and crimp tightly.

4. Cut a 3-ft. piece of foil in half lengthwise. Fold each piece to make a long, flat 2-in.-wide strip. Crisscross on a work surface and set cake pan in center. Draw strips together and lower cake pan onto steamer.

5. Cover pan and return water to a boil. Reduce heat to medium to maintain a steady boil; you should see constant steam coming from pot. Meanwhile, heat a saucepan of water to simmering. Cook brownies, covered, lifting them and replenishing water every 30 minutes flush with steamer, 1¼ hours total for a molten center (a skewer inserted has large moist crumbs adhering) or 1½ hours for a firmer center (smaller moist crumbs).

6. Let cool 15 minutes, then spoon brownies from pan.

PER SERVING 495 CAL., 66% (326 CAL.) FROM FAT; 6.3 G PROTEIN; 37 G FAT (18 G SAT.); 45 G CARBO (3.7 G FIBER); 146 MG SODIUM; 100 MG CHOL. LS/V

1. Fold 12 sheets of foil (each 12 by 20 in.) in half cross-wise; then oil tops. Center 1 graham cracker on each oiled doubled sheet, then top with a chocolate piece, marshmallow, and another cracker. Gently fold foil over s'mores and crimp to seal.

IN CAMP

2. Heat packets on a cooking grate over glowing coals in a campfire or on a charcoal grill over medium heat (about 350°; you can hold your hand 5 in. above cooking grate about 7 seconds), turning often just until chocolate softens, 2 to 3 minutes. Or, using tongs, grasp packets on sides and heat over a low fire.

Make ahead: Through step 1, up to 3 days, chilled airtight.

PER S'MORE 485 CAL., 45% (218 CAL.) FROM FAT; 7.5 G PROTEIN; 25 G FAT (12 G SAT.); 65 G CARBO (3.3 G FIBER); 201 MG SODIUM; 31 MG CHOL. LS

HOMEMADE GRAHAM CRACKERS

MAKES 24 ★ 1 HOUR AT HOME

Though these buttery, cookie-like crackers were designed for the Ultimate S'mores, they taste good enough to eat on their own.

¾ cup butter, at room temperature
⅓ cup packed light brown sugar
¼ cup granulated sugar
1 tbsp. honey
1¼ cups all-purpose flour
⅓ cup whole-wheat flour
½ tsp. *each* baking soda and cinnamon
¼ tsp. salt

1. Beat butter, sugars, and honey in a large bowl with a mixer until smooth. In another bowl, mix dry ingredients. Add to butter mixture and beat until blended.

2. Divide dough in half and roll each half between 2 sheets of parchment paper into an even 10- by 12-in. rectangle. Slide each dough and parchment packet onto a baking sheet and freeze until firm, about 10 minutes. Preheat oven to 300°.

3. Pull off top parchment. Cut dough on sheets into 2½- by 4-in. rectangles. Bake until deep golden brown, 13 to 18 minutes; swap pans halfway through. Cut crackers again on lines.

THE ULTIMATE S'MORES

MAKES 12 ★ 20 MINUTES AT HOME; 5 IN CAMP

What does a grown-up Girl Scout turned chef serve in camp? The ultimate in campground dessert, made with homemade graham crackers and marshmallows. This recipe comes from Cindy Pawlcyn (chef-owner of Mustards Grill and two other restaurants in California's Napa Valley), and it's actually far easier than it looks. You make the bundles at home and then just heat them in camp.

Vegetable oil
Homemade Graham Crackers (recipe follows)
4 bars (each 3.5 oz.) dark chocolate with almonds
   (such as Lindt), each broken into 3 pieces
Homemade Marshmallows (recipe follows)

4. Let crackers cool on sheets 2 to 3 minutes. Separate pieces and transfer to cooling racks.

Make ahead: Up to 1 week, airtight; or up to 2 months, frozen.

PER CRACKER 103 CAL., 50% (52 CAL.) FROM FAT; 1 G PROTEIN; 5.9 G FAT (3.7 G SAT.); 12 G CARBO (0.4 G FIBER); 92 MG SODIUM; 15 MG CHOL. LC/LS/V

HOMEMADE MARSHMALLOWS

MAKES 12 ★ 35 MINUTES, PLUS 2 HOURS TO STAND, AT HOME

A 9- by 13-in. pan makes flat rectangular marshmallows that are ideally sized for the Ultimate S'mores, but you could also use a 9-in. square pan to create fewer, thicker marshmallows.

Cooking-oil spray
¼ cup *each* cornstarch and powdered sugar
3 large egg whites
2 envelopes unflavored gelatin
1 cup granulated sugar
2 tbsp. light corn syrup
½ tsp. vanilla extract

1. Coat a 9- by 13-in. pan with cooking-oil spray. Stir cornstarch and powdered sugar together in a large bowl, then dust pan with half of mixture, tipping to coat. Set remaining cornstarch mixture aside.

2. Put egg whites in the large bowl of a mixer. Stir together ¼ cup cool water and the gelatin in a glass measuring cup; let stand to soften while you make syrup.

3. Stir granulated sugar, corn syrup, and ⅔ cup water in a small saucepan. Insert a candy thermometer. Boil over high heat, tipping pan occasionally to cover thermometer bulb, until mixture reaches 240°, 6 to 10 minutes. Remove from heat and immediately microwave gelatin mixture until it dissolves, about 30 seconds, and also beat egg whites on high speed into soft peaks. Stir steaming gelatin into hot syrup.

4. Pour about 3 tbsp. syrup at a time into egg whites (stop mixer if needed to keep syrup from flying up onto inside of bowl), beating on high speed 20 to 30 seconds after each addition. Continue to beat until meringue holds soft peaks and underside of bowl is completely cool, 5 to 7 minutes. Beat in vanilla.

S'MORE S'MORES

While the Ultimate S'mores (at left) are amazing, sometimes a store-bought option fits in better with the schedule. These updated combinations give you plenty of delicious ways to experiment with toasted marshmallows beyond the plain graham cracker and chocolate-square sandwiches of childhood.

CLASSIC PLUS: Graham crackers, dark chocolate, and sliced strawberries

BLACK FOREST: Chocolate wafer cookies and cherry jam

THE ELVIS: Peanut-butter sandwich cookies (twist cookies into two halves), dark or milk chocolate, and sliced bananas

GIANDUJA: Gaufrettes, pizzelle (French and Italian waffle cookies), or wafer cookies and Nutella

LEMON MERINGUE PIE: Shortbread cookies and lemon curd

NEOCLASSIC: Digestive biscuits and squares of bittersweet chocolate

PIÑA COLADA: Coconut cookies and grilled slices of pineapple

PLAYING HOOKY: Chocolate-topped butter cookies, such as Petit Ecolier

THIN MINT: Chocolate wafer cookies and thin after-dinner mints, such as After Eight

5. Spread marshmallow mixture in coated pan, using an oiled metal spatula. Let stand until firm enough to cut, 2 hours. Sprinkle with 2 tbsp. reserved cornstarch mixture, then cut with a pizza cutter or scissors into 12 rectangles to fit graham crackers; you may have leftover marshmallows.

6. Toss marshmallows in bowl with remaining cornstarch mixture to coat.

Make ahead: Up to 4 days, chilled airtight with plastic wrap between layers; coat with more cornstarch mixture if they get sticky.

PER MARSHMALLOW 103 CAL., 0% (5 CAL.) FROM FAT; 2.2 G PROTEIN; 0.1 G FAT (0 G SAT.); 25 G CARBO (0 G FIBER); 16 MG SODIUM; 0 MG CHOL. LS

CLASSIC COCOA

MAKES 1 QT. MIX; SERVES 12 ★ 5 MINUTES AT HOME; 5 IN CAMP

Few camping trips are complete without hot chocolate, and it's even better made from your own mix. Feel free to add a splash of vanilla to mugs in camp.

1 cup *each* granulated sugar, unsweetened cocoa powder, and powdered milk
½ tsp. salt
½ cup *each* miniature chocolate chips and miniature marshmallows

AT HOME

1. Combine all ingredients in a large bowl, then transfer to a 1-qt. container.

IN CAMP

2. For each serving, spoon ⅓ cup cocoa mix into a mug and stir in 1 cup boiling water.

Make ahead: Up to 1 month, airtight.

PER SERVING 142 CAL., 20% (28.4 CAL.) FROM FAT; 3.7 G PROTEIN; 3.2 G FAT (1.9 G SAT.); 30 G CARBO (2.6 G FIBER); 131 MG SODIUM; 1 MG CHOL.

CANELA TEA

MAKES 4½ CUPS; 6 SERVINGS ★ 30 MINUTES IN CAMP

This cozy, spiced drink comes from photographer Shelly Strazis of Long Beach, California, who serves it to friends around an outdoor fire after dinner. It's equally good virgin or with tequila.

1½ Mexican cinnamon sticks*, plus 6 regular cinnamon sticks for garnish (optional)
2½ tbsp. honey
2 to 3 drops almond extract
¾ cup tequila (optional)

Heat 4½ cups water and 1½ Mexican cinnamon sticks in a large pot until boiling. Reduce heat and simmer 10 minutes. Remove cinnamon. Stir in honey and almond extract. Ladle into mugs. If you like, add about 2 tbsp. tequila and a regular cinnamon stick to each.

*Buy loosed-barked Mexican cinnamon at Latino markets, or use regular cinnamon sticks.

PER ¾-CUP SERVING WITHOUT TEQUILA 31 CAL., 0% (0.1 CAL.) FROM FAT; 0.1 G PROTEIN; 8.4 G CARBO (0 G FIBER); 0.5 MG SODIUM; 0 MG CHOL.

MARGARITA 1, 2, 3

SERVES 4 OR 5 ★ 10 MINUTES IN CAMP

We call this classic margarita "1, 2, 3" because it's three ingredients in equal parts and because it goes together in a snap. It's especially good with the Yucatecan Pork on page 61. You'll need some clean ice cubes from your cooler.

½ cup *each* lime juice, Cointreau or other orange-flavored liqueur, and tequila (preferably silver)
Lime wedges
Coarse salt (optional)

Combine lime juice, Cointreau, and tequila in a pitcher or small bowl. Rub edge of each glass with a lime wedge, then dip in salt if you like. Fill glasses with ice cubes and pour lime mixture on top. Garnish each glass with a lime wedge.

PER SERVING 131 CAL., 0% (0 CAL.) FROM FAT; 0.1 G PROTEIN; 9.2 G CARBO (0.1 G FIBER); 0.7 MG SODIUM; 0 MG CHOL.

NEGRONIS

SERVES 6 ★ 5 MINUTES IN CAMP

With its bitter component from Campari, an Italian aperitif, a negroni invites slow sipping, making it the perfect campground happy hour drink. If you aren't bringing a cocktail shaker or pitcher, just fill cocktail glasses with ice and add 2 tbsp. *each* gin, Campari, and vermouth, then stir. (See photo on page 70.)

¾ cup *each* gin, Campari, and sweet vermouth
6 strips orange zest (each about ½ in. by 3 in.)

In a large cocktail shaker or pitcher, combine gin, Campari, and vermouth. Add 1 cup ice cubes and shake or stir until mixture is cold. Strain into 6 cocktail glasses. Over each glass, twist an orange zest strip to release its oils and drop into glass.

PER SERVING 210 CAL., 1% (3 CAL.) FROM FAT; 0 G PROTEIN; 0.3 G FAT (0 G SAT.); 6.7 G CARBO (0 G FIBER); 1.5 MG SODIUM; 0 MG CHOL.

HOME FIRES

★

IF THERE'S ANY FORM OF COOKING that sums up living in the West, it's the backyard barbecue. You don't need good plates or silverware, and you don't have to dress up. What's important are the sizzling perfume of a well-marinated steak or juicy burgers over hot coals, the breeze, the warm sun on your face, the conversation over plates of hot, smoky food—these are everyday pleasures when you have a grill in your yard.

In this chapter, we're adding some thrill to the laid-back chill of backyard grilling: exciting flavor combinations, unusual but easy techniques, and tips that will make cooking over fire more fun than ever before.

GRILLING BASICS

Gas or Charcoal?

Grillers have a lot of choices when it comes to building a fire, and choosing the fuel shapes every decision that follows. In this chapter, we've focused on the two fuels most popular with backyard grillers—gas and charcoal.

Grilling with gas versus charcoal is a little like driving an automatic versus a stick, and both have their fans. Gas is easy: Just turn it on and you're good to go. With charcoal, you have to interact with the fire to keep the food cooking at the right temperature—adjusting the airflow, moving the coals,

adding a bit more fuel, maybe doing some impromptu shifting of the food to whichever spot is at the right heat. Some cooks feel that charcoal gives food a more "grilled" flavor, but gas aficionados tend to disagree.

A third choice, cooking over wood, is like driving a very early Model T: lots of fun but there's no speedometer. For techniques for building a wood fire, see pages 18 and 177. For guidance on wood types, turn to page 178. And for entire menus cooked over wood, see "Inspired Fires," beginning on page 174.

Here's how to create the setups specified by the gas and charcoal recipes in this book.

DIRECT HEAT GRILLING

Unless they say otherwise, the grilling recipes in this book use direct heat, which means the fire is right beneath the food. This is ideal for grilling smaller items such as steaks, burgers, and kebabs, plus seafood and vegetables; they'll be cooked all the way through by the time the outside is nicely browned.

Direct Heat with Gas

Open the lid, press the ignition, turn all burners to high, and close the lid. Wait 10 minutes for the grill to get hot, then adjust the burners for the temperature you need before placing food onto the grill. As you cook, keep the lid closed as much as possible.

Direct Heat with Charcoal

Ignite the charcoal. Our favorite way to light a charcoal fire is the chimney starter. Set the chimney on the firegrate (the bottom grate) and open vents on the underside of the grill. Stash a few pieces of crumpled newspaper or a few paraffin cubes in the chimney's base, then fill with enough charcoal to cover the cooking grate in a single layer—usually to the top of the chimney. Ignite the paper or cubes and let the fire burn until all the charcoal ignites, 15 to 20 minutes. You can buy a chimney starter at hardware or barbecue stores.

Spread it out. Wearing mitts, dump the charcoal onto the firegrate and spread it out with tongs. Then put the cooking grate in place to preheat and let the coals burn to the heat specified in your recipe—usually 5 to 10 minutes for high, longer for medium to low (see "Taking Your Grill's Temperature," on page 89). If you can spare the grill space, leave about one-quarter of the firegrate clear of coals to make a cool zone where you can move foods that start to get too brown.

Add food. Arrange your food on the cooking grate; grill with the lid on (and its vents open) for the most even cooking, or keep the lid off for easy access—if, say, you're flipping a lot of burgers.

Adjust the vents. If you need to reduce the fire's temperature, partially close the vents in the lid and on the underside of the grill. (That will limit the oxygen that feeds the fire.)

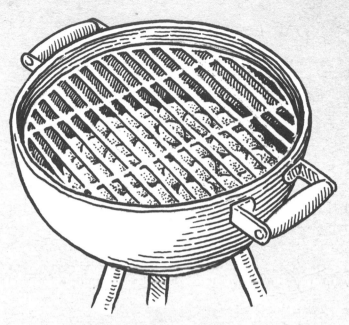

DIRECT HEAT with CHARCOAL

CHARCOAL CHOICES

BRIQUETS. This is the most common choice of fuel for charcoal grillers. These compressed pillows—made of crushed charcoal, a starch binder, and, often, coal products to make the heat last—provide reliable, even cooking. Kingsford, the major manufacturer, has in recent years reformulated its briquets, and now they light faster and burn faster. For long cooking, you will probably need to replenish the coals every 30 minutes. Hardwood, or natural, briquets (made purely from charcoal) contain no additives and burn out even faster. Avoid briquets with lighter fluid added; they're bad for the environment and give food an off flavor.

LUMP CHARCOAL. Irregularly shaped pure hardwood chunks, lump charcoal gives food a nice smokiness. Compared with standard Kingsford briquets, lump charcoal lights faster, gets hotter, and loses heat more quickly—so be generous when adding fuel if you're cooking more than 30 minutes.

BRIQUETS AND CHARCOAL. Some grillers like to use a mix of briquets and lump charcoal for high, consistent heat and good flavor.

INDIRECT HEAT with GAS

INDIRECT HEAT GRILLING

In a recipe that calls for indirect heat, the fire burns to one side of the food or all around it rather than directly beneath. Large foods such as turkey, long-cooked ones like ribs, flammable items such as grilling planks for salmon, and anything glazed in sweet barbecue sauce all benefit from the gentler, radiant heat of this method.

The drip pan. Whenever you grill indirectly, before beginning to cook, set a metal drip pan on the burner you intend to leave turned off (on a gas grill) or in the space cleared of coals (charcoal) underneath the cooking grate. The pan—ideally the same size as the food that will be above it—helps prevent flare-ups by catching flammable falling bits. For extra-incendiary fatty foods (duck, some sausages), add water to the pan to fill it at least halfway. We also add water for long-cooking foods (ribs, turkey), to help keep them moist and to even out the temperature circulating inside the grill.

Indirect Heat with Gas

Set a drip pan (see at left) on one burner, either on one side of the grill or in the middle, depending on how big your grill is and where the burners are located. With the grill lid open, ignite only the other burner or burners and turn them to high. Close the lid and wait 10 minutes or so for the grill to get hot, then adjust the temperature as needed. When the grill is at the right heat, set the food over the drip pan. As you cook, keep the lid closed.

Indirect Heat with Charcoal

Ignite the charcoal. Following the steps under "Direct Heat with Charcoal" (previous page), light charcoal—usually about 60 briquets, or two-thirds of what you would need to cover the entire firegrate.

Bank it. When coals are thoroughly ignited, after 15 to 20 minutes, bank them on opposite sides of the firegrate (bottom grate). Set a drip pan in the empty area (see "The Drip Pan," at left), add water to it if the recipe directs you to, and set the cooking grate in place to preheat. Let the coals burn to the heat specified in your recipe, usually 5 to 10 minutes for high, longer for medium to low (see "Taking Your Grill's Temperature," opposite page).

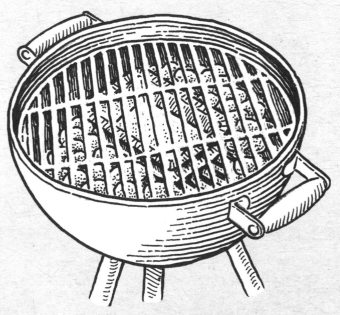

INDIRECT HEAT with CHARCOAL

Add food. The area over the section cleared of coals is the indirect-heat area; set food on the cooking grate above cleared section. Cover the grill, being sure all vents are open.

Maintain the heat. If you're cooking longer than 30 minutes, add 5 to 6 briquets to each mound of coals when the food goes on and then every 30 minutes thereafter, or more often if needed, and leave the fire uncovered for a few minutes to help them light. At the same time, sweep ash from the firegrate by moving the outside lever; this keeps vents clear and air flowing.

Adjust the vents. If needed, reduce the fire's temperature by partially closing vents in the lid and on the underside of the grill.

Brines, Marinades, and Rubs

Brines are water-based mixtures of salt, sugar, and seasonings. They add moisture to meats that tend to dry out or overcook on the grill, like pork, poultry, and certain seafoods, and they impart flavor too. Once poured over the meat, a brine should completely cover it. One quart is enough for about 3 pounds of meat; 3 quarts is enough for about 10 pounds. *Timing:* Large hunks of meat (like a turkey or a pork butt, say) can require up to a day submerged in the brine; smaller pieces, like chicken breasts or fish fillets, need at least 15 minutes and up to 2 hours, depending on their density.

Marinades also add moisture and flavor, but they are usually based on oil and an acid, and the meat isn't submerged in marinade but generously coated with it. *Timing:* Tender proteins like fish need only a few minutes, unless the marinade is gentle (i.e., less acidic and/or salty); then overnight is okay. Firmer meats like flank steak should marinate at least an hour, even in a powerful marinade, and up to a day.

Rubs, on the other hand, are dry spice mixes used to season the food at the last minute. Some recipes call for a brine and/or marinade in combination with a rub. Pack your rub generously onto the meat. The bits of fat on the surface will melt and mingle with the dry rub to form a crust.

For a collection of recipes for brines, marinades, and rubs, see page 112.

FLANK STEAK with ANCHOVY HERB MARINADE (see marinade recipe, page 112)

TAKING YOUR GRILL'S TEMPERATURE

Some grills have built-in thermometers to guide you, but if not, use the following "hand test." Measure the temperature more than once; on a charcoal grill, it can fluctuate a bit (your cue to move the food to a hotter or cooler spot, or to add coals).

VERY HIGH 550° TO 650°. You can hold your hand 5 in. above the cooking grate only 1 to 2 seconds.

MEDIUM 350° TO 450°. You can hold your hand 5 in. above the cooking grate only 5 to 7 seconds.

HIGH 450° TO 550°. You can hold your hand 5 in. above the cooking grate only 2 to 4 seconds.

LOW 250° TO 350°. You can hold your hand 5 in. above the cooking grate only 8 to 10 seconds.

CARAMELIZED TOMATO
BRUSCHETTA

CARAMELIZED TOMATO BRUSCHETTA

SERVES 6 ★ 40 MINUTES

We borrowed this tomato technique from *Seven Fires: Grilling the Argentine Way* by Francis Mallmann (Artisan Books, 2009). If you have the real estate on your grill, you can do steps 2 and 3 at the same time.

1 slender baguette (8 oz.)
3 tbsp. extra-virgin olive oil, divided
1 pt. large cherry tomatoes, halved
About ¼ tsp. *each* kosher salt and pepper
¾ cup whole-milk ricotta cheese
1 cup small fresh basil leaves

1. Heat a grill to medium (350° to 450°). Cut 18 thin diagonal slices from baguette, angling knife so each slice is 3 to 4 in. long. Save remaining bread for another use. Set baguette slices on a tray to carry to grill, and brush all over with about 1 tbsp. oil.

2. Grill bread with grill lid down, turning once with tongs, until browned, 1 to 3 minutes total. Transfer to a platter.

3. Heat a large cast-iron skillet or other ovenproof frying pan on cooking grate, with grill lid down, until water dances when sprinkled on skillet, 8 to 10 minutes. Add 1½ tbsp. oil and spread with a heatproof brush. Pour tomato halves into pan, then quickly turn with tongs so all are cut side down. Sprinkle with ¼ tsp. *each* salt and pepper. Cook with grill lid down, without stirring, until juices evaporate and tomatoes are blackened on cut side, 10 to 15 minutes. Gently loosen tomatoes from pan with a wide metal spatula as they're done and transfer to a bowl.

4. Spoon ricotta into a bowl and drizzle remaining ½ tbsp. oil on top. Put basil in another bowl. Set out toasts with tomatoes, ricotta, basil, salt, and pepper so people can build and season their own bruschetta.

PER 3-TOAST SERVING 216 CAL., 45% (98 CAL.) FROM FAT; 8.2 G PROTEIN; 11 G FAT (3.6 G SAT.); 22 G CARBO (1.7 G FIBER); 321 MG SODIUM; 16 MG CHOL. LS/V

MAXIMIZE YOUR GRILL

You can take your grilling to a whole new level by using a few unexpected tools that you may already have in your kitchen.

CAST-IRON SKILLET. With a large cast-iron skillet or other ovenproof frying pan (or even a paella pan), you can caramelize foods such as cherry tomatoes (above and at left) or apricots (page 167); otherwise these soft foods would just stick to the grill grate. Another technique: Try a skillet for browning the bottom of Grilled Potato Rosemary Cake, page 163, while the hot air inside the covered grill cooks the top.

CAST-IRON GRIDDLE. In Argentina it's known as a *plancha*, and cooking on it involves setting meats such as steak or pork chops on the hot surface for a quick, even sear (for a recipe, see page 129). You get meat that's crusty on the outside and juicy on the inside. Try cooking fish and vegetables this way too.

RIMMED BAKING SHEET. Lightly oiled, it's ideal for grilling thinly sliced vegetables. The vegetables won't fall through the grate, and they still end up with a nice smoky flavor (see page 160).

METAL MUFFIN PAN. A covered grill can act just like an oven when you pour batter into hot muffin cups, as in the Grilled Apricot Puffs (page 167).

SALSA & GUACAMOLE

ROASTED GARLIC AND CHIPOTLE SALSA

MAKES ABOUT 3 CUPS ★ ABOUT 1 HOUR

This spicy, smoky salsa, from *Sunset* reader Tina Williams of Pasadena, California, is thickened with a toasted corn tortilla. She serves it with simple quesadillas made with white cheddar cheese and corn tortillas.

1 head garlic
4 tomatoes (each about 8 oz.), stemmed and cored
3 dried New Mexico or California chiles (each about 5 in. long), rinsed, stemmed, seeded, and coarsely chopped
2 dried chipotle chiles (each about 1 in. long), stemmed
1 corn tortilla (about 6 in.)
1 cup cilantro sprigs
3 tbsp. lime juice
½ cup diced red onion
Salt

1. Preheat oven to 400°. Cut garlic head in half crosswise and wrap both halves in one piece of foil. Cut 3 tomatoes in half crosswise and place, cut side up, on a baking sheet. Bake garlic and tomatoes until garlic is soft when squeezed (unwrap to test) and tomatoes are shriveled, about 45 minutes. Dice remaining tomato and set aside.

2. Meanwhile, place dried chiles in a small bowl and add 1 cup boiling water. Let stand until chiles are soft, about 10 minutes.

3. Cook tortilla in a nonstick frying pan over medium heat, turning once, until crisp and browned on both sides, 5 to 6 minutes total. When cool enough to handle, break into 2-in. pieces.

4. When garlic is cool enough to handle, squeeze cloves from skin into a blender or food processor; discard skin. Add roasted tomatoes, chiles and soaking water, tortilla, cilantro, and lime juice. Whirl until smooth. Stir in onion and reserved diced tomato. Add salt to taste.

Make ahead: Up to 1 week, chilled.

PER ¼ CUP 37 CAL., 17% (6.3 CAL.) FROM FAT; 1.4 G PROTEIN; 0.7 G FAT (0.1 G SAT.); 7.8 G CARBO (1.9 G FIBER); 13 MG SODIUM; 0 MG CHOL. GF/LC/LS/VG

MEXICAN-STYLE SALSA VERDE

MAKES 1¾ CUPS ★ 30 MINUTES

Tomatillos and fresh chiles give this salsa a bright "green" flavor, and toasting the ingredients contributes a smoky element (plus it loosens the chiles' skins). Mexican cooks traditionally use a griddle (*comal*) to toast ingredients, but a broiler chars the chiles more evenly.

½ lb. tomatillos*, husked and rinsed
1 thick onion slice
1 large poblano* chile
1 to 1½ medium serrano chiles
½ ripe avocado (optional)
2 tbsp. coarsely chopped cilantro
1 garlic clove
2 tbsp. lime juice
About ¾ tsp. kosher salt

1. Preheat broiler and set a rack 3 in. from heating element. Line a rimmed baking pan with foil and set tomatillos, onion, poblano, and serranos in it.

2. Broil the vegetables, turning as needed, until tomatillos and onion are speckled brown and chiles are black all over, 12 to 15 minutes; as vegetables are done, transfer to a bowl. Cover vegetables with a plate or foil and let stand about 5 minutes for chile skins to loosen.

3. Pull off stems and blackened skins from the chiles; for best flavor, don't rinse chiles (a few blackened bits are okay to leave on). Open poblano and remove seeds.

4. In a food processor, pulse vegetables and any juices; avocado, if using; cilantro; and garlic until coarsely puréed. Scrape into a bowl and stir in ¼ cup water, lime juice, and ¾ tsp. salt. Season to taste with more salt.

*Tart-tasting tomatillos look like green tomatoes with papery husks. Poblanos (sometimes mislabeled as pasillas) are large, meaty, deep green chiles with a fairly mild flavor; find both in your grocery store's produce section.

Make ahead: Chill up to 2 days; if using avocado, package with as little air space as possible (so avocado does not darken) and chill up to 1 day only.

PER ¼ CUP 20 CAL., 14% (2.7 CAL.) FROM FAT; 0.7 G PROTEIN; 0.3 G FAT (0 G SAT.); 4.2 G CARBO (0.9 G FIBER); 126 MG SODIUM; 0 MG CHOL. GF/LC/VG

SALSA FRESCA

MAKES ABOUT 4 CUPS ★ 15 MINUTES

Also called pico de gallo, this salsa is all about simplicity. Use fresh, in-season produce for the best possible flavors.

4 firm-ripe tomatoes (1½ lbs. total), chopped
½ cup diced red onion
2 to 3 tbsp. chopped jalapeño chile
About 1 tbsp. lime juice
About 1 tsp. salt

In a large bowl, mix together tomatoes, onion, and chile. Stir in lime juice and 1 tsp. salt; then taste and add a little more of either if you like .

PER ¼ CUP 12 CAL., 0% (0 CAL.) FROM FAT; 0.4 G PROTEIN; 3 G CARBO (0.8 G FIBER); 212 MG SODIUM; 0 MG CHOL. GF/LC/LS/VG

GABRIEL'S GUACAMOLE

MAKES 2 CUPS ★ 10 MINUTES

At Gabriel's restaurant in Santa Fe, the guacamole is made tableside in a traditional Mexican *molcajete* (lava rock mortar) and is seasoned to suit each customer. In your kitchen, that's the best way to get the flavors just right too.

2 firm-ripe medium Hass avocados, pitted, peeled, and diced
About ¼ tsp. *each* minced garlic and jalapeño chile
¼ cup chopped tomato
About 1 tsp. finely chopped onion
Salt
About 2 tsp. *each* lime juice and finely chopped cilantro
Tortilla chips

In a medium bowl or a *molcajete*, coarsely mash avocados, garlic, and jalapeño with a wooden spoon or a pestle until avocados are creamy but still very chunky. Add tomato, onion, and salt to taste, and stir. Sprinkle with lime juice and cilantro, then stir and add more seasonings if you like. Serve with chips.

PER ¼ CUP WITHOUT CHIPS 75 CAL., 80% (60 CAL.) FROM FAT; 1.0 G PROTEIN; 6.7 G FAT (0.9 G SAT.); 4.3 G CARBO (3 G FIBER); 17 MG SODIUM; 0 MG CHOL. GF/LC/VG

BOMBAY GUACAMOLE

SERVES 6 TO 8 ★ 20 MINUTES

Mustard seeds, cumin, turmeric, and coriander give this Western classic an Eastern spin.

BOMBAY GUACAMOLE

2 ripe large avocados, halved and pitted
1 tbsp. lemon juice
½ to 1 tsp. minced Thai or serrano chile
½ tsp. *each* kosher salt and minced garlic
1 tbsp. vegetable oil
2 tsp. brown mustard seeds
¾ tsp. cumin seeds, coarsely ground with a mortar and pestle or a spice mill
½ tsp. *each* ground coriander and turmeric
1 tbsp. chopped cilantro
Pappadums* or tortilla chips

1. Scoop avocados into a bowl. Add lemon juice, chile, salt, and garlic. Coarsely mash with a pastry blender or fork.

2. Cook oil and mustard seeds in a small covered saucepan over medium heat until seeds pop, 1½ to 3 minutes. Remove from heat. Stir in cumin, coriander, and turmeric and let stand 2 minutes. Stir spice mixture and cilantro into guacamole. Serve guacamole with pappadums.

*Find pappadums (wafer crackers made from lentils) in the international aisle of well-stocked grocery stores; cook according to package directions.

PER ABOUT ¼ CUP WITHOUT CRACKERS 94 CAL., 83% (78 CAL.) FROM FAT; 1.1 G PROTEIN; 8.8 G FAT (1.1 G SAT.); 4.5 G CARBO (3.1 G FIBER); 99 MG SODIUM; 0 MG CHOL. GF/LC/VG

HONEY SESAME GRILLED CHICKEN WINGS

SERVES 6 TO 8 AS AN APPETIZER ★ 45 MINUTES

These are great for summer potlucks, since they are quick to make and small enough to suit all appetites.

½ cup soy sauce
1 tbsp. *each* minced ginger, garlic, and Asian chili paste
2 lbs. chicken wings, tips removed, cut apart at joint
½ cup honey
1½ tsp. hoisin sauce
2 tbsp. toasted sesame seeds
1 green onion, sliced

1. Combine soy sauce, ginger, garlic, and chili paste in a bowl. Add chicken and marinate about 15 minutes, stirring often.

2. Heat a grill to medium (350° to 450°). Grill chicken, covered, turning often, until golden brown, 10 to 15 minutes.

3. Combine honey and hoisin. Generously brush chicken with mixture. Grill, covered, until glaze starts to caramelize, about 3 minutes. Turn wings over and baste with more glaze. Cook 3 minutes more, being careful not to let glaze burn, and removing pieces from grill to a platter as they're done.

4. Sprinkle chicken with sesame seeds and onion. Serve with any remaining honey glaze.

PER SERVING 213 CAL., 41% (87 CAL.) FROM FAT; 13 G PROTEIN; 9.7 G FAT (2.5 G SAT.); 20 G CARBO (0.5 G FIBER); 513 MG SODIUM; 37 MG CHOL. LC

TAMIL CHICKEN WINGS

**SERVES 8 AS AN APPETIZER OR 2 AS A MAIN DISH
★ ABOUT 35 MINUTES, PLUS 1 HOUR TO MARINATE**

Sunset reader Elagupillai Mageswari of Harbor City, California, seasons chicken wings with a garlicky, fragrant Sri Lankan paste. They come together quickly and are equally good as an appetizer and a main dish.

1 stalk lemongrass; or 3 strips (each 3 by ½ in.) lemon zest, chopped
¾ cup cilantro sprigs
8 garlic cloves, peeled
1 tsp. *each* salt and turmeric
½ tsp. pepper
8 chicken wings (about 1¾ lbs. total)

1. Remove stem end and tough outer leaves from lemongrass. Cut inner stalk into chunks; whirl in a food processor with cilantro, garlic, salt, turmeric, and pepper until finely minced. Pat mixture over chicken wings. Cover and chill at least 1 hour and up to 1 day.

2. Heat a grill to medium (350° to 450°). Oil cooking grate, using tongs and a wad of oiled paper towels. Grill chicken, covered, turning occasionally, until no longer pink at the bone (cut to test), about 15 minutes total.

PER APPETIZER SERVING 92 CAL., 60% (55 CAL.) FROM FAT; 7.2 G PROTEIN; 6.1 G FAT (1.6 G SAT.); 1.4 G CARBO (0.2 G FIBER); 320 MG SODIUM; 28 MG CHOL. GF/LC/LS

TAMIL CHICKEN WINGS

BARBECUED
OYSTERS
3 WAYS

BARBECUED OYSTERS 3 WAYS

SERVES 8 AS AN APPETIZER ★ ABOUT 15 MINUTES, PLUS 1 HOUR TO CHILL TOPPER

Barbecued oysters are synonymous with Tomales Bay, just north of San Francisco. Hog Island Oyster Co., one of several oyster companies edging the bay, serves the bivalves hot off the grill at its San Francisco seafood bar, with a rotating lineup of toppings. Ian Marks, formerly executive chef at Hog Island, shared three he particularly likes.

24 large oysters on the half-shell*, such as Hog Island
    Sweetwaters or Fanny Bays
Hog Island Topper (choices and recipes follow)
Rock salt
Lemon wedges

1. Heat a grill to medium-high (about 450°). Set oysters in shells on cooking grate and top each with about 1½ tsp. of a Hog Island Topper (about a ¼-in.-thick slice of log). Cook oysters, covered, just until juices are bubbling around the edges, 4 to 5 minutes.

2. Meanwhile, line a platter with rock salt. With tongs, carefully lift oysters from grate, keeping them level so the juices don't spill, and nestle them in salt. Garnish with lemon wedges and serve hot.

*If you'd rather not shuck the oysters yourself, ask your seafood purveyor to do it for you, taking care not to spill the juices from the shells. Keep them cold and as level as possible in transport, and eat them as soon as you can.

HOG ISLAND TOPPERS

EACH MAKES ENOUGH TO TOP ABOUT 24 OYSTERS

BAGNA CAUDA BUTTER

Garlicky, salty Italian *bagna cauda*, a traditional dip for fresh vegetables, is delicious with hot oysters.

Mash 1 large **garlic clove** with ¼ tsp. **kosher salt** into a paste in a mortar with a pestle, or on a cutting board using a fork. Add 1 canned **anchovy fillet** and continue mashing until incorporated. Scrape into a bowl and add

½ cup room-temperature **butter**, ¼ cup chopped **flat-leaf parsley**, and 1 tbsp. chopped drained **capers**. Mix well. Spoon across a piece of waxed paper and roll up into a 1½-in.-thick log. Chill at least 1 hour and up to 1 week. Unwrap and cut with a sharp knife into slices about ¼ in. thick to top oysters. Makes about ¾ cup; enough to top about 24 oysters.

PER OYSTER, WITH 1½ TSP. TOPPING 49 CAL., 82% (40 CAL.) FROM FAT; 1.6 G PROTEIN; 4.4 G FAT (2.5 G SAT.); 1 G CARBO (0 G FIBER); 97 MG SODIUM; 22 MG CHOL. GF/LC/LS

CASINO BUTTER

This delectable bacon-studded butter is a riff on the topping for clams casino.

Cook 2 slices **thick-cut bacon** in a medium frying pan over medium-high heat, turning as necessary, until browned but not completely crisp, 4 to 5 minutes. Transfer to paper towels to drain; when cool, finely chop. Mix chopped bacon in a bowl with ½ cup room-temperature **unsalted butter**, 3 tbsp. minced **shallots**, 1 tsp. chopped **fresh thyme** leaves, and 2 tsp. **sweet smoked Spanish paprika** (*pimentón dulce*; find at well-stocked grocery stores or see Resource Guide, page 244) or regular paprika. Spoon across a sheet of waxed paper and roll up into a 1½-in.-thick log. Chill at least 1 hour and up to 1 week. Unwrap and cut with a sharp knife into slices about ¼ in. thick to top oysters. Makes about ¾ cup, enough to top about 24 oysters.

PER OYSTER, WITH 1½ TSP. TOPPING 55 CAL., 78% (43 CAL.) FROM FAT; 1.8 G PROTEIN; 4.8 G FAT (2.7 G SAT.); 1.1 G CARBO (0 G FIBER); 38 MG SODIUM; 23 MG CHOL. GF/LS

LANGOSTA BUTTER

Langosta is Spanish for "lobster," and its sweetness pairs well with the brine of oysters.

Mix ½ cup room-temperature **butter** in a bowl with ⅓ cup chopped **cooked lobster meat** (2 oz.), ¼ cup chopped **cilantro**, and 2 tsp. **Meyer** or regular **lemon zest**. Spoon across a piece of waxed paper and roll up into a 1½-in.-thick log. Chill at least 1 hour and up to 3 days. Unwrap and cut with a sharp knife into slices about ¼ in. thick to top oysters. Makes about 1 cup, enough to top about 32 oysters.

PER OYSTER, WITH 2 TSP. TOPPING 51 CAL., 78% (40 CAL.) FROM FAT; 2 G PROTEIN; 4.4 G FAT (2.5 G SAT.); 0.9 G CARBO (0 G FIBER); 72 MG SODIUM; 24 MG CHOL. GF/LS

GRASS-FED BURGERS WITH CHIPOTLE BARBECUE SAUCE

SERVES 4 ★ 35 MINUTES, PLUS 30 MINUTES TO CHILL

Grass-fed beef is very lean and cooks more quickly than regular, more marbled, beef, so keep an eye on the burgers as they cook. You will have plenty of the tangy sauce left over for another round of burgers, or even grilled chicken or ribs.

SAUCE
¼ cup packed light brown sugar
½ cup ketchup
2 tbsp. canned chipotle chiles in *adobo* sauce (about 3 chiles), plus 1 tbsp. sauce
1 tbsp. Worcestershire sauce
2 tbsp. molasses
2 tbsp. orange juice concentrate
1 tsp. minced garlic

BURGERS
1¼ lbs. grass-fed ground beef
2 tsp. *each* kosher salt and pepper, divided
1 red onion, sliced ¼ to ½ in. thick crosswise
1 tbsp. vegetable oil, divided
4 slices Swiss cheese
4 sesame-seed hamburger buns
4 slices ripe tomato
4 leaves butter or romaine lettuce

1. Make sauce: Purée all sauce ingredients in a food processor until very smooth.

2. Make burgers: In a bowl, combine beef and 1½ tsp. *each* salt and pepper. Shape into 4 patties, each about ¾ in. thick, making a slight depression in each to help keep burgers flat (they'll shrink as they cook). Let burgers rest at least 30 minutes in the refrigerator; they'll hold together better and stay juicier when cooked.

3. Heat a grill to medium (350° to 450°).

4. Sprinkle onion with remaining salt and pepper and 1 tsp. oil. Grill, covered, turning once, until softened, 8 minutes total.

5. Meanwhile, rub burgers with 2 tsp. oil and grill, covered, turning once, about 6 minutes total for medium-rare. In the last few moments of cooking, lay a slice of cheese on each burger. Lay buns on grill to toast slightly.

6. Transfer buns to a platter and fill with burgers and onion. Spoon about 1½ tbsp. barbecue sauce on top of each and add a slice of tomato and a lettuce leaf.

Make ahead: Sauce, up to 1 week, chilled.

PER BURGER, WITH 1½ TBSP. SAUCE AND TRIMMINGS 612 CAL., 50% (306 CAL.) FROM FAT; 36 G PROTEIN; 34 G FAT (14 G SAT.); 41 G CARBO (2.3 G FIBER); 1,175 MG SODIUM; 112 MG CHOL.

BEER AND BISON BURGERS WITH PUB CHEESE

SERVES 4 ★ 30 MINUTES, PLUS 30 MINUTES TO GRILL

Bison, beer, and a garlicky cheese spread add up to something special, but this recipe is also delicious when made with beef.

1 lb. ground bison or beef
¼ cup quick-cooking rolled oats
¼ cup amber ale, such as Fat Tire, divided
1 tsp. kosher salt
½ tsp. pepper
1 large garlic clove
4 oz. cream cheese
1 cup shredded sharp white cheddar cheese
2 tsp. olive oil
4 whole-wheat hamburger buns
2 cups alfalfa sprouts

1. Mix bison, oats, 2 tbsp. ale, the salt, and pepper in a large bowl until just combined. Shape into four ½-in. patties with a slight depression in the center of each to help keep burgers flat (they'll shrink as they cook). Let burgers rest at least 30 minutes in the refrigerator; they'll hold together better and stay juicier when cooked. Heat a grill to medium (350° to 450°).

2. Whirl garlic in a food processor until minced. Add cheeses and remaining 2 tbsp. ale and whirl until smooth.

3. Brush burgers with oil. Grill them, covered, turning once, until cooked the way you like, 6 minutes for medium. In last few minutes, grill split buns, turning once, about 2 minutes.

4. Arrange burgers on bottom of buns and top with sprouts. Spread bun tops with cheese mixture.

PER BURGER 531 CAL., 53% (280 CAL.) FROM FAT; 36 G PROTEIN; 31 G FAT (15 G SAT.); 29 G CARBO (4.2 G FIBER); 1,020 MG SODIUM; 121 MG CHOL.

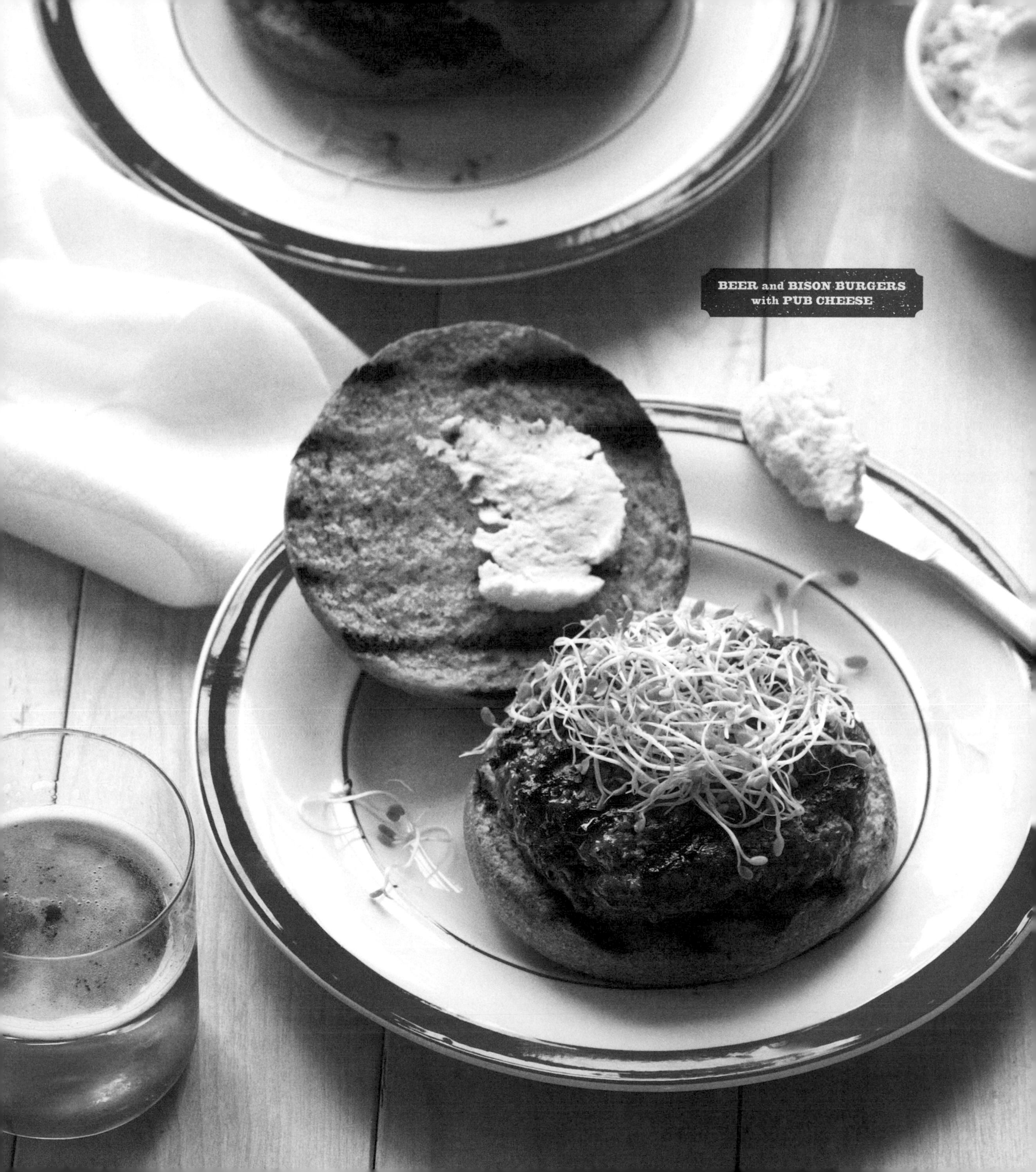

BEER and BISON BURGERS with PUB CHEESE

THE HATCH BURGER

SERVES 4 ★ 50 MINUTES, PLUS 30 MINUTES TO CHILL

At Umami Burger restaurants in Southern California and the San Francisco Bay Area, these juicy, full-flavored burgers are seasoned with Umami Dust and Umami Master Sauce (see Resource Guide, page 244). Soy sauce makes a good substitute for both Dust and Master Sauce.

3 Anaheim chiles
3 poblano chiles
¾ tsp. kosher salt, divided
½ cup mayonnaise
1 tsp. minced garlic
1½ lbs. ground beef chuck
4 to 6 tsp. soy sauce
4 slices white American cheese
About ¼ cup butter
4 slightly sweet rolls, such as Hawaiian sandwich or kaiser

1. Broil chiles on a rimmed baking sheet, turning as needed, until blackened on all sides, about 10 minutes. Let cool. Peel, then cut open and remove stem and seeds. Finely chop chiles. Put in a medium bowl and stir in ¼ tsp. salt. Mix mayonnaise with garlic in another medium bowl.

2. Mix beef with remaining ½ tsp. salt in a large bowl until just combined. Divide into 4 portions and shape each into a ½-in.-thick patty with a slight depression in the center to help keep burgers flat (they'll shrink as they cook). Let burgers rest at least 30 minutes in the refrigerator; they'll hold together better and stay juicier when cooked. Heat a grill to medium (350° to 450°).

3. Oil cooking grate, using tongs and a wad of oiled paper towels. Grill burgers, covered, turning once and sprinkling with about ½ tsp. soy sauce on each side, until done the way you like, 7 to 8 minutes for medium. During the last minute, lay a cheese slice on each burger to melt it.

4. Meanwhile, lightly butter cut sides of rolls and toast on grill, about 2 minutes.

5. Spread garlic mayo on cut sides of rolls. Add burgers, topping each with about 2 tbsp. chile mixture.

PER BURGER 800 CAL., 56% (446 CAL.) FROM FAT; 42 G PROTEIN; 50 G FAT (20 G SAT.); 46 G CARBO (2.3 G FIBER); 1,707 MG SODIUM; 159 MG CHOL.

"KIMCHI" BURGERS

SERVES 4 ★ 35 MINUTES, PLUS 30 MINUTES TO CHILL

These burgers are flavored with garlic and ginger and topped with a chile-spiked cabbage relish. For a shortcut, omit the relish and use kimchi—Korean-style pickled spicy cabbage—from an Asian market, farmers' market, or grocery store.

3 cups finely shredded napa cabbage
½ cup thinly sliced green onions, divided
3 tbsp. seasoned rice vinegar
4 tsp. *each* minced garlic and fresh ginger, divided
1 tbsp. toasted sesame oil, divided
1½ tsp. Asian chili garlic sauce, divided
¼ cup mayonnaise
1½ lbs. ground beef chuck
2 tbsp. soy sauce
4 hamburger buns, split

1. Mix cabbage, ¼ cup green onions, the vinegar, 1 tsp. *each* garlic and ginger, 2 tsp. sesame oil, and ½ tsp. chili sauce in a large bowl. Set relish aside, stirring occasionally. In another bowl, mix mayonnaise with remaining 1 tsp. chili sauce.

2. Combine beef, soy sauce, remaining ¼ cup green onions, 1 tbsp. *each* garlic and ginger, and 1 tsp. sesame oil. Shape into 4 patties, each about ½ in. thick, making a slight depression in the center to help keep burgers flat (they'll shrink as they cook). Let burgers rest at least 30 minutes in the refrigerator; they'll hold together better and stay juicier when cooked. Heat a grill to high (450° to 550°).

3. Oil cooking grate, using tongs and a wad of oiled paper towels. Grill burgers, covered, turning once, 7 to 8 minutes for medium. In the final minutes, toast buns.

4. Spread bun bottoms with chili mayonnaise. Set burgers on buns. With a slotted spoon, put some cabbage relish on each. Serve with remaining relish.

PER BURGER 607 CAL., 55% (336 CAL.) FROM FAT; 35 G PROTEIN; 37 G FAT (10 G SAT.); 27 G CARBO (1.8 G FIBER); 1,049 MG SODIUM; 110 MG CHOL.

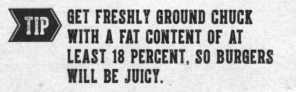 **TIP** GET FRESHLY GROUND CHUCK WITH A FAT CONTENT OF AT LEAST 18 PERCENT, SO BURGERS WILL BE JUICY.

GARDEN PARTIES

Bring your garden right to the table with these fresh ideas. You'll have the most choices in summer, but in any other season, substitute with whatever harvest you have on hand.

ELEGANT SIP
Steep lemongrass, lemon verbena, lemon balm, and lemon zest with tea, then pour over ice (get the recipe for the *Sunset* Palmer on page 171).

EASY APPETIZER
Serve just-picked ripe fruit (figs, peaches, or strawberries) with a salty cheese like parmesan or cotija. The combination is great alone or over toasts for bruschetta.

U-PICK GREEN SALAD
Send guests out to the garden with a colander to harvest their own mix of lettuces and herbs, while you whisk up a nice vinaigrette.

EDIBLE CENTERPIECE
Decorate the table with a bowl of ripe multicolor tomatoes. When it's time to eat, cut them into wedges and set out a bowl of salt, some fresh herbs, and a bottle of good olive oil so guests can season to taste.

CRAZED MOM'S EASY STEAK and
GARAM MASALA NAAN-WICHES

CRAZED MOM'S EASY STEAK AND *GARAM MASALA* NAAN-WICHES

SERVES 6 ★ 20 MINUTES, PLUS 1 HOUR TO MARINATE

Sunset associate food editor Elaine Johnson created this recipe one harried weeknight at home. The timing of it allowed her to prep the meat, race off to do a week's grocery shopping while it marinated, and arrive home (her husband having lit the grill and kids having set the table) with enough time to cook dinner. Make the sauce while the steak grills, and let everyone assemble their own sandwiches.

¼ cup olive oil
1½ tbsp. lemon juice
1½ tsp. *garam masala**
About ½ tsp. salt
½ tsp. pepper
1 flank steak (about 1 lb.), fat trimmed
6 naan breads* (each about 3½ in. by 8 in.; 18 oz. total)
3 cups loosely packed watercress sprigs

1. In an 8- or 9-in. glass dish, mix oil, lemon juice, garam masala, ½ tsp. salt, and the pepper. Turn steak in mixture and let marinate at room temperature 1 hour.

2. Heat a grill to very high (550° to 650°). While grill heats, preheat cooking grate for at least 10 minutes.

3. Pour marinade into a small pan and bring to a simmer; remove from heat. Pour 1 tbsp. water into a blender, turn on, drizzle in marinade, and whirl to emulsify.

4. Grill steak, covered, turning once, about 5 minutes for medium-rare (cut to test). Lift to a cutting board and loosely cover with foil.

5. Grill naan, turning once, until hot and slightly crusty, 1 to 2 minutes. Lift to board.

6. Thinly slice steak across the grain. Let each person arrange meat and watercress over half of each naan. Drizzle sauce on top, sprinkle with salt to taste, and fold naan in half to make a sandwich.

*Find garam masala, an earthy Indian spice mixture, and naan, an Indian flatbread, at well-stocked grocery stores and Indian markets.

PER NAAN-WICH 457 CAL., 41% (189 CAL.) FROM FAT; 25 G PROTEIN; 21 G FAT (6.9 G SAT.); 28 G CARBO (2.9 G FIBER); 764 MG SODIUM; 38 MG CHOL. LC

CHILE AND LIME MINI STEAK *TORTAS*

SERVES 4 TO 8 ★ 30 MINUTES, PLUS 30 MINUTES TO MARINATE

Here's a four-bite version of the classic Mexican sandwich. We used *arracheras* (flap meat), a thin steak available at Latino markets that marinates and grills quickly, but skirt steak is a good substitute. And we drizzled the sandwiches with *crema*, a pourable Mexican-style sour cream; regular sour cream tastes good too.

Juice of 1 lime
1½ tsp. ancho chile powder*
4 tsp. vegetable oil
½ tsp. kosher salt
1 lb. flap meat or skirt steak, cut into 3- to 4-in.-wide strips
8 small dinner rolls, split
1 cup shredded Jack cheese
1 avocado, sliced thinly
2 cans (each 4 oz.) sliced jalapeños, drained
About ¼ cup Mexican *crema* or sour cream

1. Mix lime juice, chile powder, oil, and salt in a medium bowl. Add steak, turning to coat evenly with marinade. Chill at least 30 minutes and up to 3 hours.

2. Heat a grill to high (450° to 550°). Cook steak, covered, turning once, until grill marks appear and steak is slightly pink in the center, about 4 minutes. Transfer to a cutting board, tent with foil, and let rest 10 minutes; then slice thinly to fit in rolls.

3. Open rolls and sprinkle each with about 2 tbsp. cheese. Grill rolls, cut sides up and covered, until crisp and cheese starts to melt, about 1 minute.

4. Fill rolls with steak, avocado, half the jalapeños, and a drizzle of crema. Serve with remaining jalapeños.

*Find ancho chile powder in the spice aisle of well-stocked grocery stores and at Latino markets.

PER SANDWICH 301 CAL., 54% (163 CAL.) FROM FAT; 18 G PROTEIN; 18 G FAT (6.5 G SAT.); 17 G CARBO (3.1 G FIBER); 481 MG SODIUM; 42 MG CHOL. LC/LS

GRILLED EGGPLANT WRAPS WITH TAHINI DRESSING

SERVES 4 ★ 30 MINUTES

This sandwich of grilled vegetables, yogurt-tahini sauce, and spinach is simple but substantial. You may want to make extra, because leftovers are fantastic for lunch the next day.

1 tbsp. minced garlic
3 tbsp. lemon juice
¼ cup tahini (sesame paste)
1 cup plain low-fat Greek yogurt
1 tsp. kosher salt
1 large eggplant (1 lb.), sliced into ½-in. rounds
2 ripe tomatoes, quartered
2 tbsp. olive oil
4 naan breads*
6 cups baby spinach

1. Heat a grill to high (450° to 550°). In a small bowl, mix garlic, lemon juice, tahini, yogurt, and salt. Set aside.

2. Brush eggplant and tomatoes with oil. Grill, covered, turning often, until softened and grill marks appear, about 6 minutes. Cut tomato wedges in half. Warm naan on grill.

3. Lay each naan on a plate and top with 1½ cups spinach, a few slices eggplant, 4 tomato pieces, and a large spoonful of yogurt mixture. Fold in half.

*Find naan, an Indian flatbread, at well-stocked grocery stores.

PER SANDWICH 445 CAL., 41% (181 CAL.) FROM FAT; 17 G PROTEIN; 20 G FAT (3.9 G SAT.); 55 G CARBO (11 G FIBER); 899 MG SODIUM; 3.8 MG CHOL. LC/V

> **TIP** FOR ANOTHER VEGETARIAN MEAL FROM THE GRILL, MAKE THE RATATOUILLE ON PAGE 160. TOSS VEGETABLES WITH PENNE PASTA, EXTRA-VIRGIN OLIVE OIL, AND MORE GOAT CHEESE.

JAPANESE TOFU SKEWERS ON SOBA

SERVES 2 TO 4 ★ 40 MINUTES

Tofu holds up beautifully on the grill as long as you use the firm or extra-firm kind. You'll need four 10- to 12-in. wooden or metal skewers.

½ cup reduced-sodium soy sauce
½ cup mirin (sweet rice wine)
2 tbsp. toasted sesame oil
10 to 12 oz. firm or extra-firm tofu, cut into 1-in. cubes
16 small fresh shiitake mushroom caps
2 tbsp. vegetable oil
4 green onions, cut into 1½-in. lengths
12 oz. dried soba noodles
8 radishes, thinly sliced
⅔ cup vegetable broth
2 tsp. wasabi paste
1 tsp. lemon zest
¼ cup lemon juice

1. Heat a grill to medium (350° to 450°). Soak 4 wooden skewers in water 30 minutes, or use metal skewers.

2. Meanwhile, mix soy sauce, mirin, and sesame oil in a bowl. Add tofu and marinate 10 minutes.

3. Bring a large pot of water to a boil. In a bowl, toss mushrooms in vegetable oil to coat.

4. Drain tofu, reserving marinade. Slip tofu cubes onto skewers, alternating with green onions and mushrooms. Thinly slice any leftover onion.

5. Boil noodles until al dente, 4 minutes. Drain; rinse well with cold water. Divide noodles among dinner bowls and garnish with radishes and sliced onion.

6. Oil cooking grate, using tongs and a wad of oiled paper towels. Grill tofu skewers, covered, turning once, until lightly browned, 6 to 8 minutes. Set skewers on noodles.

7. Mix reserved marinade with broth, wasabi, lemon zest, and juice and serve alongside.

PER SKEWER PLUS ¼ OF NOODLES 595 CAL., 28% (169 CAL.) FROM FAT; 23 G PROTEIN; 19 G FAT (2.3 G SAT.); 85 G CARBO (2.2 G FIBER); 1,900 MG SODIUM; 0 MG CHOL. VG

JAPANESE TOFU
SKEWERS on SOBA

PIZZA MARGHERITA
(see recipe on page 110)

PIZZA BIANCA
(see recipe on page 110)

PIZZA DOUGH FOR THE GRILL

MAKES 6 INDIVIDUAL-SIZE PIZZAS ★ 1 HOUR, PLUS 2 HOURS FOR DOUGH TO RISE

Everybody loves pizza, and for a backyard party, guests can have the fun of topping their own and enjoying it right off the grill. Start with this dough, which produces crisp crusts every time; for the easiest party, you can partially grill the crusts before people arrive. Then set out some toppings (see next page) and the menu will practically cook itself.

1 pkg. (2¼ tsp.) active dry yeast
6 tbsp. olive oil, divided
4 cups all-purpose flour
1½ tsp. salt
Toppings (see next page)

1. In the bowl of a stand mixer, stir yeast into 1½ cups warm water (100° to 110°). Let stand until yeast dissolves, about 5 minutes. Add ¼ cup oil, the flour, and salt. Mix with dough hook on low speed to blend, then mix on medium speed until dough is very smooth and stretchy, 8 to 10 minutes. If you don't have a stand mixer, mix in the oil, flour, and salt with a wooden spoon, then turn out on a lightly floured work surface and knead for 8 to 10 minutes, until dough is very smooth and stretchy. Dough will feel tacky.

2. Cover dough and let rise at room temperature until doubled in bulk, about 1½ hours.

3. Punch down dough and let rise again until doubled, 30 to 45 minutes. Meanwhile, cut 6 pieces of parchment paper, each about 12 in. long. Heat a grill to medium (about 350°).

4. Turn dough out onto a work surface and cut into 6 portions. For each pizza, lay a sheet of parchment on work surface and rub with 1 tsp. oil. Using well-oiled hands, put each portion of dough on a parchment sheet. Flatten dough portions, then pat into 9- to 10-in. rounds. If dough starts to shrink, let rest 5 minutes, then pat out again. Let dough stand until puffy, 15 to 30 minutes.

5. Flip a round of dough onto cooking grate, dough side down. Peel off parchment. Put on 1 or 2 more dough rounds. Grill, covered, until dough has puffed and grill marks appear underneath, 3 minutes. Transfer crusts, grilled side up, to baking sheets. Repeat with remaining dough. (Grilled crusts can stand at room temperature up to 2 hours; reheat grill to continue.)

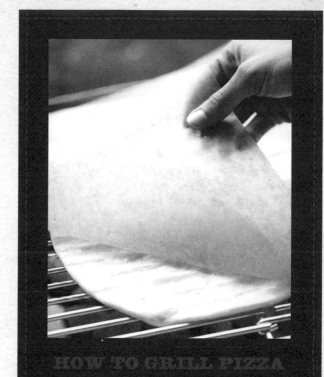

HOW TO GRILL PIZZA

Jamie Purviance, author of *Weber's Way to Grill* (Oxmoor House, 2009) and other titles, taught us these tricks for grilling pizza.

1. PAT out the dough on an oiled sheet of parchment paper.

2. FLIP the dough from the parchment paper onto the grill. Be sure the temperature isn't more than medium (about 350°), or the dough will scorch.

3. PULL off the paper and grill the first side.

4. TAKE the dough off the heat and add toppings to the grilled side. Then set the pizza back on the grill to cook the second side.

6. Arrange pizza toppings on grilled sides of crusts. With a wide spatula, return pizzas, 2 or 3 at a time, to cooking grate. Cook, covered, until browned and crisp underneath, rotating pizzas once for even cooking, 4 to 6 minutes.

Make ahead: Dough through step 1, covered and chilled, at least 3 hours and up to 2 days (dough will double in size, and flavor will develop as it chills).

continued

WHOLE-WHEAT PIZZA DOUGH

Straight whole-wheat flour makes the texture of pizza too crackerlike, but mixing it with white flour produces a crust with hearty flavor and a supple springiness. Follow directions for Pizza Dough for the Grill on the previous page, but use 2 cups **whole-wheat flour** and 2 cups all-purpose flour, and heat grill to medium-low (300° to 350°).

RIPE TOMATO PIZZA SAUCE

MAKES 1 CUP ★ 2 HOURS

Homemade tomato sauce makes the tastiest pizza. Let it cook slow and long so it gets nice and thick.

1 tbsp. olive oil
1 tbsp. minced garlic
4 large red tomatoes (2 lbs. total), chopped
1 tsp. sugar
¼ tsp. red chile flakes
½ tsp. *each* kosher salt and pepper
1 tbsp. chopped fresh oregano leaves

Heat oil in a saucepan over medium heat. Add garlic and cook, stirring, until fragrant, about 1 minute. Stir in tomatoes, sugar, chile flakes, salt, and pepper. Bring mixture to a boil, then reduce heat to low and simmer, stirring often, until very thick, about 1½ hours. Stir in oregano.

PER 2 TBSP. 44 CAL., 43% (19 CAL.) FROM FAT; 1.1 G PROTEIN; 2.1 G FAT (0.3 G SAT.); 6.4 G CARBO (1.5 G FIBER); 83 MG SODIUM; 0 MG CHOL. VG/LC/LS/GF

PIZZA MARGHERITA TOPPING

SERVES 6 ★ 10 MINUTES

Always and forever, the most popular pizza—simple and fresh.

Pizza Dough for the Grill (regular or whole wheat, previous page and above), prepared through Step 5
Ripe Tomato Pizza Sauce (above)
1 lb. water-packed fresh mozzarella cheese, drained and cut into 30 to 36 slices
Small fresh basil leaves

Spread each half-grilled crust with about 2 tbsp. pizza sauce, then evenly space 5 or 6 slices of cheese over the sauce. Grill as directed in step 6, then top each pizza with several whole or torn basil leaves.

PER SERVING WITH CRUST 725 CAL., 45% (324 CAL.) FROM FAT; 27 G PROTEIN; 36 G FAT (14 G SAT.); 73 G CARBO (4.7 G FIBER); 1,001 MG SODIUM; 67 MG CHOL. V

PIZZA *BIANCA* TOPPING

SERVES 6 ★ 10 MINUTES

The interplay of salty cheese, rosemary, and pungent onion makes this white no-sauce pizza bold and flavorful.

¼ white onion, sliced
About 12 oz. shredded mozzarella cheese
Pizza Dough for the Grill (regular or whole wheat, previous page and at left), prepared through Step 5
2 tsp. chopped fresh rosemary leaves
Salt

Evenly scatter a few onion slices and a large handful of cheese over each half-grilled crust, then sprinkle with rosemary and a little salt. Grill as directed in step 6.

PER SERVING WITH CRUST 587 CAL., 41% (243 CAL.) FROM FAT; 20 G PROTEIN; 27 G FAT (9.4 G SAT.); 66 G CARBO (2.6 G FIBER); 796 MG SODIUM; 44 MG CHOL. V

COPPA, RICOTTA, AND ARUGULA PIZZA TOPPING

SERVES 6 ★ 10 MINUTES

Coppa, sometimes called *capocollo*, is a delicious dry-cured meat made with pork neck or shoulder and eaten very thinly sliced. Its delicate flavor and rich texture are especially good paired with crisp, peppery arugula.

15 oz. ricotta cheese (about 2 cups)
Pizza Dough for the Grill (regular or whole wheat, previous page and at left), prepared through Step 5
About 5 oz. (18 slices) coppa
About 2 tbsp. extra-virgin olive oil
Squeeze of lemon juice
Salt and pepper
About 5 cups (2½ oz.) baby arugula

1. Evenly spread 2 heaping spoonfuls (⅓ cup) ricotta onto each half-grilled crust, then top with several slices of coppa. Grill as directed in step 6.

2. In a bowl, combine oil, lemon juice, and a pinch *each* of salt and pepper; toss with arugula. About 1 minute before pizzas are done, evenly scatter a generous amount of dressed arugula onto pizzas and finish grilling, covered, for about 1 minute.

PER SERVING WITH CRUST 643 CAL., 45% (288 CAL.) FROM FAT; 22 G PROTEIN; 32 G FAT (9.7 G SAT.); 67 G CARBO (2.8 G FIBER); 980 MG SODIUM; 49 MG CHOL.

COPPA, RICOTTA, and
ARUGULA PIZZA

BRINES, RUBS & MARINADES

For general information about working with brines, rubs, and marinades, see page 89.

SWEET AND SAVORY ALL-PURPOSE BRINE

MAKES ENOUGH FOR 10 LBS. MEAT, POULTRY, OR FISH (ABOUT 3 QTS. BRINE)
★ 30 MINUTES TO OVERNIGHT TO BRINE, DEPENDING ON TYPE OF MEAT

Try this for everything from turkey to trout. If you have only a few pounds of meat to brine, make a half- or even quarter-recipe.

2 cups packed light brown sugar
1½ cups kosher salt
3 garlic cloves, halved
2 tsp. peppercorns
4 dried bay leaves

1. Combine all ingredients with 3 qts. cool water in a glass, plastic, or stainless steel bowl or pot big enough to hold 10 lbs. meat, poultry, or fish. Stir briskly until sugar and salt dissolve.

2. Add meat, poultry, or fish to brine. Let fish brine 15 minutes to 30 minutes at room temperature; spareribs and small birds (such as quail, squab, or game hens) 1 hour at room temperature; and turkey breast, whole chicken, or duck 2 hours at room temperature. For a whole turkey or a roast (including rolled and tied roasts), brine at least 8 hours or overnight, chilled and covered.

3. Pat dry before grilling. If smoking, also let air-dry on a rack until the surface feels tacky (30 to 60 minutes).

Make ahead: Chill dried brined meat or poultry until the next day.

FOR CHICKEN

POMEGRANATE MOLASSES AND MINT MARINADE

MAKES ENOUGH FOR 2 LBS. CHICKEN PIECES
★ 1 DAY TO MARINATE

¾ cup chopped mint leaves
½ cup pomegranate molasses*
2 tbsp. *each* lemon juice and olive oil
3 medium garlic cloves, minced
1 tsp. kosher salt

Whisk all ingredients together. Put chicken in a nonreactive baking dish and pour marinade over, turning to coat. Marinate 1 day, covered and chilled.

*Find pomegranate molasses at well-stocked grocery stores and Middle Eastern markets.

SAGE BRINE

MAKES ENOUGH FOR 1 WHOLE CHICKEN, OR UP TO 4 LBS. CHICKEN PIECES ★ AT LEAST 2 HOURS TO BRINE

½ small bunch fresh sage
⅓ cup *each* kosher salt and packed light brown sugar
10 black peppercorns
2 dried bay leaves
10 large garlic cloves

Mix all ingredients in a large pot with 3 cups water. Bring to a boil and stir to ensure salt and sugar are dissolved. Remove from heat and mix in 9 cups cold water. Put chicken, breast side down, in a bowl or pot large enough to hold it and pour brine in. Cover, and, if using pieces, chill 2 to 3 hours; if using whole chicken, chill overnight.

FOR BEEF

ANCHOVY HERB MARINADE

MAKES ENOUGH FOR 2 LBS. BEEF OR BISON
★ AT LEAST 1 HOUR TO MARINATE

½ cup chopped flat-leaf parsley
3 tbsp. extra-virgin olive oil
1 tbsp. *each* lemon juice and chopped capers
1 tsp. *each* lemon zest and minced anchovy
½ tsp. kosher salt

Whisk all ingredients together. Put beef in a nonreactive baking dish and pour marinade over, turning to coat. Marinate 1 hour at room temperature and up to 1 day, chilled and covered.

CUMIN CHILE RUB

MAKES ENOUGH FOR 2 TO 3 STEAKS (ABOUT 2 TBSP.) ★ 10 MINUTES

2 tbsp. ground mild California or New Mexico chiles or 1½ tsp. chili powder (chile mixed with other seasonings)
1 tsp. *each* ground cumin and coriander
Rounded ¼ tsp. cayenne
1½ tsp. kosher salt

Whisk all ingredients together and pack onto meat.

Make ahead: Up to 2 months, airtight.

FOR PORK

AROMATIC HERB AND GARLIC BRINE

MAKES ABOUT 3 QTS., ENOUGH FOR 1 (5- TO 6-LB) PORK SHOULDER ★ 1 DAY TO BRINE

This flavorful brine comes from Dana Ewart and Cameron Smith, who own Joy Road Catering in British Columbia's Okanagan Valley. It's especially good with pork butt (also called pork shoulder).

⅓ cup *each* sea salt and packed light
    brown sugar
1 head garlic, cut in half
10 peppercorns
2 dried bay leaves
2 whole allspice berries
4 juniper berries
Stems from 1 bunch parsley

Simmer all ingredients in a large stockpot with 3 cups water, stirring occasionally, until salt dissolves. Remove from heat and add 9 cups cold water. Let cool. Add pork and chill, covered, at least 1 day and up to 2.

FRESH HERB
MARINADE

GREEN CHILE
and GINGER
MARINADE

POMEGRANATE
MOLASSES and
MINT MARINADE

SPICY PAPRIKA RUB

MAKES ENOUGH FOR 8 LBS. SPARERIBS OR BRISKET ★ 10 MINUTES

Celebrity chef Tyler Florence uses this recipe for pork spareribs (see page 122). It's also terrific for smoked brisket (see page 127).

1 tbsp. kosher salt
1½ tbsp. pepper
2 tbsp. garlic powder
1½ tbsp. dried oregano
2 tsp. celery seeds
6 tbsp. *each* hot paprika and chili
    powder

Whisk all ingredients together and pack onto meat.

Make ahead: Up to 2 months, airtight.

FOR SEAFOOD

GREEN CHILE AND GINGER MARINADE

MAKES ENOUGH FOR 1½ LBS. LARGE SHRIMP, PEELED AND DEVEINED; OR ABOUT 1½ LBS. FISH FILLETS ★ 15 MINUTES TO MARINATE

½ cup chopped cilantro
3 tbsp. extra-virgin olive oil
2 tbsp. lemon juice
3 serrano chiles, seeded and minced
1 tbsp. minced fresh ginger
½ tsp. kosher salt

Put all ingredients in a nonreactive bowl and stir to combine. Add seafood and turn to coat. Marinate 15 minutes at room temperature.

FOR VEGETABLES

FRESH HERB MARINADE

MAKES ENOUGH FOR 2 LBS. VEGETABLES ★ 15 MINUTES TO MARINATE

For a grilling chart, and the best ways to cut vegetables for cooking on the grill, see page 159.

2 tbsp. chopped fresh thyme, rosemary,
    oregano, or tarragon leaves, or a
    combination
½ tsp. *each* kosher salt and pepper
⅓ to ½ cup olive oil, vegetable oil,
    or melted butter

Put all ingredients in a nonreactive bowl and stir to combine. Add vegetables and turn over to coat. Marinate 15 minutes at room temperature.

CARNE ASADA CON *MOJO* (GRILLED BEEF WITH SOUR ORANGE MARINADE)

SERVES 6 ★ 30 MINUTES, PLUS 1 HOUR TO MARINATE

Carne asada is a simple dish, but a well-balanced marinade and the right cut can make it memorable. Silvana Salcido Esparza, chef of Barrio Café in Phoenix and Barrio Queen in Scottsdale, Arizona, recommends using skirt steak. It grills up tender, juicy, and very flavorful. The marinade for asada is traditionally made with Seville (sour) oranges, but since they can be hard to find, we've used a combination of orange and lime juices instead.

½ cup freshly squeezed orange juice (save the
    juiced halves)
½ cup Mexican lager beer, such as Modelo Especial
¼ cup olive oil
3 tbsp. lime juice
2 tsp. kosher salt
1½ tsp. *each* pepper and Mexican oregano, crumbled
5 garlic cloves, minced
2 dried bay leaves
1 sprig (6 in.) fresh rosemary
1 large red onion, cut in half lengthwise, then sliced
    into half-moons
2 lbs. skirt steak
Warm corn tortillas*
Guacamole
Hot sauce, such as Tapatío, or salsa

1. Combine orange juice, beer, oil, lime juice, salt, pepper, oregano, garlic, bay leaves, and rosemary in a glass 9- by 13-in. baking dish. Add juiced orange halves, onion, and steak and mix with your hands to coat evenly. Let stand at room temperature 1 hour, or chill, covered, 2 hours (no longer, or the citrus will "cook" the meat), turning meat occasionally.

2. Heat a grill to very high (550° to 650°). Discard rosemary, bay leaves, and orange halves. Drain meat and onions. Put onions on a doubled sheet of foil and turn up edges just a little to make a shallow 6- by 9-in. container.

3. Grill onions on the foil, covered, stirring occasionally with tongs, until edges start to char, 8 to 10 minutes. Set steak on cooking grate and grill, covered, turning once, until well browned and done the way you like, 8 minutes for medium-rare.

4. Transfer steak and onions to a cutting board; slice steak. Serve with tortillas, guacamole, and hot sauce.

*Warm directly on the grill just until hot, turning once; stack and wrap in a towel.

PER SERVING 285 CAL., 50% (143 CAL.) FROM FAT; 30 G PROTEIN; 16 G FAT (5.6 G SAT.); 3.6 G CARBO (0.5 G FIBER); 213 MG SODIUM; 68 MG CHOL. LC/LS

THE BEGINNER'S GUIDE TO GRILLING STEAK

Buy the right cuts and follow our simple tips, and you'll pull off steak you can be proud of.

1. CHOOSE THE RIGHT STEAK. Flank and New York strip taste great and aren't too expensive, so they're ideal for practicing your grilling skills.

2. GIVE IT A TRIM. With a sharp knife, remove any silverskin (the thin, shiny connective tissue on the outside of the meat that gets stringy when it cooks), or ask a butcher to do it. Trim excess fat as well so you don't get flare-ups.

3. MARINATE (OR NOT). If you have 2 to 3 hours to let a marinade penetrate the meat, go for it. But if you're short on time, just salt and pepper the meat and whip up a sauce (such as the Salsa Verde on page 117).

4. OIL IT. No oil in the marinade, or no marinade at all? Then coat the steak with a little oil so it won't stick to the grill.

5. TAKE THE CHILL OFF. For the most even cooking, let cold steaks sit at room temp about 30 minutes before grilling.

6. BE PATIENT. Let steaks brown on the grill before you try to turn them. They will usually release easily.

7. LET IT REST. Put the finished steak on a board and tent with foil for 5 minutes or so, allowing the juices to go back into the meat.

CARNE ASADA con MOJO

BEEF, BROCCOLINI, and BREAD SALAD with ITALIAN SALSA VERDE

BEEF, BROCCOLINI, AND BREAD SALAD WITH ITALIAN SALSA VERDE

SERVES 6 ★ 40 MINUTES, PLUS 2 HOURS TO MARINATE

Robust, briny, and herbaceous, Italian-style salsa verde works beautifully as both a marinade and a table sauce.

SALSA VERDE
5 garlic cloves
4 anchovy fillets
2 cups loosely packed flat-leaf parsley sprigs
⅓ cup capers
1 cup extra-virgin olive oil
¼ cup white wine vinegar
1 tsp. kosher salt
1 tsp. pepper

STEAK AND SALAD
1½ lbs. boneless New York strip steaks, fat trimmed
1½ lbs. broccolini, ends trimmed
5 slices (each ½ in. thick; 9 oz. total) *pain au levain* or other rustic bread
1½ tbsp. olive oil
2½ qts. loosely packed watercress sprigs

1. Make salsa verde: Whirl garlic and anchovies in a food processor until finely chopped. Add remaining salsa ingredients and pulse until herbs are chopped.

2. Prepare steak and salad: Pour about ⅓ cup salsa verde into a medium bowl. Chill remaining salsa verde, covered. Add steaks to bowl, turn over to coat, cover, and chill at least 2 and up to 24 hours; let stand at room temperature during last 30 minutes.

3. Heat a grill to medium (about 350°). Put broccolini on a rimmed pan and brush with about ¼ cup reserved salsa verde. Brush bread with oil.

4. Grill bread, broccolini, and steak, covered, turning once, until bread is browned and crisp (5 to 8 minutes), broccolini is tender-crisp and tops are lightly charred (about 10 minutes), and steaks are medium-rare (12 to 17 minutes). Transfer to a cutting board as done; tent steaks with foil and let rest 5 minutes.

5. Cut bread into small chunks and cut each broccolini into 2 or 3 pieces on a diagonal. Slice steaks diagonally across the grain about ½ in. thick, then cut pieces in half.

6. Toss watercress in a large bowl with enough of reserved salsa verde to coat lightly, then transfer to a platter or plates. Toss bread, broccolini, and steak with remaining dressing and arrange over watercress.

PER SERVING 704 CAL., 61% (427 CAL.) FROM FAT; 36 G PROTEIN; 49 G FAT (8.8 G SAT.); 33 G CARBO (4.1 G FIBER); 951 MG SODIUM; 51 MG CHOL.

TARRAGON-MUSTARD T-BONE STEAKS

SERVES 4 ★ 20 MINUTES, PLUS 30 MINUTES TO MARINATE

In a T-bone, two cuts—loin and tenderloin—are separated by the bone. The porterhouse steak is almost identical to a T-bone, except that it has a larger tenderloin portion.

⅓ cup dry red wine
3 tbsp. Dijon mustard
2 tbsp. *each* minced shallots and olive oil
1½ tbsp. chopped fresh tarragon or 2 tsp. dried tarragon
4 beef T-bone steaks (each 1½ in. thick and 1 to 1¼ lbs.), fat trimmed
2 cups (2 oz.) tender watercress sprigs
Salt and pepper

1. In a small bowl, mix wine, mustard, shallots, oil, and tarragon. Pat steaks dry, then spread mixture thickly on all sides and stack steaks on a plate. Let stand at room temperature for at least 30 minutes, or cover and chill up to 1 day.

2. Heat a grill to high (450° to 550°). Grill steaks, covered, turning once, until browned on both sides and done to your liking in center of thickest part (cut to test), 10 to 13 minutes for medium-rare.

3. Transfer steaks to plates. Let rest in a warm place for 3 to 5 minutes. Top each with ½ cup watercress. Add salt and pepper to taste.

PER SERVING 490 CAL., 48% (234 CAL.) FROM FAT; 57 G PROTEIN; 26 G FAT (9 G SAT.); 1.4 G CARBO (0.4 G FIBER); 342 MG SODIUM; 161 MG CHOL. GF/LC/LS

GRILLED BEEF RIB ROAST AND YORKSHIRE PUDDING

SERVES 5 TO 7 ★ 1½ HOURS

Sunset reader Bob House, of Scottsdale, Arizona, received an award in a *Sunset* grilling contest for this unusual recipe. House grills the herb-seasoned roast, catching the drippings. Then he pours Yorkshire pudding batter into the drip pan, where it puffs in the hot fat and browns. If you're cooking over charcoal, be sure to set up the grill in a sheltered location—wind will burn the coals too quickly.

1 tied center-cut bone-in beef rib roast (4 to 5 lbs.), surface fat trimmed to no more than ¼ in. thick
Garlic-Herb Oil (recipe follows)
1 cup *each* low-fat milk and flour
3 large eggs
¾ tsp. salt
Melted butter (if necessary)
1 large bunch watercress, tough stems trimmed

1. Pat beef dry and coat all over with garlic-herb oil. Let stand at room temperature about 45 minutes.

2. Heat a grill to medium (375° to 450°) with a charcoal area left clear or a gas burner turned off to make an indirect heat area (see "Indirect Heat Grilling," page 88, but use 80 briquets for charcoal; maintain heat as directed). Set an 8-in. square drip pan filled with 1 cup water between banks of coals or on turned-off gas burner. Set roast, bones down, on cooking grate over pan. Cook, covered, until meat starts to brown, about 45 minutes.

3. Meanwhile, in a blender, mix milk, flour, eggs, and salt until batter is smooth.

4. Transfer roast to a platter. Protecting your hands, lift off cooking grate and remove drip pan. Pour drippings through a fine-mesh strainer into a bowl. *For charcoal*, spoon 1 tbsp. fat from drippings and return to pan; discard the rest. Return pan to firegrate and pour in batter. Move briquets so they're not touching pan. Replace cooking grate, set roast back over pan, and close lid on grill (keeping vents open). Cook roast, tenting with foil if it starts to get dark, until an instant-read thermometer inserted into center of thickest part registers 135° for medium-rare, 30 to 60 minutes, or until done to your liking. Cook pudding until well browned, 40 to 60 minutes, rotating it after 30 minutes. *For gas*, spoon 3 tbsp. fat from drippings (adding melted butter, if needed, to make enough) into pan and pour in batter. Set another drip pan on firegrate, replace cooking grate, and set roast over pan. Set pudding next to roast and close lid on grill. Cook pudding until well browned, 20 to 30 minutes. Cook roast, tenting with foil if it starts to get dark, until an instant-read thermometer inserted into center of thickest part registers 135° for medium-rare, 30 to 50 minutes, or until done to your liking.

5. Transfer roast to a board; let roast rest in a warm place for juices to settle, at least 10 minutes. If pudding is done before roast is ready to carve, close charcoal grill vents and leave pudding on grill to keep warm, or turn off gas grill and keep pudding warm with lid down.

6. Carve roast. Set watercress on plates and serve beef on top of watercress, with scoops of pudding alongside.

PER SERVING 934 CAL., 68% (639 CAL.) FROM FAT; 53 G PROTEIN; 71 G FAT (27 G SAT.); 18 G CARBO (0.8 G FIBER); 426 MG SODIUM; 269 MG CHOL. LS

GARLIC-HERB OIL

In a food processor, finely chop ¼ cup **garlic cloves** with 3 tbsp. **olive oil** and 1½ tsp. *each* **dried rosemary, kosher salt, dried savory, dried thyme**, and **pepper**.

GRILLED BEEF RIB
ROAST and
YORKSHIRE PUDDING

GLAZED BABY
BACK RIBS

GLAZED BABY BACK RIBS

SERVES 8 ★ 2½ HOURS

For these juicy ribs, you'll need a sturdy drip pan.

5 lbs. pork baby back ribs
4 tsp. kosher salt
1½ tsp. pepper
1 tsp. cayenne
Sticky Brown Sugar Glaze (recipe follows)

1. Remove the membrane from underside of ribs (see at right) and cut ribs into half-racks if needed to fit on grill.

2. In a small bowl, mix salt, pepper, and cayenne. Put ribs on a baking sheet and sprinkle on both sides with salt mixture. Snugly wrap each rack in heavy-duty foil. Let sit 30 minutes at room temperature.

3. Meanwhile, heat a grill to medium-low (300° to 350°) with a charcoal area left clear or a gas burner turned off to make an indirect heat area (see "Indirect Heat Grilling," page 88, and maintain heat as directed). Set a sturdy drip pan on grate between banks of coals or on turned-off gas burner.

4. Place rib packets, bone side down, on cooking grate over indirect heat, overlapping slightly if necessary. Cook ribs, covered, until fairly tender when pierced through foil, 50 to 70 minutes. Transfer rib packets to a rimmed pan. Carefully remove ribs from foil. Set ribs, bone side up, on grill over indirect heat.

5. Spoon about ¼ cup glaze into a small bowl and set aside. Baste ribs with remaining glaze. Cover grill and cook ribs 10 minutes. Brush melted glaze from center of each rack up along sides of meat, turn ribs over, and baste with more glaze. Repeat brushing and turning every 10 minutes until ribs are browned and tender and meat has shrunk back from ends of the bones, 30 to 40 minutes total.

6. Remove ribs from grill. Tent loosely with foil and let sit about 10 minutes. Stir reserved ¼ cup glaze and brush over ribs. Cut between bones to serve.

PER 4-RIB SERVING WITH GLAZE 615 CAL., 60% (369 CAL.) FROM FAT; 33 G PROTEIN; 41 G FAT (15 G SAT.); 27 G CARBO (0.1 G FIBER); 441 MG SODIUM; 162 MG CHOL. LS

STICKY BROWN SUGAR GLAZE

In a bowl, whisk together 1½ cups packed **light brown sugar**, 3 tbsp. *each* **cider vinegar** and **beer** or water, ½ to 1½ tsp. **red chile flakes**, and 1 tsp. **dry mustard**.

SECRETS FOR FANTASTIC PORK RIBS

TRIM SPARERIBS ST. LOUIS–STYLE. Meaning, trim them into a tidy, rectangular shape that cooks evenly. Ask a butcher to trim them, or do it yourself: On the bony side, trim the flap of meat from the center, flush with the bones (above). Then cut the rack lengthwise between the 4- to 5-inch-wide rib section and the chewy 1- to 3-inch-wide rib tips (not shown). Save the flap and rib tips for soup.

REMOVE THE MEMBRANE. Pork ribs have a membrane on the underside (the bony side) that can shrink up and make the meat cook unevenly. It's easy to remove. Slide the tip of a meat thermometer under the membrane at one end to loosen an edge. Pull off the membrane with a paper towel (it may come off in pieces) while holding the rack down with your other hand.

APPLEWOOD-SMOKED SPARERIBS WITH SPICY PAPRIKA RUB

SERVES 6 TO 8 ★ 2¾ HOURS

Chef Tyler Florence uses both a dry and a wet rub on these ribs, for maximum flavor. Right before the end of cooking, he likes to sprinkle on more dry rub—"like Cheetos dust," he says.

3 cups applewood chips (see Resource Guide, page 244)
1½ slabs pork spareribs (about 8 lbs. total)
Spicy Paprika Rub (page 113)

WET RUB
⅓ cup distilled white vinegar
2 tbsp. lemon juice

1. Soak chips in water 20 to 40 minutes. Meanwhile, heat a large charcoal grill (22 in.) to low (250° to 350°) with an area left clear for indirect heat (see "Indirect Heat Grilling," page 88). Set a sturdy drip pan on grate between banks of coals and fill it halfway with warm water. When coals are at low heat (250° to 350°), sprinkle 1 cup soaked chips over them.

2. Cut the full slab of ribs in half. Rub three-quarters of the paprika rub onto both sides of ribs. Set remaining one-quarter of the paprika rub aside. Lay ribs on cooking grate over drip pan.

3. Smoke ribs, covered, 45 minutes to 1 hour. Add 8 to 10 briquets to the lit coals and 1 cup chips. Turn ribs over. Cook, covered, 45 minutes to 1 hour; add another 8 to 10 briquets and 1 cup chips. Turn ribs and cook for 30 minutes to an hour, or until meat is starting to pull away from tips of bone.

4. Meanwhile, mix vinegar, 1 tbsp. water, and the lemon juice in a small bowl to make a wet rub.

5. When meat is almost done, use a spray bottle or paper towels to thoroughly baste top of ribs with the wet rub, then sprinkle with remaining dry paprika rub. Cook ribs a few minutes more. Transfer to a cutting board and let rest 15 minutes before slicing and serving.

PER SERVING 752 CAL., 66% (500 CAL.) FROM FAT; 54 G PROTEIN; 56 G FAT (20 G SAT.); 9.8 G CARBO (2.3 G FIBER); 661 MG SODIUM; 214 MG CHOL.

GRILLED SPARERIBS WITH FENNEL SEEDS AND HERBS

SERVES 6 ★ 2¾ HOURS, PLUS 4 HOURS TO CHILL

Meat expert Bruce Aidells, author of *The Great Meat Cookbook* (Houghton Mifflin Harcourt, 2012) and other titles, drew on the Northern Italian heritage of Sonoma's founding wine families for this recipe, creating crisp-edged ribs that don't require additional sauce. He serves them on a bed of lightly charred escarole. To make this accompaniment, quarter heads of escarole, tie with kitchen twine, and generously season with olive oil, salt, and pepper. Grill, remove twine, then cut into ribbons and toss with good olive oil and balsamic vinegar.

1½ tbsp. kosher salt
1 tbsp. *each* **fennel seeds, chopped garlic, and chopped fresh rosemary leaves**
1 tsp. chopped fresh sage leaves
2 tsp. *each* **pepper, sweet Hungarian paprika, chopped fresh thyme leaves, and crushed fennel seeds***
2 racks (each 2½ lbs.) pork spareribs trimmed St. Louis–style, membrane removed (see "Secrets for Fantastic Pork Ribs," previous page), cut into 8- to 9-in. portions
2 tbsp. olive oil

1. Combine all ingredients except for ribs and oil in a bowl. Rub ribs all over with oil and smear with seasonings, putting most on meaty side. Chill airtight at least 4 and up to 24 hours; let stand at room temperature during last hour. Meanwhile, scrunch each of 5 (1½ ft.) sheets of foil into a log about 9 in. long; set aside.

2. Heat a grill to low (250° to 300°) with a charcoal area left clear or a gas burner turned off to make an indirect heat area (see "Indirect Heat Grilling," page 88, and maintain heat as directed). Set a 9- by 13-in. drip pan on grate between banks of coals or on turned-off gas burner.

3. Set ribs with bone tips upright over drip pan, arranging foil logs between ribs to hold them up. Grill, covered, until meat is very tender when pierced and shrinks back ½ in. from tips of bones, 1¾ to 2¼ hours.

4. Transfer ribs to a rimmed baking sheet and tent with foil. Let rest about 10 minutes, then cut between bones.

*Crush seeds using a mortar and pestle.

PER SERVING 736 CAL., 69% (505 CAL.) FROM FAT; 52 G PROTEIN; 56 G FAT (20 G SAT.); 2.4 G CARBO (1.2 G FIBER); 1,306 MG SODIUM; 213 MG CHOL. GF

GRILLED SPARERIBS
with FENNEL SEEDS
and HERBS

The Slow Magic of SMOKING

Cooked in a water smoker, food takes on a whole new level of flavor. It's as easy as using a charcoal grill.

If there's anything better than diving into a big platter of meat that's been smoked for hours, until it's tender and juicy and falling off the bones, it might be the fun of cooking it. Learning to smoke your own meat, fish, and poultry is partly about playing with a great piece of equipment and partly about the creative pairing of woods and foods. While there's plenty of billowing smoke to make it all seem mysterious, the process of smoking is really very simple.

THE VERTICAL WATER SMOKER

Many types of smokers are sold in hardware and outdoor supply stores, and they can be fueled by charcoal, gas, or electricity. The charcoal-powered vertical water smoker is the most popular, and it's very easy to use. It cooks with steam, which keeps the inside temperature low (below 250°) and even. Thanks to the steam and the long, slow cooking, foods remain moist and have plenty of time to absorb the swirling smoke. (You can also get good results smoking on a standard gas or charcoal grill, and you'll find those recipes in this chapter, but you have to spend more time tending the fire than on a bona fide smoker, and it's much harder to keep the temperature low.)

As the photo on page 126 shows, a vertical water smoker looks like an elongated covered charcoal barbecue. The charcoal goes in the base, and a water pan sits directly above it. Two or three cooking racks go above that and a domed lid with a temperature gauge fits on top. (If your smoker doesn't have a gauge, you'll need to purchase a smoking/grilling thermometer to insert into the top vents to measure the internal temperature.)

The smoking directions that follow and the smoking times given in our "Slow Smoke-Cooking Guide" on page 127 apply to a charcoal-fueled vertical water smoker. If you have a different type of unit, check the manufacturer's directions for cooking information.

WOODS FOR SMOKING

Your first consideration when smoking will be what type of wood to use. Each wood has a characteristic flavor, and as you experiment you'll discover what you like. Mild- to medium-flavored woods like alder, apple, cherry, and pecan are good with beef, pork, lamb, poultry, and fish; also try these milder woods for smoking times longer than 4 hours. Hickory, oak, and mesquite wood produce a fuller flavor; try them with beef, and with poultry and fish for smoking times under 4 hours.

Woods for smoking are sold in 2- to 3-inch chunks. These smolder longer than smaller chips, so are better for a water smoker. (Either chunks or chips work well on a regular gas or charcoal grill.) Avoid cedar, fir, pine, spruce, and eucalyptus. Their smoke can give food a bitter, resinous taste.

PREPARING THE FOOD

Getting meat, poultry, or fish ready for smoking can be as simple as sprinkling them with salt and pepper. Or you can add additional flavor with a rub such as Spicy Paprika Rub on page 113 or a brine like Sweet and Savory All-Purpose Brine on page 112; brining complements the smoky flavor nicely and also helps lock in moisture.

After brining, pat foods dry, then let air-dry 30 minutes to 1 hour on a metal rack. If you're using a rub (or something as simple as salt and pepper), just pat dry. For either, brush all over with olive or vegetable oil.

continued

How to Use a Vertical Water Smoker

We used a charcoal-fueled vertical water smoker with standard briquets. If your water smoker is powered by gas or electricity, follow the manufacturer's directions. Before starting a fire, take the smoker apart so you can reach the bottom section where you'll build the fire: Lift off the smoker lid, the cooking grates and water pan from the center section, and the center section itself.

1 SOAK THE WOOD. Consult the "Slow Smoke-Cooking Guide" on the opposite page for the amount and type of wood to use; keep in mind that 1 wood chunk (about 4 ounces) is equivalent to 2 cups of wood chips. We recommend starting with the minimum amount of wood listed—the smoke should enhance, not overwhelm, the taste of the food. If you decide you want a smokier flavor, increase the amount of wood the next

time you smoke-cook. Soak chunks in a bowl of water for 45 to 60 minutes or soak wood chips 30 minutes.

2 START THE FIRE. Check the smoke-cooking guide for the smoking times of the foods you're working with. For smoking less than 5 hours, you'll need enough briquets to fill the charcoal chamber so it's level (the charcoal chamber is a tall perforated ring that sits on the smoker's firegrate in the bottom section of the smoker). For more than 5 hours, you'll need enough briquets to fill the chamber so it's slightly mounded. Heat briquets on the firegrate inside the chamber, with 4 or 5 paraffin cubes distributed in the mound, and ignite. Open all vents on the smoker's lid and near the base.

3 ADD WATER TO MAKE STEAM. Set the water pan in place on the brackets in the smoker's center section. Set the center section on the bottom section. Protecting your hands, fill the pan at least three-quarters full with hot tap water.

4 ADD WOOD FOR SMOKE. Drain the soaked wood and distribute it over the hot coals, working with tongs through the smoker's door (see photo at left). Close the door.

5 ADD FOOD. See "Preparing the Food" on page 124. Set the smoker's cooking grates in place and arrange prepared food on grates in a single layer, allowing at least 1 inch between pieces. If you want to smoke several foods with different cooking times, place the faster-cooking pieces on the top grate for easy removal. Remember that foods above will drip on those below; stack them so incompatible flavors won't mingle. Insert a meat thermometer into the center of the food. Close vents slightly and cover the smoker.

6 KEEP AN EYE ON IT. Though a water smoker functions practically unattended, you'll need to check the water level and temperature every so often. Otherwise, keep the door closed so heat and smoke don't escape.

WATER: You may need to add hot water after every couple of hours to keep the pan about half full.

TEMPERATURE: Check the smoker's gauge occasionally; it should consistently read 200° to 250°. When the heat drops too low, open the vents. If the temperature stays too cool for more than 30 minutes after opening the vents, add 10 extra lit coals. When the heat rises above 250°, close the vents slightly; leave at least a half vent open on lid and near base, or fire may go out.

7 CHECK FOR DONENESS. Test foods for doneness as the chart directs, checking the thermometer in the food or, if necessary, making a small cut into its center. Keep in mind that smoke may tint foods a bright pink just beneath the browned surface.

GREAT COMBOS

It's hard to go wrong when you're smoke-cooking, but here are a few of our favorites to get you started.

★ Turkey + Sweet and Savory All-Purpose Brine (page 112) + oak wood

★ Beef brisket + Spicy Paprika Rub (page 113) + oak wood

★ Salmon fillet or whole trout + salt and pepper + alder wood

★ Pork butt + Sweet and Savory All-Purpose Brine (page 112) + hickory or cherrywood

SLOW SMOKE-COOKING GUIDE

See "How to Use a Vertical Water Smoker," opposite. The smoker temperature should stay between 200° and 250° throughout cooking.

TYPE OF MEAT	WEIGHT OR THICKNESS	BEST WOODS* FOR SMOKING	NUMBER OF 2- TO 3-IN. WOOD CHUNKS	TEST FOR DONENESS & APPROXIMATE COOKING TIME
Beef brisket on tri-tip	2 to 5 lbs.	Alder, apple, cherry, hickory, mesquite, oak, pecan	2 to 4	Meat thermometer for brisket registers 190° (6 to 7 hours); for tri-tip, 135° to 140° for rare, about 3 hours
Beef ribs	Full rack, or 4½ lbs.	Alder, apple, cherry, hickory, mesquite, oak, pecan	2 to 4	Meat pulls easily from bone, 3 to 5 hours
Boneless pork shoulder/butt	About 3 lbs.	Alder, apple, cherry, hickory, pecan	2 to 6	Meat thermometer registers 160° 5 to 7 hours
Pork spareribs	Full rack, 4 lbs.	Alder, apple, cherry, pecan	1 to 3	Meat pulls easily from bone, 4 to 5 hours
Leg of lamb, boned and tied	3½ to 4½ lbs.	Alder, apple, cherry, pecan	2 to 4	Meat thermometer registers 135° to 140° for medium-rare, 4 to 5 hours
Chicken, whole	3½ to 4½ lbs.	Alder, apple, cherry, pecan	1 to 3	Meat near thighbone is no longer pink, 4 to 6 hours
Turkey, whole	12 to 14 lbs.	Alder, apple, cherry, oak, pecan	2 to 4	Meat thermometer inserted at breastbone registers 165°, 4½ to 6 hours
Fish**, whole, small	About 1 lb.	Alder, apple, cherry, hickory, oak, pecan	1 to 3	Flakes when prodded in thickest part, 1½ to 2½ hours
Fish**, fillets or steaks	1 to 1½ in. thick	Alder, apple, cherry, hickory, oak, pecan	1 to 3	Flakes when prodded in thickest part, 1½ to 2½ hours

*Buy wood chunks at well-stocked grocery stores, hardware stores, and barbecue supply stores, as well as online; see Resource Guide, page 244.

**Salmon, albacore and yellowfin tuna, trout, sturgeon, sablefish (black cod), bonito (skipjack tuna), and mackerel are all good candidates for smoking. For how to pick sustainably caught fish, see *seafoodwatch.com*

LEMON and THYME GRILLED PORK CHOPS

GRILLED POTATO ROSEMARY CAKE
(see recipe on page 163)

LEMON AND THYME GRILLED PORK CHOPS

SERVES 6 ★ 40 MINUTES, PLUS 4½ HOURS TO BRINE

Cooking meat on a hot griddle, or *plancha*, gives it a beautifully even sear. (If you don't have a griddle, you can also use cast-iron skillets or a paella pan.) On a big grill (with a cooking grate that's at least 2½ by 3 ft.), you can cook the pork chops side by side with Grilled Potato Rosemary Cake (page 163), which makes a terrific accompaniment. Keep the temperature between 350° and 400°, and start heating the griddle for the chops when the potatoes have been on for 20 minutes.

3 dried bay leaves
2 tsp. peppercorns, cracked*, plus ½ tsp. ground pepper
1 cup dry white wine, such as Sauvignon Blanc
½ cup kosher salt
½ cup plus 2 tsp. packed light brown sugar
Zest of 2 lemons, divided
6 bone-in rib-eye pork chops (3½ lbs. total), with bones frenched* if you like
2 tbsp. extra-virgin olive oil
2½ tbsp. coarsely chopped fresh thyme leaves and small, tender sprigs

1. Heat 1½ qts. water, the bay leaves, and peppercorns in a large pot until boiling. Remove from heat and stir in wine, salt, ½ cup brown sugar, and the zest of 1 lemon. Nest pan in a sink of ice water and let brine cool. Add pork to brine. Chill at least 4 and up to 12 hours.

2. Drain meat, rinse, pat dry, and set on a platter or baking sheet. In a bowl, mix oil, thyme, ground pepper, remaining 2 tsp. brown sugar, and the zest of 1 lemon. Pat mixture onto both sides of meat, pressing it in. Let meat stand at room temperature.

3. Heat a grill to medium (350° to 450°). Heat a large cast-iron griddle, 12-in. paella pan, or 2 large cast-iron skillets on cooking grate with grill lid down until water dances when sprinkled on cooking surface, 8 to 10 minutes.

4. Grill chops on griddle, grill lid closed, turning once, until meat is well browned and done the way you like, 8 to 10 minutes total for medium-rare (cut to test). Transfer to a platter.

*Crack peppercorns in a mortar, or seal in a plastic bag and smash with a rolling pin. Rib-eye chops are also called bone-in center-cut pork rib chops; if they aren't already frenched (that is, some meat trimmed from the bone ends to make the chops look neater), ask a butcher to do it, or do it yourself by sliding a sharp knife along the bones.

PER SERVING 328 CAL., 53% (174 CAL.) FROM FAT; 32 G PROTEIN; 19 G FAT (6.2 G SAT.); 4.5 G CARBO (0.3 G FIBER); 395 MG SODIUM; 88 MG CHOL. GF/LC/LS

THAI BARBECUED PORK

SERVES 4 ★ 30 MINUTES

A Thai restaurant's amazing chicken-wing dish with fresh lemongrass provided the inspiration for this dish, says *Sunset* reader Karen Fukui of Olympia, Washington, who created the recipe. The marinade is intense, so it takes only a few minutes to impart flavor. Serve with rice and vegetables.

1 stalk fresh lemongrass, stem and coarse leaves trimmed, cut into chunks
1 tbsp. sugar
2 tbsp. reduced-sodium soy sauce
1 tbsp. Thai or Vietnamese fish sauce
1 quarter-size slice fresh ginger
¼ tsp. pepper
A few cilantro sprigs, plus leaves for garnish
1 tbsp. Thai red curry paste*
1 garlic clove
2 tbsp. vegetable oil
1 lb. pork tenderloin, cut into ½-in. slices

1. Heat a grill to high (450° to 550°). In a food processor, pulse all ingredients except for pork into a paste, adding a bit of water if needed. In a medium bowl, mix pork with paste. Let sit 15 minutes.

2. Grill pork, covered, turning once, until browned, about 6 minutes. Garnish with cilantro leaves.

*Find Thai red curry paste in the Asian foods aisle at grocery stores.

PER SERVING 210 CAL., 41% (87 CAL.) FROM FAT; 23 G PROTEIN; 10 G FAT (1.8 G SAT.); 5.9 G CARBO (0.1 G FIBER); 846 MG SODIUM; 62 MG CHOL. LC

ACHIOTE AND ORANGE PULLED PORK

SERVES 8 TO 14, DEPENDING ON SIZE OF PORK SHOULDER
★ **5 TO 7 HOURS, PLUS 8 HOURS TO MARINATE**

Real, slow-cooked barbecue takes time, but this dish is truly worth it. Santa Fe barbecue experts Bill Jamison and Cheryl Alters Jamison pile the succulent meat on *bolillos* (hard Mexican-style rolls) or other small rolls that they've smeared with mayonnaise, then top with *queso fresco*, avocado slices, and a squeeze of lime. We also like layering the sandwiches with their Chipotle Coleslaw (page 165).

MEAT AND GRILLING
1 boned pork shoulder (also called butt; 4 to 6 lbs.)
2 to 3 cups cherry or hickory wood chips (see "Woods for Smoking," page 124)

SEASONING PASTE
3 oz. (6 tbsp.) thawed frozen orange juice concentrate
3 tbsp. achiote paste*
2 tbsp. *each* kosher or sea salt and coarsely ground pepper
1 tbsp. *each* garlic powder and crumbled dried oregano
1 tsp. cayenne

ORANGE "MOP" SAUCE
3 oz. (6 tbsp.) thawed frozen orange juice concentrate
2 cups cider vinegar or distilled white vinegar
2 tbsp. butter
1 tsp. kosher or sea salt

SERVING AND CONDIMENTS
½ cup *each* thinly sliced green onions and chopped cilantro
Chipotle Coleslaw (page 165)
Rolls, mayonnaise, crumbled *queso fresco**, sliced avocado, lime wedges, and/or hot sauce

1. The night before you plan to barbecue, cut pork shoulder lengthwise into two equal pieces (to speed up cooking), removing excess fat as needed. Combine seasoning-paste ingredients in a small bowl. Massage pork well with paste, then transfer to a large resealable plastic bag and chill at least 8 hours.

2. About 45 minutes before you're ready to begin barbecuing, remove pork from refrigerator and let stand in plastic bag at room temperature (this will speed up cooking and help the meat cook evenly).

3. Put wood chips in a bowl, cover with water, and soak at least 30 minutes.

4. Combine "mop" ingredients with 1 cup water in a saucepan and warm over low heat. Set aside ¾ cup sauce.

5. Heat a grill to low (250° to 350°) with a charcoal area left clear or a gas burner turned off to make an indirect heat area (see "Indirect Heat Grilling," page 88). Set a sturdy drip pan on grate between banks of coals or on turned-off gas burner and fill halfway with water. *For charcoal*, sprinkle coals with ⅔ cup drained wood chips. *For gas*, drain all chips and place in the metal smoking box or in a foil pan directly on the heat in a corner.

6. Lift meat from marinade and lay meat on cooking grate directly over drip pan. Grill meat, covered, 1 hour. Using a heatproof brush, baste meat all over with mop sauce. *For charcoal*, add 10 to 15 briquets to fire and another ⅓ cup drained wood chips. Check water level in drip pan for either grill type; add more water as needed to keep filled halfway. Cover grill and keep smoking meat, maintaining grill temperature. Repeat process (mopping meat and checking water level, and for charcoal, adding 10 to 15 briquets and ⅓ cup chips) every hour, turning meat occasionally, until an instant-read thermometer inserted into thickest part of each piece registers 190° and meat shreds easily, 1½ hours per lb. (3 to 5 hours total). If thermometer registers 190° but meat isn't tender, cook 30 minutes more.

7. Lift meat from grill and wrap in a double layer of heavy-duty foil, sealing tightly. Let meat steam at room temperature for about 30 minutes, then unwrap it, reserving any juices that have accumulated in foil.

8. When meat is cool enough to handle, pull it apart into large pieces. Discard excess fat. Shred meat with your fingers or a pair of forks. Toss shredded meat with green onions and cilantro and drizzle with reserved juices and reserved mop sauce to taste. Serve pork with coleslaw, rolls, and your choice of condiments.

*Achiote paste is made from ground achiote seeds (also called annatto), vinegar, salt, and spices; it's often sold in bar form. Queso fresco is a fresh Mexican cheese. Find both in Latino markets and at well-stocked grocery stores.

PER SERVING 481 CAL., 54% (261 CAL.) FROM FAT; 39 G PROTEIN; 29 G FAT (10 G SAT.); 12 G CARBO (64 G FIBER); 1,110 MG SODIUM; 165 MG CHOL. LC

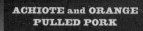

ACHIOTE and ORANGE
PULLED PORK

FENNEL-CRUSTED GRILLED
RACK of LAMB

FENNEL-CRUSTED GRILLED RACK OF LAMB

SERVES 8 TO 10 ★ 1½ HOURS, PLUS 4 HOURS TO MARINATE

Fennel seeds and rosemary perfume every bite of this tenderest of cuts.

2 tbsp. fennel seeds
1 tbsp. fresh rosemary leaves
3 large garlic cloves
1½ tbsp. kosher salt
1 tbsp. pepper
2 tbsp. extra-virgin olive oil
2 racks American lamb (each 7 to 8 ribs), bone ends
    frenched and all but a thin layer of outer fat removed*

1. Crush fennel seeds, rosemary, and garlic with salt in a mortar, or chop as finely as possible. Mix with pepper and oil.

2. Slather lamb with marinade. Chill, covered, at least 4 hours and up to 1 day.

3. Take lamb out of refrigerator 1 hour before grilling. Wrap bone ends with foil.

4. Heat a grill to medium (about 400°) with a charcoal area left clear or a gas burner turned off to make an indirect heat area (see "Indirect Heat Grilling," page 88, and maintain heat as directed). Grill lamb, meat side down, over indirect heat 5 minutes. Turn over and grill 10 minutes. Turn again; grill 10 minutes more. Move lamb to direct heat, meat side down, and grill 3 to 5 minutes, or until it's crisp and browned and a meat thermometer in thickest part registers 140° (for medium-rare).

5. Let lamb rest on a platter 15 minutes. Cut between the bones to serve.

*If the ribs aren't already frenched (that is, some meat trimmed from the bone ends to make the chops look neater), ask a butcher to do it, or do it yourself by sliding a sharp knife along the bones. Leave the barest sheath of fat on the meat—enough to crisp up on the grill but not so much that the dripping fat creates an inferno.

PER SERVING 552 CAL., 73% (404 CAL.) FROM FAT; 34 G PROTEIN; 45 G FAT (18 G SAT.); 1.5 G CARBO (0.7 G FIBER); 798 MG SODIUM; 146 MG CHOL. GF

GRILLED LAMB AND HALLOUMI KEBABS

SERVES 4 ★ 30 MINUTES

Taken off the skewers and tossed with fresh herbs, these kebabs turn into a flavorful and hearty filling for pita bread. We like to serve them with a side of hummus. The kebabs go onto 8 metal skewers.

About 5 tbsp. olive oil
3 tbsp. red wine vinegar
1 tsp. *each* kosher salt and pepper
1 tbsp. *each* chopped fresh oregano and mint leaves,
    plus ¼ cup *each* whole oregano and mint leaves
8 oz. halloumi cheese*, cut into 1-in. cubes
1 lb. cherry tomatoes
1 lb. lamb stew meat, cut into 1-in. cubes
4 white or whole-wheat pita breads, halved and warmed

1. Heat a grill to high (450° to 550°). Mix 5 tbsp. oil, the vinegar, salt, pepper, and chopped herbs in a large bowl. Measure 2 tbsp. and set aside. Add cheese, tomatoes, and lamb to remaining dressing and toss to coat. Thread cheese, tomatoes, and lamb onto 8 metal skewers.

2. Oil cooking grate, using tongs and a wad of oiled paper towels. Grill kebabs, turning once, until meat and cheese are browned, about 6 minutes.

3. Set skewers on plates, drizzle with reserved dressing, and scatter with whole herb leaves. Serve with pita.

*Find halloumi, a firm, salty cheese that keeps its shape on the grill, at well-stocked grocery stores.

PER SERVING 680 CAL., 50% (343 CAL.) FROM FAT; 43 G PROTEIN; 38 G FAT (13 G SAT.); 41 G CARBO (3 G FIBER); 1,498 MG SODIUM; 119 MG CHOL.

> **TIP** FOR A VEGETARIAN MEAL, TRY HALLOUMI AND SQUASH KEBABS: FOLLOW THE RECIPE ABOVE, BUT SUBSTITUTE CHUNKS OF SUMMER SQUASH FOR THE LAMB.

COOKING with the SUN

When we first considered trying a solar oven in the *Sunset* test kitchen, we thought the idea was a little far out, but also intriguing: We're always looking for greener, more sustainable ways to cook. And we're delighted with the results.

We bought a few different ovens, at different price levels, and tried several recipes. It took us a few failed attempts (scrambled eggs, steak, and rice among them) to understand how this type of cooking is unlike anything else, and that it needs to be approached with a different mind-set.

As we got to know the ovens and developed recipes, people would stop by our outdoor kitchen at *Sunset* to inspect the process. Inevitably, they'd ask, "Does it actually work?" We're very happy to report that it does. If you live somewhere that has a lot of sun and you use the right recipe, you can make incredibly good food without using a single drop of fossil fuel. And the smaller solar ovens are great for camping too.

CHOOSING AN OVEN

Among the several types on the market, we liked two best.

1 THE GLOBAL SUN OVEN. Looks like a giant foil-covered box—but the materials used are especially chosen for durability and efficiency (see photo at right). It's easy to set up: You just snap on the four aluminum reflectors, which open up and out from a central cooking chamber like petals on a flower, to catch the sun. An adjustable leg underneath allows you to tilt the oven toward the traveling sun as you cook, capturing as much heat as possible. It has a built-in thermometer, and gets up to about 350°.

2 THE SPORT SOLAR OVEN. Looks a lot like a cathode-ray TV. It has just two tilt positions for following the sun, but at 10 pounds is lightweight and easy to carry. The Sport only goes up to about 300°, and is smaller than the Global, but can still hold two medium pots side by side—which are included in the purchase price, along with a thermometer.

For more information on both ovens, see the Resource Guide, page 244.

TIPS FOR SUCCESSFUL SOLAR COOKING

PRACTICE. Get to know the oven and its particular ways of working before planning a solar dinner party.

PLAY TO ITS STRENGTHS. A solar oven is a moist environment, more like a steamer or Crockpot than an oven. Use it for slow-cooking recipes like braises and stews, rather than for foods that are best browned or crisp, like steak or pizza. Baked goods will be pale, not golden, but still delicious.

LIGHTEN THE LOAD. If cooking large volumes of food, divide it among multiple pots so it will cook faster.

USE DARK COOKWARE. Dark-colored metal pans and black granite-ware from an outdoor supply store attract and retain heat, aiding the process. Glass won't draw enough heat, and shiny pots reflect it.

PLAN AHEAD (and check the weather report). Cooking times will depend on how strong the sun is and how long it lasts. If cooking in winter or on a hazy day, allow extra time.

PREHEAT THOROUGHLY. It could take 30 minutes or more for the oven to reach the desired temperature.

FOLLOW THE SUN. Have the food in the oven at least an hour before the hottest part of the day, and move the oven at least once an hour to keep it in direct sunlight. Adjust the tilt of the oven too, to catch the full force of the sun.

DON'T PEEK. Cooking in a solar oven is very gentle—it's virtually impossible to burn anything—so refrain from checking on your food. Opening the door will cause the oven temperature to plummet, and it can take up to an hour to recover.

BE SAFE. That said, the oven and pots do get very hot, so use pot holders. Beware of steam when opening the oven or lifting lids. And allow the oven to cool completely, in the shade or after the sun has set, before touching the interior.

continued

SOLAR OVEN FEIJOADA

1. Set solar oven in a sunny place, reflectors up and door pointing to the sun, and preheat to 300°.

2. Drain beans. Mix with remaining ingredients except for orange wedges and add ½ cup water. Put mixture into a dark metal pan with a lid, dividing between two pans if your oven has space.

3. Bake mixture until meat and beans are tender, 4 to 5 hours. Serve with orange wedges on the side.

*Linguiça, spicy Portuguese sausage, is available at many grocery stores and online (see Resource Guide, page 244).

PER SERVING 759 CAL., 42% (321 CAL.) FROM FAT; 52 G PROTEIN; 36 G FAT (12 G SAT.); 55 G CARBO (13 G FIBER); 900 MG SODIUM; 132 MG CHOL. GF

SOLAR OVEN HERB LOAF

MAKES 1 LOAF; 12 SLICES ★ 3 HOURS

It's very important to preheat the oven for this recipe, to get a good "oven spring" in the bread—i.e., the wonderful puffy swell that happens during baking. This recipe is for a soft, tender loaf of bread, since a crisp crust isn't an option. You can also shape the dough into dinner rolls.

1 pkg. active dry yeast (about 1¾ tsp.)
3 tbsp. sugar
¼ cup mixed chopped fresh herbs, such as flat-leaf parsley, dill, chives, and rosemary
2 tbsp. melted butter, cooled
1 large egg
1½ tsp. salt
1 cup milk or half-and-half, warmed slightly
3½ to 3¾ cups flour

1. Sprinkle yeast over ¼ cup warm water (about 100°) in bowl of a stand mixer (or, if kneading by hand, in a large bowl). Let stand until dissolved, 5 minutes. Stir in sugar, herbs, butter, egg, salt, and milk; add 3¼ cups flour and stir to moisten.

SOLAR OVEN *FEIJOADA*

SERVES 4 TO 6 ★ ABOUT 45 MINUTES, PLUS 4 TO 5 HOURS TO COOK AND OVERNIGHT FOR BEANS TO SOAK

Feijoada, the national dish of Brazil, is a mix of pork cuts and black beans typically served as the main meal on weekends (and, in restaurants, Wednesdays too). The technique of cooking the stew slow and long makes it a fantastic recipe for solar ovens. We've simplified the meat options with pork shoulder and two kinds of sausage, but feel free to experiment with your favorite cuts.

For the full Brazilian spread, serve it with a side of rice and shredded kale or collard greens.

1 lb. dried black beans, soaked in water overnight
1 cup chopped onion
2 large garlic cloves
1 cup crushed tomatoes
9 oz. *linguiça**, sliced
1¾ lbs. pork shoulder, cubed
6 oz. bulk Italian sausage, formed into small balls
1 tsp. kosher salt
Orange wedges

2. Knead dough with the dough hook (or knead on a lightly floured board) until elastic and not sticky, 4 minutes; add flour as needed to prevent sticking.

3. Shape into a rectangle and, working toward you, roll dough into a loaf shape, tucking in edges as you go and sealing edge with the heel of your hand. Place seam side down in a well-greased dark 5- by 8-in. loaf pan. Cover loosely with greased plastic wrap.

4. Let dough rise in a warm place until doubled, 45 to 60 minutes. Meanwhile, set solar oven in a sunny place, reflectors up and door pointing to the sun, and preheat to about 300° or as hot as your oven will go.

5. Bake, door sealed, until bread is light golden and internal temperature reads 180° on an instant-read thermometer, 2 to 2½ hours.

6. Turn bread out of pan onto a rack and let cool completely before slicing, 1 to 1½ hours.

Make ahead: Through step 2 using cold water and milk; immediately wrap airtight (do not let rise) and chill up to 1 day. Proceed with step 3.

PER SLICE 189 CAL., 16% (30 CAL.) FROM FAT; 5.4 G PROTEIN; 3.4 G FAT (1.8 G SAT.); 34 G CARBO (1.2 G FIBER); 321 MG SODIUM; 25 MG CHOL. V

SOLAR OVEN
SHORTBREAD
COOKIES

SOLAR OVEN SHORTBREAD COOKIES

MAKES 28 COOKIES ★ ABOUT 3 HOURS

Shortbread cookies are a good choice for the solar oven because they don't need to brown or crisp. You can make the dough a day or two ahead, but before baking, let the formed cookies come to room temperature.

½ cup butter, at room temperature
¼ cup plus ½ tbsp. sugar, divided
3 tbsp. cornstarch
1¼ cups flour

1. Set up solar oven in a sunny place, reflectors up and door pointing to the sun, and preheat to 250° to 300°.

2. Whirl butter, ¼ cup sugar, cornstarch, and flour together in a food processor until smooth. (Or, in a bowl with an electric mixer on medium speed, beat butter, ¼ cup sugar, and cornstarch until smooth; stir in flour until mixture is no longer crumbly and comes together in a ball.)

3. Press dough evenly into a dark 8-in. square pan. Press edges of dough with back of a fork to make a ridged pattern.

Then, with tip of fork tines, pierce dough all over in parallel lines 1 in. apart, crossing at 2 in. intervals, creating bar shapes.

4. Bake shortbread until firm and golden at edges, about 45 minutes. Remove from oven and while hot, sprinkle with remaining ½ tbsp. sugar.

5. Cool completely in pan set on a rack. Invert, then cut into bars.

PER COOKIE 61 CAL., 49% (30 CAL.) FROM FAT; 0.1 G PROTEIN; 3.4 G FAT (2 G SAT.); 7 G CARBO (0.1 G FIBER); 26 MG SODIUM; 8.7 MG CHOL. LC/LS/V

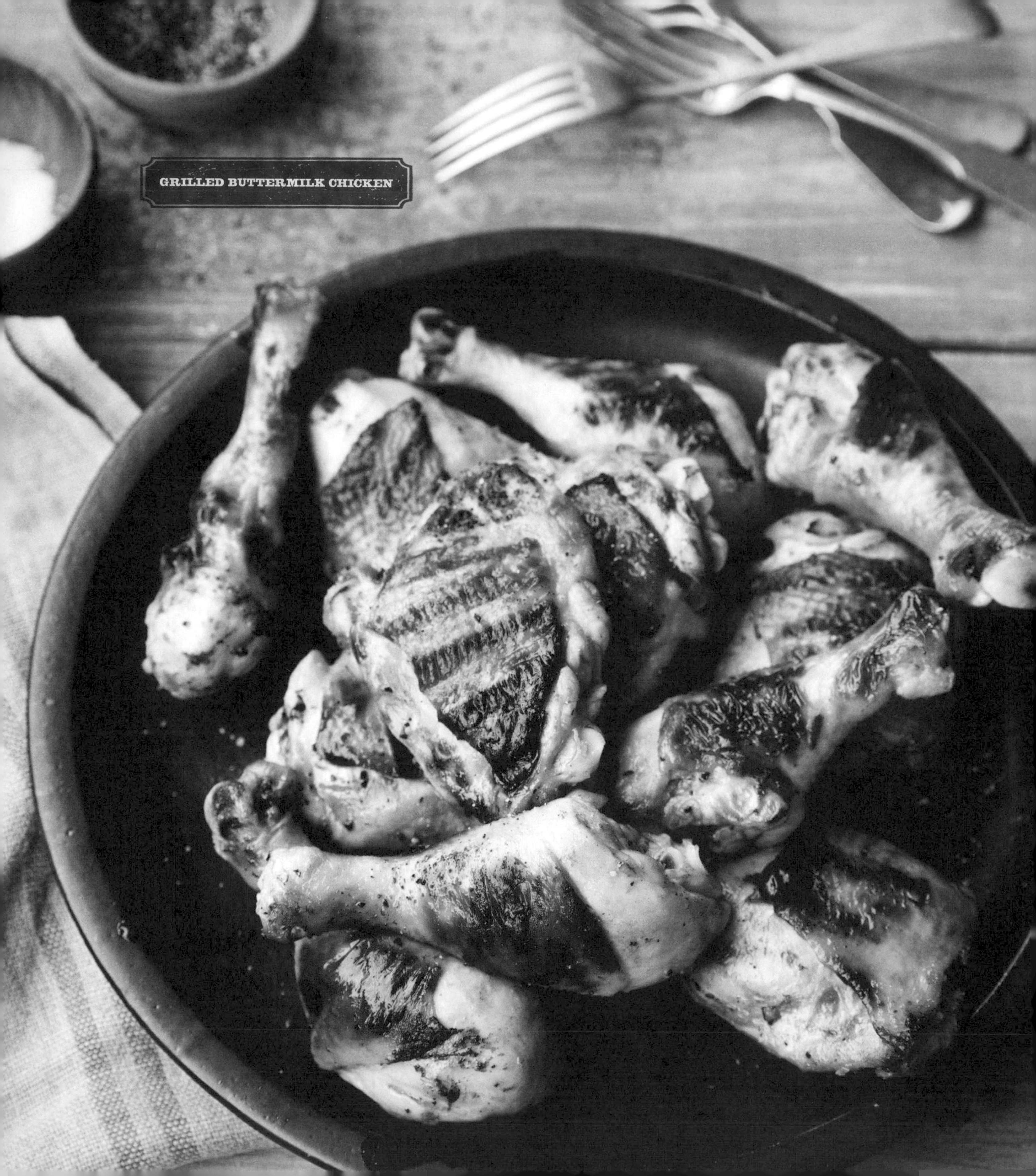

GRILLED BUTTERMILK CHICKEN

GRILLED BUTTERMILK CHICKEN

SERVES 6 ★ ABOUT 30 MINUTES, PLUS 4 HOURS TO BRINE

Brining in buttermilk and cumin keeps the meat moist and flavorful, even if you accidentally cook it a little too long.

1 qt. buttermilk
½ cup chopped shallots
2 tbsp. *each* chopped garlic, kosher salt, and sugar
1 tbsp. ground cumin
1 tsp. pepper
6 chicken thighs (about 2½ lbs. total)
6 chicken drumsticks (about 1¾ lbs. total)

1. In a large bowl, mix buttermilk, shallots, garlic, salt, sugar, cumin, and pepper. Submerge chicken pieces in buttermilk brine. Cover and chill for at least 4 hours, or up to 1 day.

2. Heat a grill to medium (350° to 450°). Lift chicken from brine; discard brine. Wipe excess from chicken with paper towels.

3. Grill chicken, covered, turning pieces frequently, until browned on both sides and no longer pink at the bone (cut to test), 20 to 30 minutes. Serve hot or cold.

Make ahead: Up to 1 day, chilled.

PER SERVING 402 CAL., 51% (207 CAL.) FROM FAT; 43 G PROTEIN; 23 G FAT (6.4 G SAT.); 4 G CARBO (0.1 G FIBER); 670 MG SODIUM; 149 MG CHOL. GF/LC

> **TIP** TO TEST CHICKEN FOR DONENESS, CUT INTO THE THICKEST PART. THE PINK SHOULD BE GONE, BUT THE FIBERS SHOULDN'T BE SEPARATING—THAT'S A SIGN OF OVERCOOKING.

SPICE-RUBBED SMOKE-ROASTED CHICKEN

SERVES 6 ★ 2 HOURS

Adding wood chips to the fire and rubbing a whole chicken with an herb and spice blend gives it loads of flavor. It's a great recipe for entertaining since it requires very little tending at the grill.

1 cup (about 3 oz.) mesquite or applewood chips (optional; see "Woods for Smoking," page 124)
12 garlic cloves, peeled
1 tbsp. chili powder
⅓ cup chopped fresh thyme leaves
⅓ cup chopped fresh rosemary leaves
¼ cup olive oil
1 tbsp. *each* salt and pepper
1 chicken (4 to 5 lbs.)

1. In a medium bowl, cover wood chips (if using) in water. Let soak at least 30 minutes; drain just before using.

2. Meanwhile, in a food processor, combine garlic, chili powder, thyme, rosemary, oil, salt, and pepper. Process until mixture forms a paste.

3. Press down on the breastbone of the chicken to flatten the bird slightly; rub the paste evenly over all the skin.

4. Heat a grill to medium (350° to 400°) with a charcoal area left clear or a gas burner turned off to make an indirect heat area (see "Indirect Heat Grilling," page 88). Set a 9- by 13-in. drip pan in place on firegrate between banks of coals or on turned off gas burner. *For charcoal*, scatter half the wood chips over the coals. *For gas*, place all the chips in the metal smoking box or in a foil pan directly on the heat in a corner.

5. Place chicken over drip pan, breast side down. For charcoal, adjust vents so that they're open halfway. Cook, covered, 30 minutes, then turn chicken over (*for charcoal*, scatter another 10 to 12 briquets over coals, along with the remaining wood chips; add 10 more briquets after 30 minutes more if needed).

6. Continue cooking chicken, covered, until a thermometer inserted through the thickest part of the breast to bone reaches 170°, 45 to 55 minutes longer. Transfer to a cutting board or platter, tent with foil, and let rest 10 minutes. Carve to serve.

PER SERVING 417 CAL., 60% (252 CAL.) FROM FAT; 38 G PROTEIN; 28 G FAT (6.8 G SAT.); 1.8 G CARBO (0.9 G FIBER); 996 MG SODIUM; 118 MG CHOL. LC

YOGURT-MARINATED CHICKEN KEBABS WITH PEARL COUSCOUS

SERVES 4 ★ 45 MINUTES

The yogurt marinade gives the chicken in this recipe—from reader Margee Berry, of Trout Lake, Washington—a delicious tang; it also tenderizes the meat. You'll need four 8-in. metal skewers.

1½ cups plain low-fat yogurt, divided
2 tsp. *garam masala**
1 tsp. Madras curry powder
2 garlic cloves, minced
1 tsp. plus 1 tbsp. salt
½ tsp. pepper
1½ lbs. boned, skinned chicken breast, cut into 1½-in. cubes
⅓ cup crumbled feta cheese
3 tbsp. minced red onion
1 tsp. lemon zest
2 tbsp. chopped fresh mint leaves, divided
1½ cups pearl couscous*
2 tsp. olive oil
2 medium red bell peppers, cut into 1½-in. pieces

1. Combine 1 cup yogurt, the garam masala, curry powder, garlic, 1 tsp. salt, and the pepper in a large resealable plastic bag. Add chicken, seal bag, and shake to coat. Let marinate 20 minutes at room temperature.

2. Meanwhile, in a small bowl, stir together ½ cup yogurt, the feta, onion, zest, and 1 tbsp. mint; set aside.

3. Bring 2 qts. water to a boil in a pot and add remaining 1 tbsp. salt. Add couscous and cook until tender, 12 to 15 minutes. Drain, return to pot, and add oil. Cover to keep warm.

4. While couscous is cooking, heat a grill to medium-high (450°). Thread chicken and bell peppers onto 4 metal skewers and discard marinade. Grill skewers, covered, turning once, until chicken is browned and no longer pink in center (cut to test), about 10 minutes. Pile couscous on a platter, sprinkle with remaining 1 tbsp. mint, and arrange kebabs around it. Serve with yogurt-feta sauce.

*Find garam masala, an earthy Indian spice mixture, and pearl (also called Israeli) couscous at well-stocked grocery stores.

PER SERVING 569 CAL., 14% (77 CAL.) FROM FAT; 55 G PROTEIN; 8.6 G FAT (3.5 G SAT.); 64 G CARBO (3.4 G FIBER); 1,275 MG SODIUM; 114 MG CHOL.

FIVE-SPICE CHICKEN NOODLE SALAD

SERVES 4 ★ 45 MINUTES

Like a cross between a noodle bowl and a salad, this dish is low in fat and has a spicy kick.

2 tbsp. *each* soy sauce and vegetable oil
2 tsp. Chinese five-spice powder
1 tsp. sugar
4 boned, skinned chicken breast halves
1 pkg. (6 oz.) rice vermicelli
1 cup coarsely shredded carrots
½ cup *each* cilantro and fresh mint leaves
¼ cup crushed peanuts
Chile Lime Dressing (recipe follows)

1. Heat a grill to medium (350° to 450°).

2. Mix soy sauce, oil, five-spice powder, and sugar in a shallow dish. Turn chicken in marinade and let stand 5 to 10 minutes. Meanwhile, heat a large pot of water to boiling.

3. Drain chicken, discarding marinade. Oil cooking grate, using tongs and a wad of oiled paper towels. Grill chicken, covered, turning once, until cooked through, 10 to 12 minutes. Transfer to a cutting board and let rest 5 minutes.

4. Add vermicelli to boiling water and turn off heat. Let stand until noodles are soft, 5 to 10 minutes; drain.

5. Divide noodles among dinner bowls. Thickly slice chicken, set on noodles, and top with carrots, herbs, and peanuts. Serve with dressing.

PER SERVING 472 CAL., 25% (119 CAL.) FROM FAT; 30 G PROTEIN; 14 G FAT (1.9 G SAT.); 58 G CARBO (2.3 G FIBER); 2,103 MG SODIUM; 76 MG CHOL. LC

CHILE LIME DRESSING

MAKES 1 CUP ★ 5 MINUTES

¼ cup *each* sugar, unseasoned rice vinegar, and Thai or Vietnamese fish sauce
6 tbsp. lime juice
1 to 2 tbsp. minced red or green jalapeño chile

Mix ½ cup hot water and the sugar in a small bowl until sugar dissolves. Stir in remaining ingredients.

PER TBSP. 16 CAL., 0% (0 CAL.) FROM FAT; 0.3 G PROTEIN; 3.9 G CARBO (0 G FIBER); 354 MG SODIUM; 0 MG CHOL.

FIVE-SPICE CHICKEN
NOODLE SALAD

We love this method. The turkey looks good because the breast is cut into thick slices against the grain. Plus, it skips the interminable and messy slicing at the table: All the meat is quickly carved in the kitchen and served neatly, ready to be eaten.

1

Slice off the breast halves lengthwise. Carve off the thighs (with legs attached) and the wings and set aside.

2

Carve each breast half across the grain into thick slices.

3

Slice the thigh meat off the bone and cut bone free from leg. Arrange sliced breasts, dark meat, and whole legs and wings on a platter (see photo, opposite).

WINE-SMOKED TURKEY

SERVES 16 TO 18, WITH AMPLE LEFTOVERS ★ 3 TO 3½ HOURS

In a recipe inspired by California wine country, wine-infused wood chips, a heady herbal marinade, apples, and onions give this crisp-skinned grilled turkey fantastic flavor. Wine shows up in the velvety Zinfandel gravy too.

**4 to 6 cups lightly packed wine-infused wood chips
    or shavings***
3 tbsp. olive oil
**2 tbsp. minced fresh sage leaves or 2 tsp. dried sage,
    plus sage sprigs for garnish**
1 tbsp. minced flat-leaf parsley
**2 tsp. minced fresh marjoram leaves or ½ tsp. dried
    marjoram, plus marjoram sprigs for garnish**
½ tsp. pepper
1 turkey (16 to 18 lbs.)
1 Golden Delicious apple, cored
1 medium onion, peeled
Zinfandel Gravy (recipe follows)

1. Soak wine-infused chips or shavings in water at least 20 minutes. In a small bowl, mix oil with minced sage, parsley, marjoram, and the pepper.

2. To prepare turkey, remove and discard leg truss. Remove giblets and neck and set aside for making Zinfandel gravy. Pat turkey dry. Brush turkey all over with 2 tbsp. oil mixture. Cut apple and onion into 1-in. chunks, stir into remaining oil mixture, and spoon apple mixture into body cavity. Put foil caps on drumstick tips and wing tips. Insert a meat thermometer straight down through thickest part of breast to bone (if using an instant-read thermometer, insert later).

3. Heat a grill to medium-low (about 325°) with a charcoal area left clear or a gas burner turned off to make an indirect heat area (see "Indirect Heat Grilling," page 88; for charcoal, start with 40 briquets). Set a sturdy drip pan between banks of coals or on turned-off gas burner and fill pan halfway with warm water. *For charcoal*, add 5 briquets and ½ cup soaked wood chips or shavings to each side now and every 30 minutes while cooking; if needed, keep grill uncovered for a few minutes to help briquets ignite. *For gas*, put 1 cup soaked wood chips or shavings in grill's metal smoking box or in a small, shallow foil pan set directly on burner in a corner. Add another 1 cup wood chips or shavings every hour or so while cooking. Replace cooking grate.

4. Set turkey, breast up, on cooking grate over drip pan and cook, covered, until meat thermometer or an instant-read thermometer inserted straight down through thickest part of breast to bone registers 165°, 2½ to 3 hours (thighs should register 170°); during cooking, loosely tent turkey with foil if it starts to get too dark.

5. Drain juices and remove apple and onion from cavity; reserve for gravy. Place turkey on a platter and let rest 15 to 30 minutes, then carve (see "Carving the Bird, Beautifully," on opposite page). Remove drip pan from grill; skim and discard fat from juices. Reserve juices for Zinfandel gravy. Garnish platter with herb sprigs.

*Order wine-infused chips online (see "Woods for Smoking," page 124, and Resource Guide, page 244). Or soak mesquite or applewood chips in equal parts red wine and water in step 1.

PER ¼-LB. SERVING (WHITE AND DARK MEAT WITH SKIN) 250 CAL., 43% (108 CAL.) FROM FAT; 32 G PROTEIN; 12 G FAT (3.2 G SAT.); 1.4 G CARBO (0 G FIBER); 82 MG SODIUM; 93 MG CHOL. GF/LC/LS

ZINFANDEL GRAVY

MAKES 6 CUPS; 18 SERVINGS ★ 2 HOURS

Giblets and neck from a 16- to 18-lb. turkey
2 large onions, quartered
2 large carrots, cut into chunks
1 cup sliced celery
4½ cups reduced-sodium chicken broth, divided
2¾ cups Zinfandel, divided
2 strips orange zest (3 in. each)
½ tsp. pepper
Cooked apple mixture and fat-skimmed turkey pan juices from Wine-Smoked Turkey (at left)
½ cup cornstarch
Salt

1. In a large pot, combine giblets, neck, onions, carrots, celery, and ½ cup broth. Cook, covered, over medium-high heat, 20 minutes. Uncover; cook over high heat, stirring often as liquid evaporates, until giblets and vegetables are browned and browned bits stick to bottom of pot, 5 to 8 minutes. Add another ½ cup broth and stir to loosen browned bits. Cook and brown, uncovered, as before.

2. Add remaining 3½ cups broth, 2 cups Zinfandel, the zest, and pepper to pot. Cover and simmer over low heat for 1 to 1½ hours.

3. Add apple mixture from turkey cavity; bring to a boil. Lower heat and simmer, covered, 5 minutes.

4. Pour broth mixture through a fine-mesh strainer into a bowl. Discard contents of strainer. Measure broth; if needed, add enough turkey pan juices to make 5½ cups. In pot, mix cornstarch with ¼ cup water and remaining ¾ cup wine. Stir in broth mixture and cook, stirring, over high heat until boiling, about 5 minutes. Season with salt to taste.

PER ⅓ CUP 34 CAL., 5% (1.8 CAL.) FROM FAT; 1.8 G PROTEIN; 0.2 G FAT (0 G SAT.); 6.1 G CARBO (0 G FIBER); 163 MG SODIUM; 3.8 MG CHOL. GF/LC

CEDAR-PLANKED
SALMON

CEDAR-PLANKED SALMON

SERVES 6 ★ 45 MINUTES, PLUS 2 HOURS TO SOAK PLANK

Based on a Northwest Native American method of roasting salmon on a wood frame, grilling salmon on a cedar plank gives the fish a deep, woodsy taste and keeps it moist by protecting it from the flames. You will need an untreated cedar board, ½ to ¾ in. thick and big enough to accommodate your fish. Find planks at a well-stocked fishmonger, barbecue store, or online (see Resource Guide, page 244).

2 tbsp. table salt
1 tsp. vegetable oil
1 skin-on, boned salmon fillet* (2 to 2½ lbs.)
½ tsp. kosher or sea salt
¼ tsp. pepper
1 tsp. butter

1. Put 2 qts. hot water and table salt in a pan big enough to hold the plank (such as a roasting pan); stir to dissolve salt. Soak plank at least 2 hours.

2. Meanwhile, heat a grill to medium-high (about 450°) with a charcoal area left clear or a gas burner turned off to make an indirect heat area (see "Indirect Heat Grilling," page 88).

3. Wipe water off plank and rub it with oil. Set it over direct heat and toast it, covered, until it starts to smoke and char, 5 to 10 minutes.

4. Meanwhile, season salmon fillet with kosher salt and pepper. Turn plank over, set over indirect heat, and set fillet, skin side down, on charred side. Dot with butter.

5. Cook salmon on plank, covered, until center of fillet flakes, 30 to 40 minutes.

*Look for a long, narrow fillet that fits your board. If all you can find is a short, wide fillet, just divide it down the center and lay the pieces end to end on the board to fit.

PER SERVING 322 CAL., 55% (176 CAL.) FROM FAT; 34 G PROTEIN; 20 G FAT (4.3 G SAT.); 0.1 G CARBO (0 G FIBER); 258 MG SODIUM; 98 MG CHOL. GF/LC/LS

SALMON *SHIOYAKI*

SERVES 4 ★ 15 MINUTES, PLUS 2 HOURS TO SALT FISH

Add *shioyaki*—Japanese for "salt-grilled"—to your repertoire. The technique (which is also the name of the dish) creates salmon with an umami-rich crust and a crispy skin. Taichi Kitamura, chef of Sushi Kappo Tamura restaurant in Seattle, shared the recipe with us. When he was growing up in Kyoto, it was his favorite fish dish, and still is.

4 sockeye salmon fillets (each ½ to 1 in. thick and
    5 to 6 oz.), with skin
1½ tsp. fine sea salt
1 tbsp. vegetable oil
Hot cooked sushi rice such as Nishiki or other short-
    to medium-grain rice
4 sheets nori (about 8 in. square), each cut into 6 pieces
Lemon wedges
*Furikake** (Japanese rice seasoning)

1. Set salmon on a cooling rack in a rimmed pan, sprinkle fillets all over with sea salt, and chill uncovered at least 2 hours and as long as 5 hours.

2. Heat a grill to medium-high (about 450°). Fold a 12-by 20-in. sheet of heavy-duty foil in half crosswise. With a knife tip, poke dime-size holes through foil about 2 in. apart. Oil one side of foil. Rub fish all over with oil.

3. Set foil with oiled side up on cooking grate. Set fillets, slightly separated and skin side down, on foil. Grill, covered, until fish is barely cooked through, 7 to 12 minutes. With a wide spatula, slide fish off skin onto a platter and tent with foil. Cook skin on foil until crisp, 2 to 3 more minutes. Remove foil from grill, then gently peel off skin, using fingers or a wide spatula (skin may break into pieces).

4. Serve salmon immediately with crispy skin, rice, nori, lemon, and furikake.

*A salty-sweet shake-on condiment, furikake can be found at Asian markets or ordered online (see Resource Guide, page 244).

PER SERVING 292 CAL., 50% (145 CAL.) FROM FAT; 33 G PROTEIN; 16 G FAT (2.6 G SAT.); 1 G CARBO (0.5 G FIBER); 967 MG SODIUM; 101 MG CHOL. LC

1. Heat a grill to medium-low (300° to 350°). Snip off salmon fins. To remove salmon scales and help skin crisp up when cooked, liberally sprinkle fish, including head and tail, with kosher salt. Let sit 10 minutes. Rub salt (wearing dishwashing gloves if you like, to protect your hands) in a somewhat rough manner, then wipe off scales and salt with a towel.

2. Generously sprinkle Porcini Rub inside fish cavity and all over outside. Stuff cavity with orange and bay.

3. Brush cooking grate well with a wire brush. Oil grate, using tongs and a wad of oiled paper towels. Set fish toward back of grill with its belly away from you, on a diagonal if needed for fit.

4. Cover grill and cook fish 5 minutes without moving it. Then, using 2 wide spatulas, roll fish to other side over the top of the fish (not the belly; see photo at left). Every 10 minutes, roll fish over its back to the opposite side. For moist fish that is easy to separate from bones, don't cook past medium-rare (it should no longer feel soft when pressed with a finger), 25 minutes total for a 7-lb. fish, 35 minutes total for an 11-lb. fish.

5. Have a helper hold a board larger than the fish at the edge of grill. Using 2 wide spatulas, carefully lift fish to board. Cover with foil and let rest 15 minutes; it will continue to cook. Lift crisp skin off one side of salmon and set skin aside. Slide fingers or a wide spatula between flesh and bones to loosen flesh; transfer it (in sections, if necessary) to a platter. Discard bay and orange. Turn fish over; repeat on other side. Serve with pieces of crisp skin.

PER SERVING 411 CAL., 56% (229 CAL.) FROM FAT; 44 G PROTEIN; 25 G FAT (4.1 G SAT.); 1.2 G CARBO (0.3 G FIBER); 256 MG SODIUM; 132 MG CHOL. GF/LC/LS

PORCINI RUB

Working in batches in a spice grinder or clean coffee grinder, grind 3 tbsp. *each* **fennel seeds**, **kosher salt**, and **sugar**; 2 oz. **dried porcini mushrooms**; and 4 tsp. **pepper** until finely ground.

WHOLE SALMON WITH BAY, ORANGE, AND PORCINI

SERVES 8 TO 15 ★ 1 HOUR

This aromatic and impressive dish, created by John Fink, chef/owner of Bay Area catering company The Whole Beast, is big enough to feed a crowd. He uses homegrown fresh bay leaves, but dried leaves work too. A 7-lb. fish serves 8 generously and it just fits on a standard charcoal kettle grill. If you want to cook a bigger fish, measure your grill first to be sure it will fit.

1 whole king salmon with head, 7 to 11 lbs., gutted
Kosher salt
Porcini Rub (recipe follows)
1 large orange, sliced
24 fresh California or Mediterranean bay leaves; or use dried bay leaves, soaked in water 30 minutes

Make a
FRESH-BAY "CAGE"

This dramatic variation for grilling the whole salmon opposite was inspired by Native American salmon bakes.

Inspired by the Northwest Native American technique of cooking whole salmon on a wood frame over an open fire, John Fink devised a fragrant cage for a whole fish, using long, slender branches of fresh bay. The cage infuses the fish with flavor, helps keep its skin from sticking to the grill, and makes it easy to flip the fish for even cooking. Plus, it's wonderful to look at and fun to create.

If you don't have bay branches, you can try slender fruit-tree branches. You'll also need some baling wire (sold at craft stores), wire cutters, and preferably a charcoal or wood-fired grill. If you use a gas grill, be careful during cooking that the charred leaves don't fall into the grill's inner workings, where they could damage it.

Follow the recipe for Whole Salmon with Bay, Orange, and Porcini (opposite), but omit bay leaves in the cavity.

1 START THE CAGE. Cut 4 strong, slender bay branches (with side shoots) that are a bit longer than the fish. Following the illustration below left (leaves and side shoots have been omitted for clarity), lay branches 1 and 2 flat, in an oval a little wider than the fish, and join with wire at point A, with a skinny end meeting a fatter end. Let the side shoots just be messy.

2 SET FISH IN PLACE. Lay the fish on its side between branches 1 and 2 with its head at point A. If possible, thread one of the branches' ends through the fish's mouth to help secure the fish.

3 SECURE THE TAIL. Tie branches 1 and 2 with wire at point B. Then wrap the wire several times around point B and the fish's tail, and tie securely; this is your "handle" for turning the fish on the grill.

4 FINISH THE CAGE. Center branch 3 underneath the fish and branch 4 on top of it. Secure with wire at points A and B.

5 NEATEN IT UP. Fold or weave all the side shoots across the fish through the main branches—no need to secure with wire.

6 GRILL THE FISH. Cook salmon as directed, then snip off the bay cage and remove skin and flesh.

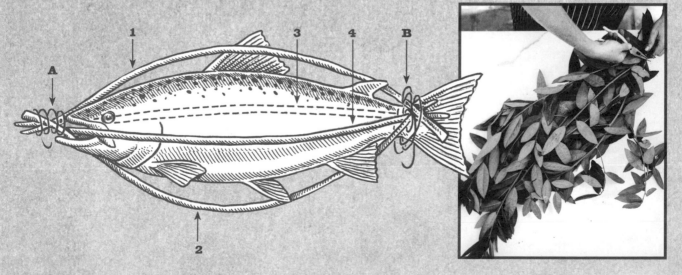

GRILLED HALIBUT, LETTUCE, AND TAPENADE BUNDLES

SERVES 4 ★ 40 MINUTES

Though extremely simple to put together, these bundles offer several "wow" factors—the surprise of the lettuce wrappers, the delicious contrast of mild, sweet halibut with briny tapenade, and the very moist texture of the fish, thanks to the romaine. To make them come out perfectly, choose large lettuce leaves that will wrap around the fish; cook the lettuce briefly so it's flexible, then plunge it into ice water to keep the emerald green color.

12 very large romaine lettuce leaves
½ cup green olive tapenade
1 lb. halibut fillets (1 in. thick)
Olive oil
Lemon wedges

1. Heat a grill to medium (about 375°). Meanwhile, bring a pot of water to a boil; add lettuce leaves 2 or 3 at a time and cook until ribs are flexible, 1½ to 3 minutes for each batch. As lettuce is done, transfer to a bowl of ice water. Lay leaves flat, with smooth sides up, on kitchen towels and pat dry.

2. Spread the 8 largest leaves with tapenade. Cut fish into 8 pieces, each about 2½ in. wide; set 1 at base of each leaf. If leaf isn't big enough to enclose fish, overlap leaf with another. Roll up each bundle from leaf's base,

folding in sides (gently crack lettuce ribs if needed). Brush bundles with oil. Discard any extra leaves.

3. Grill, turning once, until fish is just opaque (cut through a bundle with a small knife to check), 8 minutes. Serve with lemon.

PER SERVING 325 CAL., 69% (223 CAL.) FROM FAT; 18 G PROTEIN; 25 G FAT (4 G SAT.); 7.1 G CARBO (2.5 G FIBER); 417 MG SODIUM; 52 MG CHOL. GF/LC/LS

HALIBUT KEBABS WITH GRILLED BREAD AND PANCETTA

SERVES 4 ★ 30 MINUTES

You won't believe how outrageously yummy these halibut skewers are. Crusty Italian bread and halibut are seasoned with fresh rosemary, and then skewered with a ribbon of pancetta woven around them. As the skewers cook, the sizzling, crisping pancetta bastes both bread and meat. You'll need four 10-in. metal skewers.

¼ cup olive oil
1 tbsp. coarsely chopped fresh rosemary leaves
1 tsp. *each* salt and pepper
1½ lbs. boned and skinned halibut, cut into 2-in. chunks
4 cups 1½-in. cubes crusty bread, such as ciabatta
3 oz. pancetta*, sliced paper-thin

1. Heat a grill to medium (350° to 450°).

2. Meanwhile, in a large bowl, combine oil, rosemary, salt, and pepper. Add halibut and bread. Toss to coat, then set aside 5 minutes.

3. If the pancetta is rolled, unroll into strips. Skewer one end of a pancetta strip, then alternate fish and bread cubes on the skewer, weaving (and skewering) pancetta between them. Repeat with 3 remaining skewers.

4. Grill kebabs, turning frequently, until fish is cooked through and bread is charred in places, about 6 minutes.

*You could try very thinly sliced bacon if you don't have pancetta; prosciutto is too lean and will burn.

PER SERVING 516 CAL., 56% (288 CAL.) FROM FAT; 42 G PROTEIN; 32 G FAT (6.9 G SAT.); 22 G CARBO (1.2 G FIBER); 1,117 MG SODIUM; 66 MG CHOL.

GRILLED CHEESE FROM THE GRILL

The Culinary Institute of America in St. Helena, California, created one of our favorite takes on grilled cheese, called *Spiedini di Mozzarella*. Layer three ½-in.-thick slices of well-buttered **sourdough bread** with ¼-in.-thick slices of **fresh mozzarella**. Cut the stack into quarters, then push the woody end of a **rosemary sprig** through each mini stack to hold the layers together. Sprinkle with **salt** and **pepper**. Grill over high heat, turning, until lightly toasted. Serve as an appetizer or main dish.

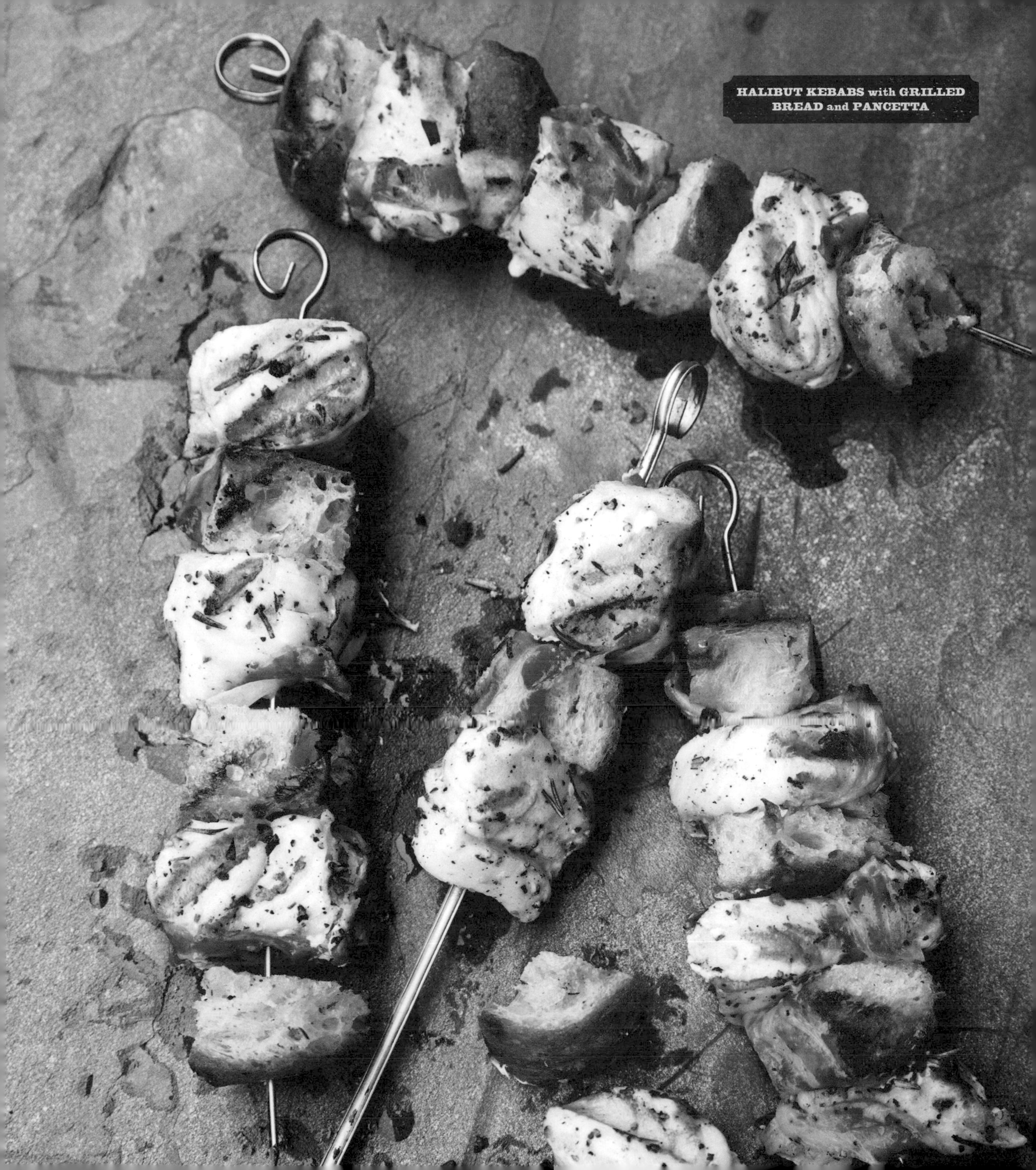
HALIBUT KEBABS with GRILLED
BREAD and PANCETTA

FISH TACOS

JAPANESE FISH TACOS

**MAKES 12 TO 14 ★ 45 MINUTES,
PLUS 1 HOUR TO MARINATE**

Food historians suggest that Mexico's fish tacos originated with Japanese fishermen in Baja, since the batter is very similar to that for tempura. This is our grilled tribute, with ponzu-wasabi mayonnaise and a sesame-flavored slaw.

FISH AND TORTILLAS
½ cup ponzu sauce*
1½ lbs. boned, skinned albacore* tuna loin (about 1 in. thick)
1 tbsp. vegetable oil
12 to 14 corn tortillas* (5 to 6 in.), wrapped in foil and warmed over direct low heat on grill (turn often)

PONZU-WASABI MAYO
1 cup mayonnaise
2 tbsp. ponzu sauce
About 2 tsp. wasabi paste or powder

TOASTED SESAME SLAW
3 cups napa cabbage, cut in fine shreds
½ cup red cabbage, cut in fine shreds
⅓ cup finely shredded carrot
1 large green onion, cut in 3-in.-long slivers
¼ cup toasted sesame seeds
1 tbsp. vegetable oil
1 tbsp. seasoned rice vinegar

1. Prepare fish: Pour ponzu into a large resealable plastic bag. Add albacore, seal bag, and turn fish to coat. Chill 1 hour, turning once.

2. Meanwhile, make mayo: Stir all ingredients together in a bowl, including wasabi to taste. Chill until used.

3. Make slaw: In a bowl, combine cabbages, carrot, and onion. Just before serving, stir in sesame seeds, oil, and vinegar.

4. Heat a grill to very high (550° to 650°). Oil cooking grate, using tongs and a wad of oiled paper towels.

5. Drain ponzu from bag. Add oil and turn bag to coat fish. Grill fish, covered, turning once, until grill marks appear and fish is rare, 3 minutes. Slice albacore crosswise. Fill tortillas with slaw and fish, then top with a drizzle of the mayo.

*Find ponzu, a Japanese citrus-soy sauce, in the Asian foods aisle. Look for pole- or troll-caught albacore, which is sustainably fished. If tortillas are very thin, buy double the amount and stack 2 per taco.

PER TACO WITH 1 TBSP. SAUCE 214 CAL., 37% (80 CAL.) FROM FAT; 13 G PROTEIN; 8.9 G FAT (1.1 G SAT.); 20 G CARBO (1.8 G FIBER); 333 MG SODIUM; 25 MG CHOL. LC/LS

BAJA LIGHT FISH TACOS

MAKES 12 TO 14 ★ 1 HOUR

These Baja-style tacos are grilled instead of deep-fried, and served with a trim version of tartar sauce.

CHIPOTLE TARTAR SAUCE
2 tbsp. canned chipotle chiles, seeded, deveined, and rinsed
8 oz. (1 cup) plain low-fat Greek yogurt
¼ cup sweet pickle relish
¼ cup chopped onion

CABBAGE-CILANTRO SLAW
3 tbsp. lime juice
2 tbsp. vegetable oil
¼ tsp. red chile flakes
½ tsp. kosher salt
1 bag (10 oz.) very finely shredded cabbage
⅓ cup chopped cilantro

FISH AND TORTILLAS
1 tbsp. ancho chile powder
2 tsp. dried oregano, preferable Mexican
¼ tsp. *each* kosher salt and pepper
1½ lbs. skinned Pacific cod fillets
1 tbsp. olive oil
12 to 14 corn tortillas* (5 to 6 in.), wrapped in foil and warmed over direct low heat on grill (turn often)

1. Make sauce: Purée all ingredients in a blender. Chill until used.

2. Make slaw: Put lime juice, oil, chile flakes, and salt in a large bowl. Just before serving, toss with cabbage and cilantro.

3. Prepare fish: Heat a grill to high (450° to 550°). Combine chile powder, oregano, salt, and pepper in a small bowl. Set fish on a rimmed baking sheet. Rub all over with olive oil, then sprinkle with chile mixture. Oil cooking grate, using tongs and a wad of oiled paper towels.

4. Grill fish, covered, turning once, until just cooked through, 4 to 6 minutes. Break fish into large chunks. Fill tortillas with slaw and fish. Serve with tartar sauce.

*If tortillas are very thin, buy double the amount and stack 2 per taco.

PER TACO WITH 1 TBSP. SAUCE 151 CAL., 27% (41 CAL.) FROM FAT; 10 G PROTEIN; 4.7 G FAT (0.6 G SAT.); 18 G CARBO (1.9 G FIBER); 10 MG SODIUM; 17 MG CHOL. GF/LC/LS

GOLDEN STATE FISH TACOS

MAKES 12 TO 14 ★ 1½ HOURS

Inspired by the top-quality avocados
and lemons of California, these halibut
tacos are finished off with a yogurt
sauce. You'll need 6 to 8 slender metal
skewers.

AVOCADO AND SALTED LEMON SALAD

½ lemon, cut lengthwise
½ tsp. kosher salt
2 small avocados, chopped
2 tbsp. diced white onion
1 red Fresno chile, seeded and minced
2 tsp. lemon juice
2 tsp. olive oil

YOGURT SAUCE

1 cup plain whole-milk yogurt
½ tsp. kosher salt
2 tbsp. chopped flat-leaf parsley

FISH AND TORTILLAS

¼ tsp. *each* kosher salt and pepper
Zest of 1 lemon
1½ tsp. ground coriander
1½ lbs. boned, skinned halibut fillets
    (each 1 in. thick), cut into 1½-in.
    chunks
1 tbsp. olive oil
12 to 14 corn tortillas* (5 to 6 in.),
    wrapped in foil and warmed over
    direct low heat on grill (turn often)
3 cups iceberg lettuce cut in fine shreds

**GOLDEN STATE
FISH TACOS**

1. Make salad: Slice lemon crosswise
paper thin, discarding seeds and ends.
Cut each slice in half. In a bowl, mix
lemon with salt. Let stand until wilted,
45 to 60 minutes. Rinse, drain, and
return to bowl. Stir in remaining salad
ingredients.

2. Make sauce: Stir together all ingredients in a bowl. Chill until used.

3. Prepare fish: Heat a grill to high
(450° to 550°). Mix salt, pepper, zest,
and coriander in a small bowl. Put
halibut on a rimmed baking sheet;
coat with olive oil. Sprinkle with zest
mixture. Thread fish onto slender

metal skewers. Oil cooking grate, using
tongs and a wad of oiled paper towels.

4. Grill fish, covered, turning once,
until just cooked through, 3 to 4 minutes. Fill tortillas with lettuce, fish,
and salad. Serve with yogurt sauce.

*If tortillas are very thin, buy double
the amount and stack 2 per taco.

PER TACO WITH 1 TBSP. SAUCE 235 CAL., 54%
(126 CAL.) FROM FAT; 9.3 G PROTEIN; 14 G FAT (2.3 G
SAT.); 18 G CARBO (3.5 G FIBER); 190 MG SODIUM;
24 MG CHOL. GF/LC/LS

TIP FOR PERFECT FISH TACOS,
HAVE THE SAUCE, SALAD,
AND TORTILLAS READY
SO THE TACOS CAN BE
EASILY ASSEMBLED AS
SOON AS THE FISH COMES
OFF THE GRILL.

GRILLED SARDINES with
COLD BEAN SALAD

GRILLED SARDINES WITH COLD BEAN SALAD

SERVES 4 ★ 30 MINUTES

If only all sardine dishes tasted as good as this one, everyone would be a fan of this delicious and sustainable Western fish, which is full of healthful oils. Using the dressing as a marinade for both the sardines and the bean salad brings the two elements together.

1 tsp. minced garlic
¼ cup lemon juice
About ½ cup extra-virgin olive oil
1 tsp. kosher salt
½ tsp. pepper
8 whole sardines (1¼ lbs. total), cleaned and spines removed (leave fish whole)
2 cans (each 15 oz.) cannellini beans, drained
1 cup halved grape tomatoes
1 cup curly parsley leaves

1. Heat a grill to high (450° to 550°). In a medium bowl, whisk together garlic, lemon juice, ½ cup oil, the salt, and pepper. Pour ¼ cup dressing over sardines in another medium bowl and let stand 10 minutes.

2. Meanwhile, add beans, tomatoes, and parsley to remaining dressing and toss to coat.

3. Oil cooking grate, using tongs and a wad of oiled paper towels. Starting with skin side down, cook sardines, turning once, until cooked through and dark grill marks appear, about 5 minutes.

4. Divide bean salad among plates. Top each with 2 sardines.

PER SERVING 520 CAL., 49% (252 CAL.) FROM FAT; 22 G PROTEIN; 30 G FAT (12 G SAT.); 28 G CARBO (9.5 G FIBER); 1,019 MG SODIUM; 39 MG CHOL. GF

GRILLED MARINATED CALAMARI

SERVES 4 ★ 30 MINUTES, PLUS 1 HOUR TO MARINATE

Though people in this country are less familiar with grilled calamari than in Greece, say, where it's a specialty at seaside towns, it's an excellent dish to add to your repertoire. Plenty of lemon, olive oil, and chiles; a little smoke from the grill; and a brief cooking time (so the calamari stays tender) add up to delicious results.

2 lbs. cleaned calamari (squid), tubes and tentacles separated but whole
1 tbsp. minced garlic
1½ tsp. red chile flakes
¼ cup chopped flat-leaf parsley
⅔ cup extra-virgin olive oil, divided
¼ cup lemon juice, divided
1 tsp. sea salt, divided
½ loaf crusty bread, such as ciabatta, cut in half horizontally

1. In a medium bowl, combine calamari, garlic, chile flakes, parsley, ⅓ cup oil, 2 tbsp. lemon juice, and ½ tsp. salt. Chill, stirring often, 1 to 5 hours.

2. Pour calamari and marinade into a colander over a bowl. Brush marinade over cut sides of bread.

3. Heat a grill to high. Grill bread on each side until grill marks appear, 3 to 5 minutes. Cut into slices.

4. Set calamari tubes perpendicular to cooking grate and grill, turning once, just until firm, about 3 minutes. Meanwhile, using tongs, drop tentacles in clumps onto grill just to firm up, then spread out to cook evenly, 4 minutes total.

5. Put calamari in a dish and drizzle with remaining ⅓ cup oil, 2 tbsp. lemon juice, and ½ tsp. salt. Serve with bread.

PER SERVING 707 CAL., 57% (402 CAL.) FROM FAT; 39 G PROTEIN; 46 G FAT (7.4 G SAT.); 36 G CARBO (1 G FIBER); 998 MG SODIUM; 500 MG CHOL.

GRILLED SEAFOOD AND CHORIZO PAELLA

SERVES 12 ★ 2 HOURS

Few dishes are as dramatic as an enormous paella, rich with saffron-scented rice and a variety of shellfish. Building it layer by layer at the grill is pure theater, and your guests can join in the fun. Serve it with generous spoonfuls of *allioli*, a garlicky Spanish mayonnaise. You'll need a 17- to 18-in. paella pan* (or use two 12-in. cast-iron frying pans).

2 lbs. ripe tomatoes, cut in half
1 medium onion, chopped
1 *each* red and green bell pepper, seeds and ribs
    removed and chopped
2 tbsp. minced garlic
5 tsp. sweet smoked Spanish paprika *(pimentón dulce)**
2 tsp. kosher salt
4 cups Spanish Valenciano or Arborio rice*
24 mussels, scrubbed and "beards" pulled off
24 small littleneck clams, scrubbed
¾ lb. peeled, deveined medium shrimp (32 per lb.),
    with tails left on
1¼ lbs. Spanish chorizo*, cut into thin diagonal slices
1 tsp. saffron threads
9 cups chicken broth, divided
2 cups dry white wine
7 tbsp. olive oil, divided
Coarsely chopped flat-leaf parsley
Allioli (recipe follows)

1. Coarsely grate tomatoes into a bowl and discard skins. Put onion and bell peppers in another bowl. Measure garlic, paprika, and salt into a small bowl. Put rice in a bowl, seafood in another, and chorizo in a third.

2. Heat a grill to medium (350° to 450°). Meanwhile, toast saffron in a large saucepan over medium heat on a stove, stirring, until fragrant, about 2 minutes. Add 6 cups broth and the wine, cover, bring to a boil over high heat, and keep warm. In a small saucepan, bring remaining 3 cups broth to a boil; keep warm. Carry all ingredients, a 17- to 18-in. paella pan, a long-handled wooden spoon, slotted spoon, and oven mitts to grill.

3. *For charcoal*, add 15 briquets to fire just before cooking and cook with lid off until step 7. *For gas*, keep lid closed as you cook. Heat paella pan on grill. Add 3 tbsp. oil, then chorizo, and brown, stirring, about 5 minutes. Using slotted spoon, transfer chorizo back to bowl.

4. Sauté onion and peppers in pan until onion is softened, about 5 minutes. Stir in tomatoes and cook, stirring often, until liquid evaporates and paste turns a shade darker, 10 to 12 minutes. Stir in remaining ¼ cup oil and the garlic mixture; cook, stirring, for 30 seconds. Stir in rice until evenly coated, then pat out level.

5. Carefully pour hot saffron liquid over rice and scatter chorizo on top. Check to be sure grill and liquid in pan are level. If needed, reduce gas or airflow in vents on lid and at base of grill (for charcoal grill) to maintain a steady simmer. Cook for 12 minutes.

6. Pour enough hot plain broth over paella so rice is just covered in liquid (you may not use it all). Arrange mussels around rim of pan, almost touching, pushing them into liquid. Arrange any remaining mussels, the clams, and then the shrimp over paella in liquid.

7. Cover grill and cook until clams and mussels open (discard any that are unopened) and rice is *al punto* (al dente), another 6 to 10 minutes. Carefully remove paella from grill, drape with paper towels, and let stand about 5 minutes. Sprinkle with parsley. Serve with allioli.

*Find paella pans at kitchenware stores or online. Look for Spanish paprika, rice, and chorizo (not soft Mexican-style chorizo) in well-stocked grocery stores or online. (For online ordering info, see Resource Guide, page 244.)

PER SERVING 692 CAL., 38% (262 CAL.) FROM FAT; 35 G PROTEIN; 29 G FAT (8.7 G SAT.); 63 G CARBO (3.6 G FIBER); 1,162 MG SODIUM; 123 MG CHOL. GF

ALLIOLI

MAKES 1⅔ CUPS ★ 5 MINUTES

1 cup extra-virgin olive oil
⅓ cup canola oil
4 large garlic cloves
1 large egg plus 1 egg yolk
About 2 tbsp. lemon juice
About 1 tsp. kosher salt

Pour oils into a container with a spout. In a food processor, whirl remaining ingredients, including 2 tbsp. lemon juice and 1 tsp. salt, into a smooth paste. With motor running, add oil in a slow stream until incorporated. Add more lemon juice and salt if you like.

Make ahead: Up to 1 week, chilled.

PER 2 TBSP. 209 CAL., 98% (204 CAL.) FROM FAT; 0.8 G PROTEIN; 23 G FAT (3 G SAT.); 0.7 G CARBO (0 G FIBER); 154 MG SODIUM; 32 MG CHOL. GF

GRILLED SEAFOOD and
CHORIZO PAELLA

COCONUT
LIME SHRIMP
SKEWERS

COCONUT LIME SHRIMP SKEWERS

SERVES 12 AS AN APPETIZER ★ 30 MINUTES, PLUS 1 HOUR TO MARINATE

Lime adds zing and toasted coconut gives crunch to this make-ahead crowd-pleaser. You'll need at least 24 wooden skewers (each 6 in.).

1 tbsp. *each* minced fresh ginger, minced garlic, and lime zest
2 tbsp. lime juice
1 can (14 oz.) coconut milk
2 lbs. peeled, deveined large shrimp (26 to 30 per lb.)
¼ tsp. kosher salt
Lime wedges
½ cup toasted, sweetened shredded coconut

1. In a medium bowl, combine ginger, garlic, lime zest and juice, and coconut milk. Add shrimp, tossing to coat, then chill, covered, at least 1 hour and up to 1 day.

2. Meanwhile, soak skewers in water at least 30 minutes. Heat a grill to high (450° to 550°). Thread 2 or 3 shrimp onto each skewer through ends of shrimp so they look like the letter C. Cook, turning once, until flesh has just turned pink and is slightly charred, about 3 minutes on each side.

3. Arrange skewers on a serving platter and sprinkle with salt, a squeeze of lime juice, and coconut. Serve with extra lime wedges.

PER 2-SKEWER SERVING 147 CAL., 56% (82 CAL.) FROM FAT; 15 G PROTEIN; 9.1 G FAT (7.3 G SAT.); 3.6 G CARBO (0.3 G FIBER); 127 MG SODIUM; 93 MG CHOL. GF/LC/LS

SALT-CURED OUZO SHRIMP

SERVES 4 TO 6 ★ 15 MINUTES, PLUS 45 MINUTES TO CURE

We love these shrimp with their two-punch licorice hit of anise seeds and ouzo. Thread the shrimp onto 6 wooden or metal skewers.

1½ tbsp. sugar
1 tbsp. kosher salt
1½ tsp. anise seeds, divided
1½ lbs. peeled, deveined extra-large shrimp (16 to 20 per lb.), with tails left on

HOW TO CONTROL FLARE-UPS

If flames suddenly shoot up and around your food while you're grilling, it will not only char your food but also give it an unpleasant, greasy flavor. If you can spare the space, try to have a "cool spot" on the grill—either a turned-off burner or an area free of coals—so you can shift the food there if and when the fire flares. For more control, close the lid, cutting off the fire's oxygen supply. And if the flames are really persistent on a charcoal grill, close the vents on the lid and below, on the underside of the grill (slide the lever to adjust vents). We don't recommend squirting the fire with water because that often sprays ash onto the food.

1 tbsp. olive oil
About 2 tbsp. ouzo or other anise-flavored liqueur
1½ tsp. minced garlic

1. In a bowl, mix sugar, salt, and ¾ tsp. anise seeds. Add shrimp and stir gently to coat. Cover and chill 45 minutes to 1 hour. Rinse both the shrimp and the bowl well and drain.

2. Meanwhile, soak wooden skewers in water at least 30 minutes, or use metal skewers.

3. Return shrimp to bowl. Add remaining ¾ tsp. anise seeds, the oil, 2 tbsp. ouzo, and the garlic; mix to coat. Thread shrimp onto skewers through each end so shrimp look like the letter C, dividing them equally among skewers.

4. Heat a grill to high (450° to 550°).

5. Lay shrimp on cooking grate and cook, turning once, until shrimp are bright pink and opaque but still moist-looking in center (cut to test), 2 to 3 minutes total. Transfer to a platter. Drizzle more ouzo over shrimp if you like.

PER SKEWER 150 CAL., 26% (39 CAL.) FROM FAT; 23 G PROTEIN; 4.3 G FAT (0.7 G SAT.); 3.3 G CARBO (0 G FIBER); SODIUM N/A; 173 MG CHOL. GF/LC

The Griller's Guide to
VEGETABLES

By grilling one or two vegetables with your main course, you can serve an entire meal from the grill. Before grilling, prepare vegetables as directed on these two pages; some vegetables need to be precooked. Then coat with the Fresh Herb Marinade (see page 113)—or just use the basting sauce or marinade that you're putting on your main course—and grill as directed.

THE METHOD

1 Prepare a charcoal or gas grill for medium heat (350° to 450°; see "Direct Heat Grilling," page 87). Indirect medium-low heat (300° to 350°) works too, if that's what's needed for the protein you're grilling; turn the vegetables less often, though, and let them cook a bit longer. If you're using wooden skewers, soak them in hot water for 30 minutes first so they won't burn on the grill.

2 Put prepared vegetables in a bowl or on a rimmed baking sheet, depending on their shape and size, and drizzle with marinade. Turn vegetables to coat. If your vegetables are small or cut into pieces, thread onto skewers, making sure vegetables lie flat.

3 Oil hot cooking grate, using tongs and a wad of oiled paper towels. Set vegetables on cooking grate and grill, turning frequently, until they're streaked with brown, crisp-edged, and tender when pierced (for specific directions and cooking times, see chart opposite).

4 Serve vegetables hot or at room temperature.

VEGETABLE	PREPARATION	DIRECTIONS & COOKING TIME
ARTICHOKES	Trim away stem and coarse outer leaves; cut off top third. Trim thorny tips. Cook in boiling water to cover until stem end is tender when pierced, 20 to 40 minutes. Drain and cut in half lengthwise; scrape out fuzzy choke in center.	Grill 8 to 12 minutes.
ASPARAGUS	Trim tough stem ends.	Set crosswise on cooking grate and grill about 5 minutes.
BELL PEPPERS & CHILES	Leave whole. Peppers are good with or without seasoning.	Grill 5 to 10 minutes.
CABBAGE & RADICCHIO	Cut cabbage into quarters lengthwise; cut radicchio in half.	Grill 6 to 10 minutes.
CARROTS	Cook whole medium peeled carrots in boiling water to cover until just tender, about 10 minutes. Drain.	Set crosswise on cooking grate and grill 8 to 10 minutes.
CORN IN HUSKS	Pull off husks down to light green inner ones. Gently pull them back; remove and discard silks. Drizzle corn with marinade or butter and salt. Replace inner husks; tie with strips of husks or kitchen twine at top to enclose.	Grill 18 to 20 minutes.
CORN, HUSKED	Enclose in foil, if you like, with butter and salt or marinade.	Grill 8 to 10 minutes.
EGGPLANT	Cut off stem end. Cut Asian eggplants in half lengthwise; cut small globe (regular) eggplants crosswise into ½-in.-thick slices.	Grill until meltingly soft, 8 to 12 minutes.
FENNEL	Cut off and discard woody stems. Cut vertically into four slices.	Grill 20 to 30 minutes.
KALE (LACINATO)	Trim stems and ribs. Brush with oil.	Grill 3 to 5 minutes.
MUSHROOMS (BUTTON, CREMINI, PORCINI, PORTABELLA, SHIITAKE)	Trim any tough stem ends; remove tough stems entirely.	Grill 10 to 15 minutes (start large ones gill side down; turn halfway through).
ONIONS, GREEN	Trim root ends and 2 in. of green tops (seasoning is optional—green onions are good with or without).	Grill 3 to 5 minutes.
ONIONS (RED, WHITE, YELLOW)	Peel. Cut small onions in half lengthwise and larger ones into quarters, then marinate. Thread onto skewers with onions arranged as flat as possible.	Grill 15 to 30 minutes.
SQUASH, SUMMER (CROOKNECK, PATTYPAN, ZUCCHINI)	Leave small squash (1 in. or less in diameter) whole. Cut larger squash in half lengthwise.	Grill 15 to 30 minutes.
SQUASH, WINTER (ACORN, BUTTERNUT, KABOCHA)	Cut squash in half, scoop out seeds, and cut halves ½ in. thick.	Grill 10 to 15 minutes.
SWEET POTATOES or YAMS	Cut small sweet potatoes in half, large ones into 1-in. wedges.	Grill 18 to 20 minutes.
TOMATOES	Cut into thick slices.	Grill 8 to 12 minutes.

GRILLED RATATOUILLE

SERVES 8 ★ ABOUT 2 HOURS

Instead of stewing the vegetables, as is traditional in France, we like to grill them so they keep their shape and acquire a delicious smoky flavor. We also use a baking sheet instead of skewers, and we glaze them with balsamic vinegar, another nontraditional touch. The result: creamy, melt-in-your-mouth vegetables to serve in pita, over pasta, or with grilled meat.

2 red or yellow bell peppers, seeded and cut into ¾-in.-wide wedges
2 red onions, cut into 1-in.-wide wedges
1 large eggplant, cut into 1-in. chunks
2 small yellow zucchini or crookneck squash, cut crosswise into ¼-in.-thick slices
3 Roma tomatoes, quartered lengthwise
3 garlic cloves, chopped
1 tbsp. *each* finely chopped fresh oregano and flat-leaf parsley
5 tbsp. extra-virgin olive oil
1 tsp. pepper
About 2 tsp. kosher salt
3 tbsp. balsamic vinegar
⅓ cup toasted pine nuts
½ cup crumbled ash-coated fresh goat cheese

1. Heat a grill to medium (350° to 450°) with a charcoal area left clear or a gas burner turned off to make an indirect heat area (see "Indirect Heat Grilling," page 88).

2. In a large bowl, toss together all but the last 3 ingredients. Spread vegetables on a large rimmed baking sheet (not nonstick).

3. Cook vegetables, covered, over indirect heat, until very tender, about 60 minutes (for charcoal, add 4 briquets to each side every 30 minutes and keep measuring heat), gently stirring every 15 minutes. Drizzle with vinegar, stir, and cook 15 minutes more. Let vegetables cool. Put in a medium bowl, toss with pine nuts and salt to taste, and sprinkle with cheese.

PER ABOUT ¾-CUP SERVING 295 CAL., 46% (135 CAL.) FROM FAT; 8.9 G PROTEIN; 15 G FAT (3.5 G SAT.); 35 G CARBO (3.5 G FIBER); 547 MG SODIUM; 6.7 MG CHOL. GF/LC/V

GRILLED CAESAR SALAD

SERVES 4 ★ 20 MINUTES

Romaine brushed with olive oil–anchovy paste and grilled, then topped with manchego shavings, takes Caesar salad to a whole new level. Little Gem, a type of miniature romaine lettuce, is perfect for this recipe, but hearts of regular romaine work too.

3 canned anchovy fillets, drained and finely chopped
2 to 2½ tbsp. extra-virgin olive oil
1 tbsp. lemon juice
Salt and pepper
2 whole small Little Gem lettuce heads or 4 hearts of romaine
2 oz. manchego cheese, shaved into thin curls with a vegetable peeler
1 lemon, cut into wedges

1. Heat a grill to medium-high (450°). With the flat side of a knife, mash the anchovies to a paste. In a small bowl, whisk together oil, lemon juice, anchovy paste, and salt and pepper to taste.

2. Keeping leaves attached to cores, cut lettuce heads in half lengthwise. Brush all over with 1½ to 2 tbsp. anchovy dressing.

3. Grill lettuces, covered, turning once, until they are softened and streaked brown, about 8 minutes.

4. Place lettuces cut side up on a platter. Drizzle remaining dressing over lettuces and top with manchego curls. Serve with lemon wedges.

PER SERVING 149 CAL., 79% (117 CAL.) FROM FAT; 6.2 G PROTEIN; 13 G FAT (4.8 G SAT.); 5.2 G CARBO (2.7 G FIBER); 206 MG SODIUM; 17 MG CHOL. GF/LC/LS

 TIP TRY THE GRILLED CAESAR SALAD WITH KALE; WHEN IT'S GRILLED (SEE PAGE 159), KALE ACQUIRES A SUBTLE SMOKY FLAVOR AND LIGHT CRUNCH.

GRILLED CAESAR SALAD

SOY-FURIKAKE CORN

SOY-*FURIKAKE* CORN

SERVES 4 ★ 20 MINUTES

A Japanese-inspired topping brings hits of crunchy, salty, nutty, earthy, and briny flavor to grilled corn.

⅓ cup mayonnaise
1 tsp. *each* toasted sesame oil and reduced-sodium
   soy sauce
4 ears corn, husks removed
1 tbsp. vegetable oil
¼ cup *furikake** or toasted sesame seeds

1. In a bowl, whisk together mayonnaise, sesame oil, and soy sauce; set aside.

2. Heat a grill to medium (350° to 450°). Rub corn with vegetable oil and cut each ear in thirds. Grill corn, turning occasionally, until grill marks appear on most sides, 10 to 20 minutes. Spread mayonnaise mixture on corn. Over a plate, sprinkle corn with furikake, turning to evenly coat.

*Find furikake, a mix of sesame, seaweed, and dried fish, at well-stocked grocery stores and Asian markets.

PER SERVING 220 CAL., 55% (122 CAL.) FROM FAT; 3.9 G PROTEIN; 14 G FAT (1.6 G SAT.); 23 G CARBO (2.9 G FIBER); 363 MG SODIUM; 5.1 MG CHOL. LC

GRILLED CORN POBLANO SALAD

MAKES 3½ CUPS; 6 TO 8 SERVINGS ★ 30 MINUTES

This simple combination is always a hit.

3 ears corn, husks removed
1 poblano chile
3 tbsp. canola oil, divided
1 tbsp. lime juice
1 tsp. finely chopped canned chipotle chile
½ tsp. kosher salt
1 avocado, cut into chunks
¼ cup cilantro leaves
½ cup slivered sweet onion, such as Walla Walla or Maui,
   rinsed and patted dry

1. Heat a grill to high (450° to 550°). Rub corn and poblano with 1 tbsp. oil. Grill both, turning occasionally, until poblano is mostly blackened, 5 to 10 minutes, and some corn kernels have browned, 10 to 20 minutes. Let cool.

2. Cut corn kernels from cobs into a large bowl. Peel and seed poblano, cut into ½-in. pieces, and add to corn. In a small bowl, whisk remaining 2 tbsp. oil with lime juice, chipotle chile, and salt.

3. Stir avocado, cilantro, and onion into corn mixture along with chipotle dressing.

PER ½-CUP SERVING 283 CAL., 35% (99 CAL.) FROM FAT; 5.7 G PROTEIN; 11 G FAT (1.2 G SAT.); 43 G CARBO (1.7 G FIBER); 171 MG SODIUM; 0 MG CHOL. GF/LC/LS/VG

GRILLED POTATO ROSEMARY CAKE

SERVES 6 ★ 1 HOUR

Keep an eye on the heat when making this rustic grilled alternative to potatoes au gratin (pictured on page 128)—if the temperature climbs past 400°, the potatoes may scorch.

About 1 tbsp. chopped fresh rosemary leaves
1 tsp. kosher salt
½ tsp. pepper
2½ lbs. Yukon Gold potatoes
¼ cup extra-virgin olive oil, divided

1. Heat a grill to medium (350° to 400°).

2. Combine 1 tbsp. chopped rosemary, the salt, and pepper in a small bowl. Peel potatoes and put in a bowl of water. Coat a large cast-iron skillet with 1 tbsp. oil. Using a mandoline or knife, cut half the potatoes into ⅛-in. slices and arrange them in tightly overlapping circles in skillet. Sprinkle with half of salt mixture. Repeat with remaining potatoes and salt mixture, making a second layer. Drizzle remaining 3 tbsp. oil over potatoes, shaking skillet to distribute it well. Press potato cake with hands to compact.

3. Cook potatoes in skillet on cooking grate, grill lid closed, until well browned on bottom (lift edge with a spatula to check), 35 to 40 minutes. Remove from grill. Loosen potatoes with a wide spatula. Invert a platter over skillet, hold both together (use mitts), and invert potato cake. Scatter rosemary on top and cut into wedges.

Make ahead: Potato cake, kept warm in skillet or on platter in a 200° oven, up to 1 hour.

PER SERVING 221 CAL., 36% (80 CAL.) FROM FAT; 4 G PROTEIN; 9.4 G FAT (1.3 G SAT.); 30 G CARBO (2.1 G FIBER); 330 MG SODIUM; 0 MG CHOL. GF/LC/LS/VG

POTATO SALADS & SLAWS

BREAD-AND-BUTTER PICKLE POTATO SALAD

**MAKES ABOUT 11 CUPS; 12 TO 14 SERVINGS
★ ABOUT 1 HOUR**

A classic potato salad, with the tang of chopped pickle, this is a potluck must-have—reliable, easy, and universally beloved.

**4 lbs. Yukon Gold potatoes (about
   2¼ in. wide), scrubbed
2 tbsp. mustard seeds
1 cup finely chopped bread-and-butter
   pickles, plus ½ cup juice strained
   from jar
1 cup reduced-fat or regular mayonnaise
¼ cup cider vinegar
2 red bell peppers (each 8 oz.), seeded
   and diced
¾ cup minced parsley
Salt and pepper**

1. In a large pot, combine potatoes and 3 qts. water. Cover and bring to a boil over high heat. Reduce heat and simmer until potatoes are tender when pierced, 20 to 30 minutes. Drain well and let stand until cool enough to touch, 15 to 25 minutes.

2. Meanwhile, in a small bowl, soak mustard seeds in about ½ cup hot water until soft, 5 minutes. Drain.

3. In a large bowl, mix mustard seeds, chopped pickles, pickle juice, mayonnaise, and vinegar. Peel warm potatoes, cut into about ¾-in. cubes, and drop into dressing. Add bell peppers; mix gently. Let cool to room temperature, at least 15 minutes. Add ½ cup parsley and salt and pepper to taste; mix gently. Scrape into a serving bowl and sprinkle with remaining ¼ cup parsley.

Make ahead: Up to 1 day, covered and chilled; mix before serving.

PER SERVING 151 CAL., 17% (25 CAL.) FROM FAT; 3.6 G PROTEIN; 2.8 G FAT (0.6 G SAT.); 28 G CARBO (2.2 G FIBER); 307 MG SODIUM; 0 MG CHOL. LC/LS/V

CUCUMBER POTATO SALAD

MAKES 8 CUPS; 8 SERVINGS ★ 30 MINUTES

For delicate, thin cucumber slices, use a Japanese-style handheld slicer.

**1½ lbs. small red thin-skinned potatoes
½ cup plain low-fat Greek yogurt
½ cup olive oil mayonnaise or regular
   mayonnaise
½ cup roughly chopped fresh dill
2 tbsp. red wine vinegar
1 tsp. kosher salt
½ tsp. pepper
1½ cups slivered red onion, rinsed and
   patted dry
1 English cucumber, very thinly sliced**

1. Bring 1 in. water to a boil in a large saucepan. Set whole potatoes in a steamer basket and steam in pan, covered, until tender, 15 to 20 minutes. Cool in ice water, then pat dry.

2. Whisk yogurt, mayonnaise, dill, vinegar, salt, and pepper in a bowl.

3. Quarter potatoes and put in a large bowl. Add onion, cucumber, and half the dressing; gently stir to coat. Add more dressing if you like, or save to use as a dip.

Make ahead: Through step 2, up to 2 days. Chill potatoes and dressing separately and slice cucumber just before serving.

PER 1-CUP SERVING WITHOUT EXTRA DRESSING
154 CAL., 32% (49 CAL.) FROM FAT; 3.9 G PROTEIN; 5.5 G FAT (0.5 G SAT.); 21 G CARBO (2.1 G FIBER); 425 MG SODIUM; 5.8 MG CHOL. LC/V

CREAMY LIME SLAW

SERVES 8 ★ 30 MINUTES

A great side for grilled fish or shrimp.

**4 green onions
½ head napa cabbage, sliced thinly
½ head red cabbage, sliced thinly
½ cup cilantro leaves
2 limes
½ cup nonfat Greek yogurt
1½ tbsp. sugar
1 tsp. kosher salt
½ tsp. pepper**

1. Slice green onions long and on the bias so you have pieces similar in shape to the cabbage. Toss together onions, cabbages, and cilantro in a large bowl.

2. Zest both limes and juice 1 lime. In a bowl, mix zest and juice, yogurt, sugar, salt, and pepper. Pour dressing over cabbage mixture; stir to combine.

PER 1-CUP SERVING 49 CAL., 2% (1 CAL.) FROM FAT; 2.9 G PROTEIN; 0.1 G FAT (0 G SAT.); 9.5 G CARBO (2.2 G FIBER); 268 MG SODIUM; 0 MG CHOL. GF/LC/LS/V

SPICY-SWEET ASIAN SLAW WITH PICKLED DAIKON

**MAKES 3 QTS.; 8 SERVINGS ★ 15 MINUTES,
PLUS 6 HOURS TO PICKLE**

To create this refreshing salad, we started with an easy recipe for pickled daikon from executive chef Alexander Ong of Betelnut restaurant in San Francisco. Try it with the Thai Barbecued Pork on page 129.

**1½ lbs. daikon, peeled
¼ cup kosher salt
1 cup *each* sugar and distilled white
   vinegar**

2 tbsp. toasted sesame oil
4 Thai or serrano chiles, cut into
    wide slices
1½ qts. thinly sliced napa cabbage
3 green onions, cut into 2-in. lengths,
    then into long slivers
3 tbsp. toasted sesame seeds
2 cups thinly sliced red cabbage

1. Cut daikon lengthwise into ½-in. slices, then stack and cut into ½-in. cubes. Toss with salt in a medium bowl. Let stand about 2 hours, stirring occasionally, to draw out moisture. Rinse daikon well and drain. In bowl, stir sugar with vinegar until dissolved, then stir in daikon, oil, and chiles. Chill, covered, at least 4 hours.

2. Drain daikon, reserving pickling liquid, and discard chiles.

3. In a large bowl, toss together napa cabbage, onions, sesame seeds, and daikon. Add ½ cup pickling liquid (or more if you like) and toss to coat. Mix in red cabbage with a quick toss so its color doesn't bleed.

Make ahead: Through step 2, covered and chilled, up to 1 week.

PER SERVING 115 CAL., 26% (30 CAL.) FROM FAT; 2.3 G PROTEIN; 3.4 G FAT (0.3 G SAT.); 19 G CARBO (2.8 G FIBER); 224 MG SODIUM; 0 MG CHOL. GF/LC/LS/VG

CHIPOTLE COLESLAW

SERVES 6 TO 8 ★ ABOUT 10 MINUTES, PLUS 30 MINUTES TO CHILL

Created by outdoor cooking experts Bill Jamison and Cheryl Alters Jamison, this feisty coleslaw makes an excellent side dish. It's even better piled on sandwiches made with Achiote and Orange Pulled Pork (page 130).

½ cup *each* mayonnaise and sour cream
3 tbsp. white vinegar
1 tbsp. molasses (not blackstrap)
1½ tsp. sugar
1 small canned chipotle chile, minced,
    plus 2 tsp. adobo sauce from the can
About 1 tsp. kosher salt

CHIPOTLE COLESLAW

6 cups *each* packed shredded green
    and red cabbage
7 green onions, sliced into thin rounds
1 cup tightly packed chopped cilantro
    leaves, plus whole leaves for garnish

1. Prepare the dressing: In a medium bowl, stir together mayonnaise, sour cream, vinegar, molasses, sugar, minced chile, adobo sauce, and 1 tsp. salt.

2. In a large bowl, toss together cabbages, green onions, and ¾ cup chopped cilantro. Pour dressing over vegetables, toss well, and chill at

least 30 minutes. Before serving, add more salt if you like and scatter remaining ¼ cup chopped cilantro, plus leaves, over the top.

Make ahead: Through step 2, before scattering with remaining cilantro, up to 4 hours, chilled.

PER SERVING 215 CAL., 67% (144 CAL.) FROM FAT; 3.7 G PROTEIN; 16 G FAT (4.0 G SAT.); 17 G CARBO (4.7 G FIBER); 473 MG SODIUM; 16 MG CHOL. LC/V

GRILLED APRICOT PUFFS with
HONEY CRÈME FRAÎCHE

GRILLED APRICOT PUFFS WITH HONEY CRÈME FRAÎCHE

SERVES 6 ★ 35 MINUTES

These beautiful pastry puffs bake in a muffin pan on the grill while the apricots and sugar caramelize in a cast-iron skillet nearby. Keep an eye on the puffs as they cook, and rotate the pan if it looks like your grill has hot spots. (If a puff gets a scorched spot anyway, scrape it off with a serrated knife.)

1 cup crème fraîche
3 tbsp. honey
2 large eggs
6 tbsp. *each* flour and milk
¼ tsp. kosher salt
½ to ¾ cup packed light brown sugar
¾ tsp. dried culinary lavender
9 apricots, halved and pitted
1 tbsp. butter, cut into 6 pieces
Lavender sprigs for garnish (optional)

1. Heat a grill to medium-low (350° to 400°; if you'll be using a nonstick muffin pan, don't let grill go over 450°). Stir together crème fraîche and honey in a bowl. Chill.

2. Whirl eggs, flour, milk, and salt in a food processor until smooth. Pour batter into a glass measuring cup.

3. Combine sugar (use ½ cup if fruit is very sweet, ¾ cup if it's more tart) and lavender in a large cast-iron or other ovenproof frying pan and pat out evenly. Arrange apricots in sugar, cut side down.

4. Set a muffin pan on one side of cooking grate and set pan with fruit on other side; cook with grill lid down, 5 minutes. Put a piece of butter in each of 6 muffin cups and cook with lid down until butter starts to brown, 30 to 60 seconds. Pour batter into cups with butter, filling about halfway. Grill, lid closed, until puffs are golden and syrup around apricots forms big, shiny bubbles and is deep golden brown, 10 to 15 minutes.

5. Loosen puffs from pan with a small metal spatula and set on plates; they'll sink a bit and form a depression. Turn fruit over in syrup, using a wide metal spoon. Fill puffs with some crème fraîche and an apricot and syrup. Spoon remaining apricots and syrup next to puffs, and serve warm with more crème fraîche and a lavender sprig if you like.

PER SERVING 372 CAL., 47% (173 CAL.) FROM FAT; 5.6 G PROTEIN; 19 G FAT (11 G SAT.); 45 G CARBO (1.3 G FIBER); 131 MG SODIUM; 111 MG CHOL. LS/V

GRILLED STRAWBERRY SHORTCAKE KEBABS

SERVES 8 ★ 30 MINUTES

For this twist on strawberry shortcake, cubes of angel food cake are skewered along with strawberries, then grilled. The strawberries become slightly tender and glazed and the cake gets a little toasted. You'll need 32 bamboo skewers (each 8 in.); there's no need to soak them before they go on the grill, because they don't cook long enough to char.

½ cup *each* whipping cream and crème fraîche
2 tbsp. packed dark brown sugar
Zest of ½ lemon
1 angel food cake (1 lb.)
32 strawberries (2 lbs.), preferably about 1½ in. wide, hulled to create a V-shaped hollow
6 tbsp. strawberry jam

1. Beat whipping cream, crème fraîche, sugar, and lemon zest in a bowl with a mixer until thick enough to hold a soft shape. Chill.

2. Cut cake into 1½-in.-wide slices, then into 32 chunks, each 1½ in. Save remaining cake for other uses.

3. Heat a grill to medium-low (300° to 350°). Put strawberries in a large bowl. Microwave jam in a glass measuring cup until bubbling, about 30 seconds. Using a pastry brush, dab hulled insides of berries with jam, then brush remaining jam over berries and turn gently to coat all over.

4. Hold a pair of bamboo skewers so they're slightly separated and thread a chunk of cake onto them, then a berry crosswise, then another chunk of cake and another berry. Repeat to make 15 more kebabs.

5. Grill kebabs, covered, turning once with tongs, until grill marks appear, 3 to 4 minutes; cake should release from grate when it's toasted, but if not, nudge with tip of tongs. Serve with cream mixture.

Make ahead: Through step 4, up to 2 hours, covered and chilled.

PER SERVING 302 CAL., 35% (106 CAL.) FROM FAT; 4 G PROTEIN; 12 G FAT (7.1 G SAT.); 47 G CARBO (2.8 G FIBER); 326 MG SODIUM; 33 MG CHOL. LC/LS/V

GRILL-BAKED BLACKBERRY SKILLET COBBLER

SERVES 6 TO 8 ★ 1½ HOURS

When it's warm outside, why heat up the house by turning on the oven? Cobbler bakes beautifully on the grill, as this recipe proves. It's adapted from one by cookbook author Carolyn Beth Weil. Give it a jump start over direct heat, then move it to indirect to cook the buttery, rich biscuit topping until golden. For the best flavor, use a gas grill—charcoal makes it too smoky.

¾ cup plus 3 tbsp. sugar
2 tbsp. cornstarch
6 cups blackberries
1 tsp. lemon zest
1 tbsp. lemon juice
1½ cups flour
2 tsp. baking powder
½ tsp. salt
⅓ cup cold butter, cut in chunks
⅔ cup whipping cream
Vanilla ice cream

1. Heat a gas grill to medium (350° to 400°) with a burner turned off to make an indirect heat area (see "Indirect Heat Grilling," page 88).

2. In a large bowl, combine ¾ cup sugar, the cornstarch, blackberries, and lemon zest and juice. Mix gently to coat. Pour into a 10-in. cast-iron skillet or other oven-proof frying pan.

3. In another bowl, mix flour, baking powder, salt, and remaining 3 tbsp. sugar. With your fingers or a pastry blender, rub or cut butter into flour mixture until coarse crumbs form. Add cream and stir just until mixture forms a soft, crumbly dough.

4. Pat ¼-cup portions of dough into flat disks ½ in. thick and arrange evenly over fruit.

5. Grill cobbler over direct heat, with grill covered, until berry mixture begins to bubble, 5 to 10 minutes. Slide to indirect heat and cook, with grill covered, until topping is golden brown and fruit is bubbling in center, 40 to 45 minutes more. Let cool on a rack at least 10 minutes. Serve warm or at room temperature with ice cream.

PER SERVING 369 CAL., 38% (141 CAL.) FROM FAT; 4.4 G PROTEIN; 16 G FAT (9.5 G SAT.); 55 G CARBO (6.1 G FIBER); 331 MG SODIUM; 48 MG CHOL. LS/V

PINEAPPLE SATAY WITH COCONUT CARAMEL

SERVES 4 ★ ABOUT 1 HOUR

Pineapple holds up to skewering, doesn't fall apart on the grill, and makes an elegant, surprising dessert—especially when drizzled with a simple-to-make caramel sauce. You'll need 16 wooden skewers for this recipe.

1 ripe pineapple
1 cup sugar
¾ cup coconut milk
¼ cup unsweetened shredded coconut, toasted

1. Soak skewers in water 30 minutes. Meanwhile, trim ends from pineapple, then stand it on one end and cut off peel. Quarter pineapple lengthwise and cut out core. Reserve half the pineapple for another use. Cut each remaining quarter into 4 lengthwise slices, then cut each slice in half crosswise to make 16 thin wedges. Skewer each lengthwise.

2. In a small saucepan, combine sugar with ½ cup water. Bring to a boil, swirling to dissolve sugar; boil, swirling occasionally (do not stir), just until golden and honeylike. Remove from heat and slowly whisk in coconut milk (mixture will bubble furiously).

3. Heat a grill to high (450° to 550°). Using a pastry brush, coat pineapple pieces with caramel sauce. Grill just until marks appear, then turn to mark other side, 4 to 5 minutes total. Put skewers on a platter, sprinkle with toasted coconut, and serve with remaining caramel sauce for dunking.

PER SERVING 299 CAL., 30% (89 CAL.) FROM FAT; 1.4 G PROTEIN; 9.9 G FAT (8.3 G SAT.); 56 G CARBO (1.9 G FIBER); 7.3 MG SODIUM; 0 MG CHOL. GF/LC/LS/VG

 TIP IN ADDITION TO THE PINEAPPLE ABOVE, TRY OTHER STURDY FRUITS ON THE GRILL INCLUDING CANTALOUPE WEDGES, NECTARINES, AND PEACHES (HALVES OR WEDGES).

PINEAPPLE SATAY with
COCONUT CARAMEL

POMEGRANATE-ORANGE COOLERS

SERVES 8 TO 10 ★ ABOUT 10 MINUTES, PLUS 1 HOUR TO CHILL

For the best flavor, use freshly pressed pomegranate juice, sold chilled in grocery stores and, in fall and winter, at farmers' markets.

5 cups pomegranate juice
⅓ cup fresh orange juice
⅓ cup fresh lime juice
5 cups chilled ginger ale
Thin orange slices for garnish (optional)

In a pitcher, combine pomegranate juice, orange juice, and lime juice. Cover and chill until very cold, at least 1 hour. Just before serving, stir in ginger ale. Pour into ice-filled glasses. If desired, garnish glasses with thin orange slices.

Make ahead: Juice mixture, up to 1 day, chilled airtight.

PER SERVING 115 CAL., 0% (3.5 CAL.) FROM FAT; 0.3 G PROTEIN, 0.4 G FAT, 29 G CARBO (0.2 G FIBER); 20 MG SODIUM; 0 MG CHOL.

MELON *AGUA FRESCA*

MAKES ABOUT 2½ QTS.; 10 SERVINGS ★ 10 MINUTES, PLUS 1 HOUR TO CHILL

Lightly sweetened and full of fruit, an *agua fresca* is the perfect summertime refresher. Be sure to use very ripe melons for the best texture and flavor.

5 cups cubed peeled, seeded watermelon, cantaloupe, or honeydew melon (from about 3 lbs. melon)
½ to ¾ cup sugar
⅓ to ½ cup fresh lime juice

1. In a blender, purée melon, ½ cup sugar, and 1 cup water until very smooth.

2. Pour into a large pitcher (at least 3 qts.). Whisk in ⅓ cup of lime juice and 7 cups water, then more sugar and lime juice to taste. Chill until cold, at least 1 hour. Serve over ice.

Make ahead: Before adding ice, chilled, up to 1 day.

PER 1-CUP SERVING 64 CAL., 3% (1.8 CAL.) FROM FAT; 0.6 G PROTEIN; 0.2 G FAT (0 G SAT.); 16 G CARBO (0.5 G FIBER); 7.5 MG SODIUM; 0 MG CHOL.

STRAWBERRY LEMONADE

MAKES 7½ CUPS; 6 SERVINGS ★ ABOUT 20 MINUTES

This beautiful lemonade is as much about the strawberries as it is the lemons.

2 pts. strawberries, hulled
¾ cup honey
1 cup lemon juice (from 5 or 6 lemons)

1. In a blender, purée the strawberries and honey. Pour purée through a fine-mesh strainer set over a bowl, pressing mixture with a spoon to extract as much liquid as possible. Discard contents of the strainer.

2. Pour the strawberry juice into a pitcher and stir in the lemon juice and 4 cups water. Serve over ice.

Make ahead: Up to 4 days, chilled.

PER SERVING 83 CAL., 3% (2.5 CAL.) FROM FAT; 0.8 G PROTEIN; 0.3 G FAT (0 G SAT.); 22 G CARBO (2.1 G FIBER); 1.9 MG SODIUM; 0 MG CHOL.

SUNSET PALMER

SERVES 2 ★ 5 MINUTES, PLUS 20 MINUTES TO STEEP

A play on the classic iced tea and lemonade drink made popular by legendary golfer Arnold Palmer. The combination of lemon-scented ingredients gives a gentler citrus flavor than lemon juice.

2 stalks fresh lemongrass, ends trimmed, chopped
½ cup *each* fresh lemon verbena* and lemon balm leaves*, plus lemon verbena for garnish
Zest of 1 lemon
1 tbsp. sugar
1 cup brewed black tea, such as English breakfast, cooled

1. Put lemongrass, lemon verbena, lemon balm, and zest in a heatproof container. Pour 2 cups boiling water over herbs and steep 20 minutes. Strain, then stir in sugar.

2. Divide liquid between 2 ice-filled glasses. Top each with about ½ cup black tea. Garnish with lemon verbena leaves.

*Grow your own lemon verbena and lemon balm, or look for them at a farmers' market.

PER SERVING 32 CAL., 0% (0.3 CAL.) FROM FAT; 0.1 G PROTEIN; 0 G FAT; 8.3 G CARBO (0.1 G FIBER); 0.6 MG SODIUM; 0 MG CHOL.

MAI TAI

SERVES 1 ★ 10 MINUTES

This classic rum-based cocktail is infused with three kinds of citrus flavors. Add a tiny paper umbrella for the full tropical-vacation effect.

2 tbsp. *each* light rum and orange curaçao
¼ cup fresh orange juice
1 tbsp. fresh lime juice
1 dash *each* orgeat* and simple syrup*
1 tbsp. dark rum
Mint sprig and pineapple slice for garnish

1. Fill an 8-oz. glass with ice. Pour in the light rum, orange curaçao, orange juice, lime juice, orgeat, and simple syrup.

2. Drizzle dark rum on top. Garnish with mint and pineapple.

*Find orgeat, an almond-flavored syrup, and simple syrup at liquor stores.

PER SERVING 212 CAL., 0% (1.2 CAL.) FROM FAT; 0.5 G PROTEIN; 0.1 G FAT (0 G SAT.); 17 G CARBO (0.2 G FIBER); 1.4 MG SODIUM; 0 MG CHOL.

MOJITO

SERVES 1 ★ 10 MINUTES

The secret to a good mojito is lots of fresh mint.

20 fresh mint leaves (each about 1½ in. long), plus mint
    sprig for garnish
2 tsp. superfine sugar
4 to 5 tbsp. light rum
3 tbsp. fresh lime juice
4 to 6 tbsp. chilled club soda

In an 8- to 10-oz. glass, combine mint leaves and sugar. With a wooden spoon, pound to coarsely crush. Add rum and lime juice; mix well. Fill glass with ice cubes and chilled club soda. Garnish with mint sprig.

PER SERVING 209 CAL., 0% (0.4 CAL.) FROM FAT; 0.3 G PROTEIN; 0.1 G FAT (0 G SAT.); 12 G CARBO (0.3 G FIBER); 2.1 MG SODIUM; 0 MG CHOL.

ST-GERMAIN FIZZY

SERVES 6 TO 8 ★ 10 MINUTES

Here's our favorite excuse to sip St-Germain, a liqueur that's infused with freshly picked, fragrant white elderflowers and tastes of litchi and pear.

1 cup halved and thinly sliced strawberries
1 cup chopped apricots or peaches
1 cup chilled St-Germain liqueur
1 bottle prosecco (750 ml.), chilled

Put strawberries, apricots, and liqueur in a pitcher. Pour in prosecco, stir gently, and pour into Champagne flutes.

PER SERVING 184 CAL., 0.7% (1.3 CAL.) FROM FAT; 0.4 G PROTEIN; 0.1 G FAT (0 G SAT.); 15 G CARBO (0.8 G FIBER); 0.4 MG SODIUM; 0 MG CHOL.

CALIFORNIA-STYLE PIMM'S CUP

SERVES 8 ★ 20 MINUTES

Valerie Aikman-Smith, a California food stylist born in Great Britain, shared with us this supremely summery drink, which is a must at English cricket matches. Her version is packed with California citrus, cucumbers, and mint.

2 oranges, cut into half-moons
2 lemons, cut into half-moons
1 Persian cucumber or one 3-in.-long piece English
    cucumber, sliced
2 cups Pimm's No. 1*
4 cups Sprite or other lemon-lime soda
6 to 8 large sprigs mint, crushed gently, plus a few
    loose leaves

Fill 2 pitchers a quarter full with ice. To each, add a layer of orange slices, a few lemon slices, and a layer of cucumber slices. Repeat the layering. Pour in the Pimm's No. 1 and Sprite, dividing between pitchers, and mix with a long-handled spoon. Poke mint down into drink. Divide drink among tall glasses, with a few slices of fruit and cucumber in each glass, along with some mint leaves.

*Find Pimm's No. 1, a bottled gin-based drink, at well-stocked liquor stores.

PER SERVING 226 CAL., 0.01% (1.8 CAL.) FROM FAT; 1.3 G PROTEIN; 0.2 G FAT (0 G SAT.); 21 G CARBO (2.9 G FIBER); 16 MG SODIUM; 0 MG CHOL.

INSPIRED FIRES

WHAT IS LIFE WITHOUT A WELL-CONSIDERED RISK? Even if you fail, you've at least learned something. And if you succeed, it's thrilling.

This chapter is all about the fun of trying things you've never ventured to do before—cooking exploits that lead to utterly delicious food (and bragging rights). Some are practically child's play, like the firepit you can build in 15 minutes using loose bricks (think Legos). Others are more of a leap, and show off live fire for the incredible force of nature that it is—and how it can be tamed by the cook. Let the flames begin!

PLAY WITH FIRE

With nothing more than a few bricks, some sand, and some foil, Bay Area chef Michael Chiarello proves that you don't need fancy equipment to grill great food.

LONG BEFORE HE BECAME A CELEBRITY, Michael Chiarello loved cooking over fire. As a boy, with everything still ahead of him—including the Emmy award–winning TV shows, the family winery, and the restaurants (Bottega, in the Napa Valley, and San Francisco's Coqueta)—he helped his Italian grandparents light the woodstove every morning at their ranch near Mt. Shasta. "It wasn't just starting a fire; it was a ritual," he says. "It's where I learned to cook."

As he got older, he cooked in a wood-burning oven outside too, with his *nonna*, aunts, and mother. A live fire's need to be fed and stoked appealed to him: "There's a relationship in tending it," he says. And it could be simple to create. "When my uncle would go mushroom hunting with us, he'd bring four bricks and a Weber grill grate, set up a firepit, and grill the mushrooms we'd found." In his 2013 book *Live Fire* (Chronicle Books) and recently with us, Chiarello drew on those memories to create a homemade firepit in less than 15 minutes—and from it, produce an entire rustic Italian menu.

Michael Chiarello grills the crust for pizza-like *piadine* on his homemade firepit.

THE DIY FIREPIT

BUILD THE PIT: ABOUT 15 MINUTES ★ LIGHT A TIPI-STYLE FIRE: 1¾ TO 2 HOURS

BUILD THE PIT

STEPS 1–2 Plan the size of your pit to fit whichever cooking grate you'd like to use. On bare ground (not grass), spread a double layer of heavy-duty foil to extend a foot beyond the grate. Stack 3 layers of bricks in a rectangle, arranging bricks in each layer so they overlap the ends of the bricks beneath. (For a standard 21-in. round Weber grate, build it 2 bricks by 3 bricks.) Leave a couple out of the top layer on opposite sides to encourage airflow, and fill pit with an inch of sand.

BUILD THE FIRE

STEPS 3–5 Arrange kindling in a tipi over paraffin fire-starter cubes or newspaper. Lean larger kindling against tipi, then 5 or 6 small logs. Light the cubes or newspaper.

Once the logs have caught, add several larger logs to the perimeter, and let it all burn down to ashy chunks with low flames (1½ to 2 hours). Then you'll be ready to cook. Because there's less smoke and char than cooking over high flame, Chiarello says, "it makes your food taste much cleaner."

START COOKING

STEP 6 Keep another log burning at the back of the pit. When it's ashy chunks, rake it into the main fire to maintain heat and set the grate in place.

To make the menu on the following pages, grill in this order:

- Prosciutto (page 179)
- *Piadine* (page 183)
- Chicken (page 184)
- Potatoes (page 187)
- Roasted garlic (for a future meal; page 187)

Choosing Your
FIREWOOD

Food grilled over actual logs, rather than over charcoal or a gas burner topped with wood chips or chunks, is a primary form of cooking, irreducible and deeply satisfying. A good, aromatic firewood will perfume your entire yard as you cook—and infuse the food with deep flavor.

Different woods have different intensities, from mild to pungent, and you can usually find a selection at a hardware store, garden center, or barbecue supply place (see Resource Guide, page 244). The logs will be seasoned (i.e., sufficiently dried to burn well) and ideally no thicker than 4 or 5 inches—and all about the same size, so the heat stays constant. If you have trimmings from your own trees, let them air-dry for several months or more before using; wet wood will steam, be overly smoky, and stall the fire.

When it comes to choosing types of wood, your own taste is your ultimate guide, but in general, milder firewood like fruitwood is best suited to delicate foods like fish and poultry, and smokier wood to dense meats like beef and pork. To get some sense of what the smoke will be like, just sniff the logs you're contemplating buying; mild wood won't be very aromatic unlit, but the medium to pungent woods will have detectable aromas. The only woods you should steer clear of are ones that are treated or painted, because they may be toxic; and softwoods, which contain a lot of sap and produce a bitter, resinous smoke: These types include pine, fir, cedar, aspen, and eucalyptus.

WOODS FOR COOKING: A FLAVOR SPECTRUM

MILD	MEDIUM	INTENSE
Alder, apple, ash, cherry, citrus, olive	Almond, hickory, pecan, red oak, white oak (burns faster than red oak)	Mesquite, walnut
Good for: vegetables, chicken, fish, turkey, desserts	Good for: sturdy vegetables, chicken, turkey, duck, pork, lamb, beef, oilier fish such as salmon	Good for: beef, lamb

GRILLED PROSCIUTTO

MAKES HOWEVER MANY YOU WANT ★ 3 MINUTES, PLUS ABOUT 1½ HOURS FOR FIRE

Before and while grilling the *piadine* (page 183), Michael Chiarello grilled several of these crisp, meaty slices. "It's a little something for everyone to snack on. It takes the pressure off the cook," he says. They're great with a glass of prosecco. On a gas or charcoal grill, cook over direct medium-high (400°) heat.

As many slices of prosciutto as you like

1. Build a fire and let burn to ashy chunks with low flames (see "The DIY Firepit," page 177).

2. Using tongs and a wad of oiled paper towels, oil the hot cooking grate well. Arrange sliced prosciutto perpendicular to rack and grill until crisp and browned on the edges, turning often, about 3 minutes. Stack on a small plate and serve.

PER OZ. (2 SLICES) 60 CAL., 45% (27 CAL.) FROM FAT; 8 G PROTEIN; 3 G FAT (1 G SAT.); 0 G CARBO; 770 MG SODIUM; 15 MG CHOL. LC

ASPARAGUS, ARUGULA, and
ROASTED GARLIC PIADINE
(see page 183)

MICHAEL CHIARELLO'S PIZZA DOUGH

MAKES TEN 6-OZ. BALLS OF DOUGH ★ OVERNIGHT FOR SPONGE, 30 MINUTES TO MIX AND KNEAD, AND 3 TO 4 HOURS TO REST AND RISE

This recipe produces some of the lightest, tastiest pizza dough we've had. Roll or stretch these balls thinly to make pizza, and a little thicker for *piadine*. Grill both over medium-high heat (450°; use a pizza stone if it's a gas grill) or bake in a 450° to 500° oven on a pizza stone.

SPONGE
2¼ tsp. active dry yeast (regular, not fast-acting)
1 tbsp. sugar
2 cups bread flour

DOUGH
Olive oil
1 cup unbleached all-purpose flour
4 cups bread flour, divided
2 tbsp. sea salt, preferably gray salt

1. Make sponge: In a large bowl, mix yeast with 2 cups warm water (105° to 115°), sugar, and bread flour with a wooden spoon until smooth. Cover with plastic wrap and let rest in a warm place (80° to 90° is ideal) overnight.

2. Make dough: Lightly oil a large bowl and set aside. In a stand mixer fitted with the dough hook, combine sponge, 1 cup warm water, the all-purpose flour, 3 cups bread flour, and the salt. Mix at low speed until dough is soft, sticky, and smooth, 6 to 8 minutes.

3. Increase speed to medium and gradually sprinkle in remaining 1 cup bread flour. Mix until smooth, then cover bowl with a kitchen towel and let rest 30 minutes.

4. Mix dough at low speed a couple of minutes, or until it begins to pull away from the sides of the bowl. If it doesn't, let it rest another 15 minutes; then mix again.

5. Turn dough out onto a floured work surface and sprinkle with more flour. With floured hands, knead dough several times until smooth and slam the dough hard onto work surface a few times to help the gluten develop and make dough more elastic.

6. Put dough in oiled bowl, cover tightly with plastic wrap, and let rise at room temperature until doubled in size, 2 to 4 hours. Divide into 10 equal portions and roll each into a tight ball.

7. Let balls rise about 20 minutes covered with a kitchen towel. They are ready to use now, but if you want to store them, put them side by side in a lightly oiled shallow container with a lid. Drizzle tops with oil to keep a skin from forming.

Make ahead: In container, covered and chilled, overnight or frozen up to 6 months. Let dough come to room temperature before proceeding.

PER DOUGH BALL 369 CAL., 5% (18 CAL.) FROM FAT; 12 G PROTEIN; 2.1 G FAT (0.3 G SAT.); 74 G CARBO (2.7 G FIBER); 914 MG SODIUM; 0 MG CHOL. VG

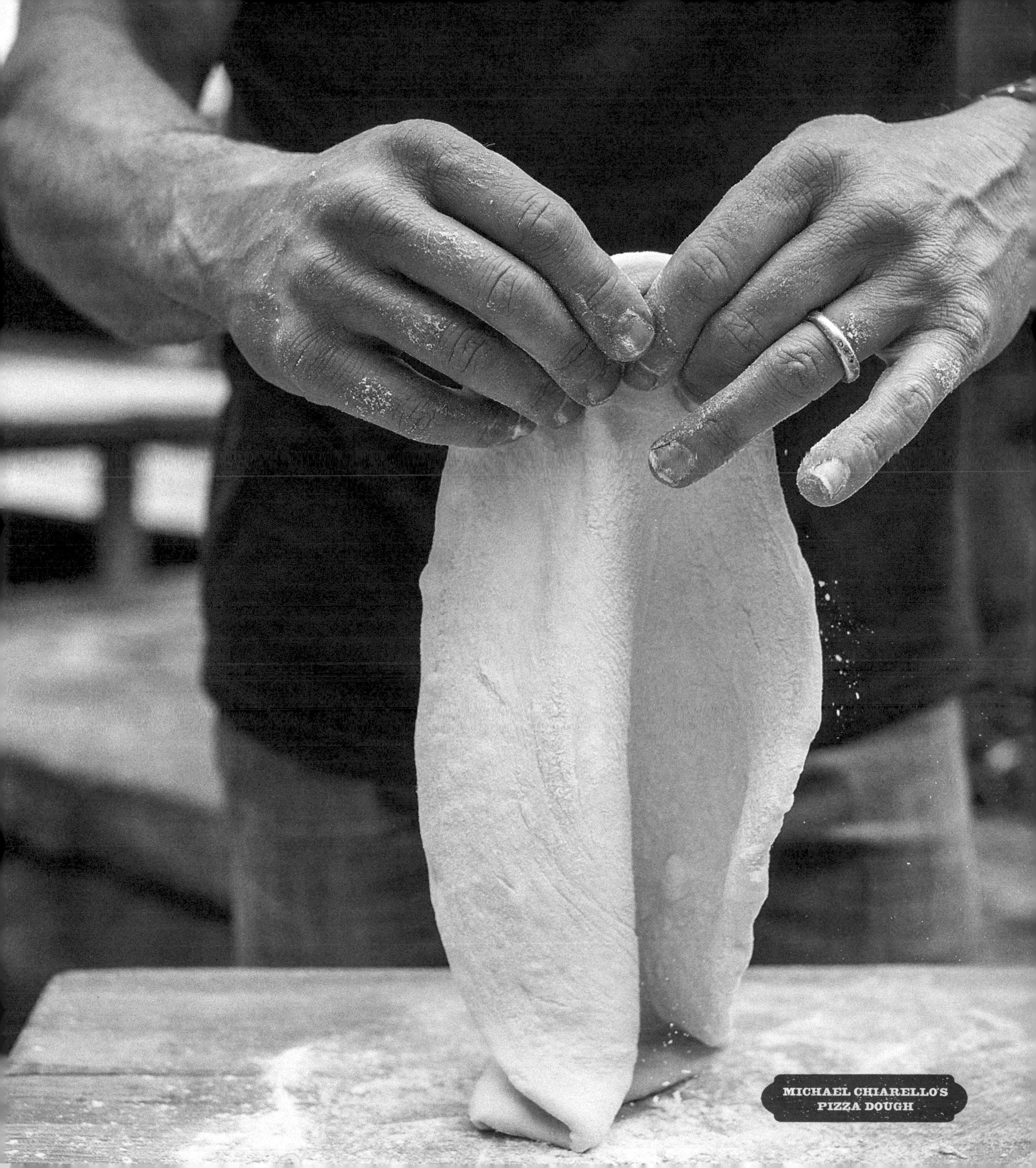

MICHAEL CHIARELLO'S PIZZA DOUGH

ASPARAGUS, ARUGULA, and
ROASTED GARLIC PIADINE

ASPARAGUS, ARUGULA, AND ROASTED GARLIC *PIADINE*

MAKES 2 (9 IN.) PIZZAS; SERVES 8 ★ 3 HOURS, PLUS ABOUT 1½ HOURS FOR FIRE

Chiarello describes *piadine*, flatbreads from Italy's Emilia-Romagna region, as "crisp warm dough with a highly flavored sauce and a cool salad." To make them on a gas grill, set a pizza stone on the cooking grate over high heat (450° to 550°) for at least 20 minutes, then bake right on the stone. No matter what your method, says Chiarello, "don't wait for your guests to sit down for these. You gotta make 'em and eat 'em." (They're often eaten folded like a taco; see photo on page 180.)

ARUGULA AND MEYER LEMON SALAD
2 heads garlic
About ¼ tsp. coarse sea salt, preferably gray
About ⅛ tsp. pepper
About 3 tbsp. extra-virgin olive oil, divided
2 tsp. sherry vinegar
3 cups loosely packed arugula
½ cup spring onions*, sliced thin, bulbs and pale green parts only (about 6 onions; or use ½ cup sliced regular green onions)
2 firm Meyer lemons, chilled, then sliced very thin and seeds removed

ASPARAGUS PESTO
Kosher salt
¾ lb. pencil-size asparagus, tough ends snapped off
1½ tbsp. toasted pine nuts
½ cup loosely packed chopped fresh basil
2 tsp. minced garlic
2 pinches coarse sea salt, preferably gray
Pepper
About 6 tbsp. extra-virgin olive oil
6 tbsp. freshly grated parmesan cheese

PIZZA
2 balls pizza dough (each 5 to 6 oz.), homemade (see Michael Chiarello's Pizza Dough, page 180) or store-bought
Extra-virgin olive oil
Coarse sea salt and pepper
¾ oz. pecorino cheese, shaved with a vegetable peeler (about ¼ cup)

1. Build a fire and let burn to ashy chunks with low flames (see "The DIY Firepit," page 177). Set grate in place.

2. Meanwhile, preheat oven to 400°. Make salad: Cut tops off garlic heads, sprinkle with salt and pepper, and drizzle each with 1 tsp. oil. Wrap in foil and roast in oven 1 hour. Let cool, then squeeze cloves from skin. (For Chiarello's Ash-Roasted Garlic recipe, see page 187.)

3. While garlic roasts, make pesto: Boil a large pot of water on the stove and salt generously with kosher salt. Boil asparagus about 3 minutes, or until tender; drain and spread out to cool.

4. Cut asparagus into thirds and save tips for salad. In a food processor, pulse together asparagus stalks, pine nuts, basil, garlic, sea salt, and pepper to taste. With the machine running, drizzle in 6 tbsp. oil. Add parmesan in batches, pulsing after each batch (pesto should be thick). If cheese begins to clump, add water, 1 tsp. at a time, until it loosens. Cover with plastic wrap, smoothing it against surface of pesto.

5. Finish salad: In a small bowl, whisk 2½ tbsp. oil, the vinegar, ¼ tsp. sea salt, and ⅛ tsp. pepper; set aside. Put asparagus tips, arugula, spring onions, roasted garlic cloves, and lemons in a large bowl.

6. Make pizza: On a floured work surface, dust balls of dough with flour. Working with 1 ball at a time and keeping others covered, roll or stretch until 9 to 10 in. across. "If you have trouble rolling them out, let them rest 30 seconds to relax," Chiarello says. To avoid tearing rolled-out dough when you lift it, drape it over the backs of both hands and lay it gently on grate. Brush with oil and sprinkle with salt and pepper.

7. Grill dough until it bubbles and is browned underneath, about 2 minutes. Using long tongs, flip over, brush with more oil, sprinkle with salt and pepper, and grill another 2 minutes, moving over lower heat if necessary (push coals to one side to make a lower-heat spot). Stretch and grill remaining dough round the same way. Don't worry if they're not perfectly round. "I like my crusts sort of free-form, *deformato*," Chiarello says.

8. Top each *piadina* with about ⅓ cup pesto. Toss salad with dressing and divide among piadine. Top with pecorino and cut into slices, or fold and eat taco-style.

*Buy spring onions at farmers' markets in season.

Make ahead: Pesto, 2 days chilled or 2 weeks frozen.

PER ¼ PIZZA 255 CAL., 49% (126 CAL.) FROM FAT; 6.7 G PROTEIN; 14 G FAT (2.4 G SAT.); 27 G CARBO (3 G FIBER); 386 MG SODIUM; 3.5 MG CHOL. V

1 tbsp. Calabrian chile paste or homemade chile paste*
¼ cup white balsamic vinegar
2 tsp. rosemary, chopped
½ cup extra-virgin olive oil
2 chicken halves (4 to 5 lbs. total)
About 1½ tsp. coarse sea salt, preferably gray

1. In a small bowl, mix chile paste, vinegar, rosemary, and oil. Chiarello loves the paste's flavor: "I call it Calabrian ketchup. It's fruity and a little bit smoky, with nuanced heat."

2. Put chicken in a glass dish just large enough to hold it flat. Add marinade and turn to coat. Marinate 2 hours or chill overnight, turning a few times (bring to room temperature before grilling).

3. Build a fire and let burn to ashy chunks with low flames (see "The DIY Firepit," page 177). Set cooking grate in place. Using tongs and a wad of oiled paper towels, oil the hot cooking grate well.

4. Pat excess marinade from chicken halves and season with 1½ tsp. salt. Arrange halves on grate, skin side up and touching down the middle. Oil bottom of a cast-iron skillet and set on chicken. Add a foil-wrapped brick to skillet.

5. Cook chicken until crisp and brown underneath, 10 to 13 minutes. If flames flare up, shift chicken to cooler spot on grill. Turn bird over and cook, still weighted, until brown and crisp and an instant-read thermometer registers 170° when inserted in a thigh, 11 to 13 minutes.

6. Transfer chicken to a cutting board, tent with foil, and allow to rest 5 minutes. Cut into quarters, season with salt, and serve.

*To find Calabrian chile paste (also called Silafunghi hot chili sauce), see Resource Guide, page 245. Or mix 1 tbsp. minced roasted red peppers with ½ tsp. *each* extra-virgin olive oil and lemon juice and ¼ tsp. *each* salt, red chile flakes, and smoked Spanish paprika.

PER SERVING 598 CAL., 48% (289 CAL.) FROM FAT; 71 G PROTEIN; 33 G FAT (7.1 G SAT.); 1.7 G CARBO (0.1 G FIBER); 875 MG SODIUM; 219 MG CHOL. GF

CALABRIAN CHICKEN UNDER A BRICK *(AL MATTONE)*

SERVES 4 ★ 45 MINUTES, PLUS 2 HOURS TO MARINATE AND ABOUT 1½ HOURS FOR FIRE

This chicken is seasoned with a chile paste from Calabria, where Chiarello's family is from, and cooked under a brick (*mattone* in Italian). The weight cooks the chicken evenly and keeps it juicier. Chiarello likes a good char on his bird (as in photo opposite), but if you prefer yours on the golden side, start it skin side up as directed here. To grill over gas or charcoal rather than wood, use direct medium-high heat (400°), but otherwise follow the recipe.

ASPARAGUS, ARUGULA, and **ROASTED GARLIC PIADINE** (see page 183)

CALABRIAN CHICKEN under a **BRICK**

OLIVE PESTO SMASHED POTATOES (see recipe on page 187)

OLIVE PESTO
SMASHED
POTATOES

OLIVE PESTO SMASHED POTATOES

SERVES 4 ★ 45 MINUTES, PLUS ABOUT 1½ HOURS FOR FIRE

"Smashing the potatoes gives you more surface to caramelize," says Chiarello. Spreading them evenly with pesto gives you seasoning in every bite. To make these on a gas or charcoal grill, preheat the frying pan over medium-high heat (400°), then cook as directed.

2 garlic cloves, minced
¼ cup chopped fresh basil leaves
1 cup kalamata olives, pitted and patted dry
¼ cup *each* extra-virgin olive oil and freshly grated parmesan cheese
12 small red or Yukon Gold potatoes (2 to 3 in. diameter), well-scrubbed
2 tbsp. minced flat-leaf parsley

1. Build a fire and let burn to ashy chunks with low flames (see "The DIY Firepit," page 177). Set a cooking grate in place.

2. Meanwhile, make pesto: Purée garlic and basil in a food processor. Add olives and oil and pulse to a smooth, thick paste. Transfer to a bowl and stir in cheese.

3. Put potatoes in a large pot on the stove with generously salted water to cover. Bring almost to a boil, then reduce heat and simmer until easily pierced with a knife, 15 to 20 minutes. Drain. When cool enough to handle, press each between your hands until about ¾ in. thick but still in one piece.

4. Spread each potato with 1 heaping tbsp. pesto and press to compact it. Heat a cast-iron frying pan on cooking grate, then add potatoes. Pan-roast until crisp underneath, 5 minutes. Turn pesto side down and let roast and crisp up. "Roasting the pesto adds umami to the potatoes and an interesting toastiness," Chiarello says. Put on a platter, pesto side up, and sprinkle with parsley.

Make ahead: Potatoes and pesto, up to 2 days, chilled and covered.

PER SERVING 328 CAL., 65% (214 CAL.) FROM FAT; 4.8 G PROTEIN; 24 G FAT (2.9 G SAT.); 25 G CARBO (3.7 G FIBER); 625 MG SODIUM; 4.4 MG CHOL. GF/V

ASH-ROASTED GARLIC

MAKES HOWEVER MANY YOU WANT ★ ABOUT 1 HOUR, PLUS ABOUT 2 HOURS FOR FIRE

You can use the last heat of a wood or charcoal fire to efficiently roast garlic for your next meal. (In an oven, roast the garlic at 400° for 1 hour.) Chiarello puts the soft, smoky cloves in salad, and also uses them in vinaigrettes, in marinades, under the skin of a chicken, and spread on grilled steak.

Whole garlic heads
Salt and pepper
Olive oil

Cut tops off garlic heads and set them on a doubled piece of heavy-duty foil. Sprinkle with salt and pepper and drizzle with oil. Wrap and roast on (not in) hot ash of a dying wood fire for about 1 hour, rotating occasionally. When cool, squeeze roasted garlic cloves from skins.

Make ahead: Up to 1 week, chilled; 2 months, frozen.

PER GARLIC HEAD 85 CAL., 26% (22 CAL.) FROM FAT; 2.8 G PROTEIN; 2.5 G FAT (0.4 G SAT.); 15 G CARBO (0.9 G FIBER); 7.5 MG SODIUM; 0 MG CHOL.

THINK INSIDE THE BOX

One spectacular way to feed a crowd is to cook a whole animal—or, for a range of appetites, a combination of smaller cuts. A roasting box, with the meat enclosed inside and the fire on top, makes it easy.

THE BEST-KNOWN ROASTING BOX in America is the Cuban-style Caja China (although Louisianans might disagree, having had their own version—affectionately called a Cajun microwave—for decades).

The Caja China requires no special knowledge or skills, is portable, and, unlike pit roasting, leaves your garden unscathed. And it's fast: A whole pig cooks in four hours—half the time of a pit roast. Best of all, though, are the succulent, crisp-skinned results.

Made by La Caja China, a Cuban American company in Miami, the basic Caja China looks like a box crossed with a wheelbarrow. It's made of plywood and lined with aluminum, with wheels under one end and two looping handles at the other. A drip pan sits in the bottom of the box, and the meat goes onto a rack over the drip pan. The top of the box consists of a large steel tray with a grate that you fill with burning charcoal, so the meat cooks beneath the heat rather than over it. (See the Resource Guide, page 244, for more details.)

So what is Chinese about the Caja China? According to Maricel Presilla, a Cuban American restaurateur and winner of a James Beard award for her authoritative tome *Gran Cocina Latina* (W.W. Norton, 2012), in Cuba anything especially clever or inventive is automatically dubbed "Chinese"—a likely explanation of how this ingenious device got its name. We've used our Caja China #2 model, the largest, for everything from whole lamb to whole pig (for the taco party on page 193) to a mixed grill, shown here.

Use the Caja China to cook a mixed grill—pork shoulder, chickens, tri-tips, and sausages—for a party (see recipe, page 194).

TOOLS FOR BOX ROASTING

A CAJA CHINA. The #2 size is capable of roasting a pig with a market weight of up to 100 lbs. (65 lbs. dressed) and easily handles all the meats in our Mixed Grill (page 194). The box comes in several smaller sizes too.

HEATPROOF SPOT. For resting charcoal tray.

LARGE BRINING INJECTOR FOR PIG. Find at any good butcher shop (or see Resource Guide, page 244).

2 LARGE, CLEAN TARPS. One for brining pig, one for the carving table.

HEAVY-DUTY GRILLING MITTS. To protect your hands.

DIGITAL THERMOMETERS. Handier than a meat or instant-read thermometer, because the display unit sits outside the grill; you can read the temperature without having to lift the lid and let out heat. Use at least two for the pig and two for the mixed grill. For the type that sticks magnetically to the outside of the box, see the Resource Guide.

HEATPROOF METAL BUCKET. Preferably with a lid, for collecting hot ash.

METAL DUSTPAN. For scooping ash.

METAL HOE OR RAKE. For spreading coals.

FOIL. To keep pig warm as you're carving.

A HELPER. Roasting in a large Caja China is not a job for a solo cook (in case that hasn't already occurred to you). But two people can get the job done easily.

WHOLE ROAST PIG WITH CUMIN AND OREGANO

SERVES 20 TO 25 ★ ABOUT 4 HOURS, PLUS 4 HOURS TO BRINE

Whole-animal cooking, being adopted by more and more restaurants around the country, is also appealing to home cooks who want to know more about their meat, and to eat it with less waste. With a whole roast pig, you can compare the tastes and textures of different cuts—tenderloin, belly, ham—along with the crisp skin. And it's a very affordable way to feed a crowd.

We like to brine the pig to season the meat thoroughly and keep it moist, but you can also roast it as is, or use a seasoning rub. You'll need several 10-lb. bags of ice, 50 lbs. of charcoal, and 9 paraffin fire-starter cubes. (For other materials, see "Tools for Box Roasting," page 189.)

Cumin Oregano Brine (page 193)
1 whole pig, including head (about 65 lbs. dressed weight, for a Model #2 Caja China), butterflied and spine split* so it lies flat

1. Strain brine mixture through a fine sieve. Lay pig on a large work surface, skin side down. Fill a brining syringe with brine by immersing the needle and pulling back the plunger. Inject brine into meat every 3 to 4 in.

2. Line Caja China with a large plastic tarp or a few plastic trash bags cut to open fully. Lay a few bags of ice on plastic, then set pig on top of ice. Lay another piece of plastic over pig and top with two bags of ice. Put lid on box and wheel it to an area that you won't mind getting wet if the box leaks. If you're keeping the box outdoors, put some heavy objects on top of the lid so it can't be pushed loose by animals. Brine at least 4 hours and preferably overnight.

3. Remove ice bags and pig and drain any water from the box. Lay pig skin side up on cooking rack and set inside the box over the drip pan, uncovered (**A**). Let pig sit at room temperature for about an hour before cooking.

4. Ignite 20 lbs. charcoal briquets on grate set in Caja China's top tray: Divide into three mounds, and use 3 paraffin fire-starter cubes at base of each mound (**B**). Once briquets are covered with ash, 20 to 30 minutes, spread evenly over grate with a metal hoe or rake (**C**).

5. Lift tray to a heatproof spot. Insert probe of a digital thermometer (**D**) into thickest part of meat. If you have two, put one in the butt and one in the shoulder, avoiding any bones and arranging thermometer cords over sides of the box; put digital readout underneath, on outside, or next to the roasting box (it will stay completely cool, because all the heat is on top of the box). Tent pig with foil to keep skin from overbrowning.

6. Set tray over box to close and seal. Roast pig 1 hour. Remove excess ash from charcoal tray: Lift grate of still-burning charcoal from tray (**E**), leaving ash in tray beneath, and rest on a heatproof spot. Scrape ash out of tray (**F**) and dump into heatproof bucket. Return grate of hot coals to top of tray.

7. Add 10 lbs. more charcoal to grate and roast another 1 hour. Clear ash and add charcoal the same way as before and for every hour of remaining cooking time, until digital readout reaches 165°, about 4 hours total cooking time. Check skin about 30 minutes before end of cooking; if it needs crisping, remove foil.

8. Remove pig, still on cooking rack, from box (**G**), set on a clean tarp or cutting boards laid end to end, and let rest 20 to 30 minutes covered with foil before carving.

9. Meanwhile, if you're serving the roast pig as part of a taco bar (see page 193), set up all the fixings while the pig rests. Once you start slicing, you'll want to serve immediately, so it's important to have the add-ons ready.

*Order at least a week in advance from your butcher, prepared as described.

PER SERVING 206 CAL., 51% (106 CAL.) FROM FAT; 22 G PROTEIN; 12 G FAT (4.2 G SAT.); 0.8 G CARBO (0.1 G FIBER); 603 MG SODIUM; 75 MG CHOL.

CUMIN OREGANO BRINE

MAKES 9½ CUPS ★ 15 MINUTES, PLUS 2 HOURS TO CHILL

½ cup kosher salt
1½ tsp. ground cumin
1 tbsp. dried oregano, preferably Mexican*
2 garlic cloves, chopped
Zest of 2 limes
¼ cup packed light or dark brown sugar

Mix the salt, 1 qt. water, and the remaining ingredients together in a very large pot. Heat over high heat, covered, until mixture boils and salt and sugar dissolve. Remove from heat, add another 1 qt. water and 1 cup ice cubes, and chill, stirring occasionally, until cold, about 2 hours.

*Mexican oregano is especially fragrant. Find it at well-stocked grocery stores and Mexican markets.

Make ahead. Up to 2 days, covered and chilled.

ROAST PORK TACO BAR

SERVES 20 TO 25

Roasting an entire pig generates a lot of drama and anticipation, so it's ideal for a party. Letting people serve themselves makes it easy on the cooks—who, after the heroic roasting, deserve to kick back and have a beer.

Whole Roast Pig with Cumin and Oregano (page 190)
About 50 corn or flour tortillas
1 qt. shredded lettuce
1 lb. coarsely shredded semisoft cheese such as
    Monterey jack or *queso Oaxaca**
1 qt. salsa (see page 92 for a recipe)
6 to 8 cups guacamole (see page 93 for a recipe)
2 cups Mexican *crema** or sour cream

1. While pig rests, push coals aside on Caja China cooking grate and set packet of foil-wrapped tortillas on grate to let warm; turn every few minutes. Set out toppings and tortillas buffet-style.

2. Carve pig (at right). You can do this in the kitchen or around a corner if you have squeamish guests, and then bring the heaping platters of meat to the buffet table. Invite everyone to assemble their own tacos (they'll probably be standing right there waiting).

*Find queso Oaxaca, a ribbony cheese somewhat like mozzarella, and crema, a pourable sour cream, at Latino markets.

HOW TO CARVE A WHOLE ROAST PIG

You'll want to slice and serve the meat in stages. This way you can keep it from cooling off (as it would if you sliced and served it all at once).

Start by slicing from the thickest parts of the pig—the shoulder and butt areas. Cut off large chunks and move them to a cutting board. Then cut those chunks into smaller slices. Transfer the slices to a serving platter and cover with foil to keep warm. Continue until you've cut most of the meat off those four areas.

Then, working with a back leg, locate the place where the leg attaches to the hip socket and, lifting the leg up, cut through the joint to separate it from the body. Then slice the meat off the leg bone. Repeat with other back leg, then front legs. With foil, cover the parts of the pig that aren't being cut, to try to keep the heat in. Pull or cut meat off torso, and save the head for soup or stew if you like.

MIXED GRILL TIMELINE

This timeline is a rough guide; your meats may cook faster or slower depending on the outside temperature and any wind (breezes fan fires and make them hotter). When checking temperature of the meat, especially toward the end of cooking, be sure to insert the thermometer probe into the thickest part of the meat in at least two places; chickens should be tested in both the breast and the thigh.

1 TO 2 DAYS BEFORE	Brine pork butts.
NIGHT BEFORE	Brine chicken.
NEXT DAY: 4½ HOURS BEFORE DINNER	Brine tri-tips. Take pork out of fridge.
4 HOURS BEFORE	Light 15 lbs. briquets on Caja China.
3½ HOURS BEFORE	Put pork butts in Caja China, tented with foil. Roast to 160° (about 3 hours). Take chickens and tri-tips out of fridge. Rub chickens with Sage Garlic Butter.
2½ HOURS BEFORE	Scrape ash from charcoal tray; add 10 more lbs. briquets.
2 HOURS BEFORE	Put chickens in Caja China. Roast 1 to 1½ hours (to 160° in breast, 170° in thigh).
1½ HOURS BEFORE	Scrape ash from charcoal tray; add 10 more lbs. briquets. Take sausages out of fridge. Put tri-tips in Caja China. Roast 45 minutes (to 125° to 130° for medium rare).
1 HOUR BEFORE	Put sausages in Caja China to roast until hot and cooked through, 30 minutes. Remove foil from pork. Scrape ash from charcoal tray; add 10 more lbs.
30 MINUTES BEFORE	All meats out of Caja China to rest 20 minutes. Carve and arrange on platters.

CAJA CHINA MIXED GRILL

SERVES 20 TO 25 ★ 4 TO 5 HOURS, PLUS AT LEAST 1 DAY TO BRINE

Although a little trickier, timing-wise, than roasting a whole pig, an assortment of meats carefully arranged in the Caja China means that everyone has lots of choices for dinner. The meats go into the box in sequence, depending on how long each cooks (see "Mixed Grill Timeline" at left). To see how to clear ash from the top tray, look at the photo on page 191. Two digital thermometers are ideal—one for the pork and one for the chicken. In addition, you'll need about 45 lbs. of charcoal and 9 paraffin fire-starter cubes. For other tools you'll need, see "Tools for Box Roasting," page 189. For side dishes to go with the meats, see pages 158 through 165.

2 pork butt roasts (each about 6 lbs.)
Double recipe Aromatic Herb and Garlic Brine (page 113)
2 whole chickens (each about 5 lbs.)
Double recipe Sage Brine (page 112)
Garlic Herb Rub (recipe follows)
Sage Garlic Butter (recipe follows)
2 beef tri-tips (each about 2 lbs.), marinated (buy marinated, or use Anchovy Herb Marinade, page 112)
About 3 lbs. mixed fresh sausages (such as lamb, chicken, and pork)

1. Add pork to cooled herb and garlic brine and chill, covered, at least 1 day and up to 2. Meanwhile, put chickens, breast down, in bowls or pots large enough to hold them and add sage brine. Chill, covered, overnight.

2. Remove pork from refrigerator about 1 hour before cooking, drain, and dry thoroughly with paper towels. Pat garlic herb rub all over pork. Form a deep foil "pan" under each pork butt to contain juices, using 2 or 3 layers of foil; then set each on a flat metal rack and put in a rimmed baking pan. Tent pork with a single layer of foil.

3. Ignite 15 lbs. charcoal briquets on grate set in Caja China's top tray (divide into 3 mounds, and use 3 paraffin fire-starter cubes at base of each mound; see photo on page 191). Once briquets are covered with ash, 20 to 30 minutes, spread evenly over grate.

4. Lift tray with grate and charcoal and set on a heat-proof spot. Place pork on pan in bottom of Caja China. Insert probe of a digital thermometer into thickest part of a pork butt and arrange thermometer cord over side of box; set digital readout underneath, on outside, or next to the roasting box (it will stay completely cool, because all the heat is on top of the box). Replace tray on box and roast pork 1 hour.

5. Remove excess ash from charcoal tray: Lift grate of still-burning charcoal from tray, leaving ash in tray beneath, and set on a heatproof spot. Scrape ash from tray and dump into a heatproof bucket. Return grate of hot coals to top of tray. Add 10 lbs. more charcoal to grate and roast 1 more hour. Clear ash and add charcoal the same way as before, and for every hour of remaining cooking time, even at the very end, to keep temperature constant.

6. While pork is roasting, remove chickens and tri-tips from refrigerator. Drain chickens and dry thoroughly inside and out with paper towels. Rub sage garlic butter under skin of chickens, in cavity, and over skin. Put chickens in V-shaped roasting racks and tri-tips on any kind of metal rack, and set each in a rimmed baking pan (this will make removing them easier).

7. Remove tray of charcoal and set on a heatproof spot. Set pans with chickens in roasting box and replace charcoal tray. Roast 45 minutes. Meanwhile, remove sausages from refrigerator and arrange on a metal rack in a single layer; set in a rimmed baking pan.

8. Add tri-tips to Caja China. Roast 15 minutes, then add sausages to box, remove foil from pork, and roast all the meats together for 30 minutes. Checking thermometers, remove each meat as it's done (see "Mixed Grill Timeline," opposite, for times and temperatures). Let meat rest 20 minutes (cover sausages with foil to keep warm). Slice meat and serve on platters, with sausages.

PER SERVING 907 CAL., 57% (517 CAL.) FROM FAT; 86 G PROTEIN; 58 G FAT (21 G SAT.); 6 G CARBO (0.7 G FIBER); 1,378 MG SODIUM; 324 MG CHOL.

GARLIC HERB RUB

MAKES 1¾ CUPS ★ 1 HOUR

6 heads garlic
About ⅔ cup olive oil, divided
2 bunches fresh oregano or marjoram
4 to 6 sprigs (5 in.) fresh rosemary
Leaves from 2 bunches flat-leaf parsley
½ tsp. dried culinary lavender
Sea salt and pepper

1. Preheat oven to 400°. Slice garlic heads in half crosswise and set on a sheet of foil. Drizzle with about 3 tbsp. oil and enclose in foil. Roast 45 minutes to 1 hour, or until cloves are buttery soft. Let cool.

2. Pull oregano and rosemary leaves from stems; chop finely, along with parsley leaves. Crush lavender in a mortar with a pestle (or put in a resealable plastic bag and pound with a meat mallet). Squish garlic cloves from their skins into a small bowl. Add ½ cup oil and smash garlic into a paste with a fork. Stir in herbs; season lightly with salt and pepper.

Make ahead: Up to 1 week, chilled.

SAGE GARLIC BUTTER

MAKES 2 CUPS ★ 15 MINUTES

1½ cups butter, at room temperature
⅔ cup chopped fresh sage leaves
¼ cup minced garlic
2 tsp. *each* kosher salt and pepper

Whirl all ingredients together in a food processor, scraping the insides of the bowl as needed to blend.

Make ahead: Up to 1 week, chilled.

FEAST AT THE BEACH

Two Oregon chefs fire up a seafood boil right on the sand.

THE WEST ABOUNDS IN GREAT OUTDOOR traditions, but clambakes and lobster boils have typically been the other coast's domain. "Summer was all about cookouts on the beach," remembers Jason French, who owns Ned Ludd restaurant in Portland, Oregon, but spent childhood summers in Maine. "Such freedom—running wild, with this huge ocean in front of us."

Once he had kids, French was inspired to resurrect the tradition in Oregon using the local bounty. So he and chef John Gorham, a fellow East Coast transplant and owner of Portland's Toro Bravo restaurant group, packed up their families and their 20-quart pots and headed to the coast.

After the fire got going, their method was easy: In a pot of seawater, layer seafood and vegetables in order of longest to shortest cooking time, and boil away.

The chefs served the works with homemade sauces. Then it was cake with campfire-cooked fruit for dessert, and a stroll to the waves to rinse off sticky fingers. "As much as I love a Maine lobster bake," says French, "I'd say the food is a lot better with John and me cooking."

At Rockaway Beach, French (right) and Gorham (to his right) unwrap bundles of vegetables and set them out with seafood directly on a table covered with newspaper. FACING PAGE: The day starts with a fresh seafood stop at the Jetty Fishery (top). After they've carried the gear and food onto the beach, Gorham builds the fire in a sheltered spot.

SEAFOOD COOKOUT ESSENTIALS

Here's everything you need to throw your own party on the beach.

THE INGREDIENTS. French and Gorham cleaned and cut vegetables and fruit ahead of time, packing the components for each dish in separate containers in a cooler.

THE GEAR. For cooking, they used a 20-quart canning pot with an insert. You'll also need cheesecloth, kitchen scissors, tongs, grilling mitts, some newspaper, a cutting board, a chef's knife, a dutch oven, wooden spoon, and serving dishes and tools. Plus a propane lighter ("Yup," says French, who runs a wood-fired restaurant but remembers too many events spent struggling with matches, "this is the older, wiser me.").

THE SEAFOOD. French and Gorham bought freshly caught littleneck clams, lingcod, and Dungeness crab from the Jetty Fishery in Rockaway Beach, about 60 miles from Portland.

THE FIRE. Check that your beach allows wood fires. The chefs built theirs in a pit, and used a portable grate with legs (see Resource Guide, page 244), but a charcoal-grill grate set on bricks will also work. For building the fire, follow the tipi method on page 177.

NORTHWEST SEAFOOD BOIL

SERVES 10 ★ 1¼ HOURS, PLUS 30 MINUTES FOR FIRE

It's hard to control a fire's heat precisely, but these ingredients are forgiving. The recipe can also be done on your home stove (use a 20-qt. canning pot).

Seawater (or regular water plus ½ cup kosher salt)
3 lbs. (about 30) small Red Bliss, German Butterball, or other thin-skinned potatoes
10 ears corn on the cob, ends trimmed, husks pulled down to remove silk, then pulled back up
3 lbs. (25 to 40) littleneck clams, scrubbed
2 lbs. lingcod, Pacific cod, or black cod (sablefish) fillets (about 1 in. thick)
10 small red torpedo onions*, peeled, or 2 large red onions, peeled and quartered
10 Turkish (not California) bay leaves
5 lbs. (about 3) Dungeness crabs, steamed, cleaned, quartered, and cracked
Tartar Sauce (recipe follows)
Italian-Style Salsa Verde (page 201)

1. Dig a pit and build a fire in it (see "The DIY Firepit," page 177, for setup options, or use a firepit with a built-in grate). Let fire burn to medium-high, spreading out logs as needed; if using your own grate, set it in place.

2. Fill a 20-qt. canning pot with 4 in. seawater or salted regular water. Cover and heat to simmering over fire or over high heat on stove.

3. Wrap potatoes, corn (divided into two groups of 5 ears), clams, and cod separately in cheesecloth: Cut five 30-in. lengths of cheesecloth. For each, unfold a cheesecloth length to yield a double-thick piece. Lay it on a table, pile the ingredient in the center, pull up two opposing corners, and tie loosely. Repeat with other corners, creating a pouch that's secure but loose enough for ingredients to spread out in more or less a single layer.

4. Put potato pouch, loose onions, and bay leaves in canning insert, and when water is boiling, lower into pot. Cook, covered, 10 minutes. Add cod pouch, then clams, and top with loose crabs. Cover and cook 8 to 10 minutes more; cod should be opaque, crab should be warmed through, and clams should open (though it may be difficult to check).

5. Using tongs, transfer the bundles of ingredients to a newspaper-lined table or into large bowls. Put corn bundles into canning insert and into boiling water; cook until tender, about 5 minutes. Meanwhile, drain off any water from bundles on table. Snip open cheesecloth and pour ingredients out onto platters or a fresh spot on the covered table. Throw away any unopened clams. Serve with tartar sauce and salsa verde.

*Find torpedo onions, an elongated, mild red variety, in summer at farmers' markets.

PER SERVING WITHOUT SAUCES 427 CAL., 9% (40 CAL.) FROM FAT; 52 G PROTEIN; 4.5 G FAT (0.6 G SAT.); 46 G CARBO (4.8 G FIBER); 814 MG SODIUM; 137 MG CHOL. LC

TARTAR SAUCE

Combine ¾ cup *each* **extra-virgin olive oil** and **grape-seed oil** in a glass measuring cup. Put 3 large **egg yolks**, ¾ tsp. **kosher salt**, 3 tbsp. **lemon juice**, 1 tsp. *each* **Dijon mustard** and **Champagne vinegar**, ¼ tsp. **sugar**, and a pinch of **cayenne** in a blender or food processor. With motor running, gradually add oil in a steady stream. Scrape into a bowl and fold in 1 tbsp. *each* chopped **capers** and **flat-leaf parsley** and 2 tbsp. *each* chopped **dill pickles**, fresh **tarragon**, and **chives**. Taste and adjust salt, lemon, vinegar, or cayenne; you want the flavor to be zippy. Makes 1¾ cups.

Make ahead: Up to 1 day, chilled.

PER TBSP. 110 CAL., 98% (107 CAL.) FROM FAT; 0.3 G PROTEIN; 12 G FAT (1.6 G SAT.); 0.4 G CARBO (0 G FIBER); 61 MG SODIUM; 22 MG CHOL. LS/V

ITALIAN-STYLE SALSA VERDE

In a small bowl, combine ½ cup coarsely chopped **flat-leaf parsley**; ¼ cup *each* coarsely chopped **chives**, **fennel fronds** or dill, **mint leaves**, fresh **tarragon**, and **shallots**; 2 tbsp. finely chopped **capers**; 2 tsp. coarsely chopped fresh **sage leaves**; and ¾ tsp. **kosher salt**. Whisk in 1¼ cups fruity **extra-virgin olive oil**. Taste and adjust salt. Chill overnight, if possible, so flavors can marry. Makes 1¾ cups.

Make ahead: Up to 1 day, chilled; serve at room temperature.

PER TBSP. 88 CAL., 98% (86 CAL.) FROM FAT; 0.2 G PROTEIN; 10 G FAT (1.4 G SAT.); 0.5 G CARBO(0.2 G FIBER); 60 MG SODIUM; 0 MG CHOL. GF/LS/VG

LETTUCE AND CUCUMBER SALAD WITH GOAT CHEESE

SERVES 10 ★ 30 MINUTES

For an element of surprise, Jason French spreads basil purée on the platter, rather than tossing it with the other ingredients. This also helps keep the salad crisp.

¾ cup plus 5 to 6 tbsp. extra-virgin olive oil, divided
1 qt. (4 oz.) loosely packed fresh basil leaves
About 1¼ tsp. kosher salt, divided
5 or 6 Persian cucumbers or 1½ English cucumbers, cut into chunks
5 small heads Little Gem* lettuce or 3 hearts of romaine, torn into pieces
About 2 tbsp. lemon juice
10 oz. fresh goat cheese

1. Put ¾ cup oil in a blender, add a few basil leaves, and pulse to blend. Continue pulsing as you add more leaves and 1 small ice cube (it helps move the leaves around); blend until all leaves are added and mixture is smooth. Season with about 1 tsp. salt.

2. Put cucumbers and lettuce in a large bowl, add 5 to 6 tbsp. oil and the lemon juice, and toss to coat evenly. Season with about ¼ tsp. salt and toss again.

3. Spread basil purée on plates or a large platter, top with lettuce and cucumbers, and crumble goat cheese on top. Serve right away.

*Find Little Gem lettuce, a flavorful mini romaine, at farmers' markets.

Make ahead: For basil purée, lettuce prep, and dressing, up to 1 day, chilled separately; bring basil purée to room temperature before serving.

PER SERVING 335 CAL., 86% (287 CAL.) FROM FAT; 7.6 G PROTEIN; 33 G FAT (9.4 G SAT.); 5.3 G CARBO (1.2 G FIBER); 341 MG SODIUM; 22 MG CHOL. GF/LS/V

FACING PAGE: As the sun begins to set, Gorham, French, and friends feast on salad, the seafood boil, and zingy sauces.

OLIVE OIL CAKE

SERVES 10 TO 12 ★ 1¼ HOURS, PLUS 1 HOUR TO COOL

Gorham's dense but moist cake, which he makes before heading to the beach, soaks up juice from the fruit. You'll need a 10-in. round cake pan that is 2 in. deep; look for it at well-stocked cookware stores or see the Resource Guide, page 244.

2 large eggs
1⅔ cups sugar
2 cups flour
1 tsp. baking powder
½ tsp. baking soda
¾ tsp. kosher salt
¾ cup whole milk
1 cup mild extra-virgin olive oil
1 tsp. lightly packed lemon zest
3 tbsp. lemon juice
Campfire-Glazed Peaches and Figs (recipe at right)
Sweetened whipped cream*

1. Preheat oven to 375°. Butter a 10-in. round and 2-in.-deep cake pan. Set a piece of parchment paper, cut to fit, inside, then butter parchment and dust pan with flour. Set aside.

2. Beat eggs in a large bowl with a mixer, using the whisk attachment, until frothy. Gradually add sugar and beat on high speed until mixture is pale and leaves a ribbon when you lift whisk, 6 to 8 minutes; scrape bowl halfway through.

3. Whisk together flour, baking powder, baking soda, and salt in a medium bowl. In a large measuring cup or bowl, whisk together milk, oil, and lemon zest and juice.

4. Add one-third of dry ingredients, then half of wet ingredients, to egg mixture, beating after each addition until smooth; continue, pausing a few times to scrape inside of bowl, until everything is added.

5. Pour batter into prepared pan and set in oven. Immediately turn down heat to 350°. Bake until cake pulls away from pan and a toothpick inserted in center comes out clean, 50 to 55 minutes.

6. Cool on a rack 15 minutes, then loosen cake from pan with a knife. Turn out onto a plate, remove parchment, and carefully flip cake back onto rack. Let cool completely.

7. Serve wedges of cake with fruit and whipped cream.

*To whip cream at the beach, shake cold cream in a quart-size canning jar until thick.

Make ahead: Up to 2 days, wrapped airtight.

PER SERVING OF CAKE WITH FRUIT 508 CAL., 43% (220 CAL.) FROM FAT; 4.8 G PROTEIN; 25 G FAT (6.3 G SAT.); 70 G CARBO (3.3 G FIBER); 225 MG SODIUM; 49 MG CHOL. LS/V

CAMPFIRE-GLAZED PEACHES AND FIGS

SERVES 10 TO 12 ★ 30 MINUTES, PLUS 2 HOURS FOR FIRE

This dessert has all the virtue of fresh fruit with just a hint of indulgence from browned butter and sugar. And it's equally good made on a home stove.

4 tbsp. unsalted butter
6 tbsp. sugar
Generous pinch kosher salt
1 vanilla bean, split
2½ lbs. (about 5) peaches or nectarines, pitted and cut into ½-in. wedges
1¼ lbs. (1½ pts.) figs, stems trimmed, halved or quartered if large

1. Build a fire in a pit (see "The DIY Firepit," page 177, for setup options, or use a firepit with a built-in grate). Let fire burn until embers are red-hot but there are no flames, then spread out embers. If using your own grate, set it in place.

2. Put butter, sugar, and salt in a large, heavy dutch oven or enameled cast-iron pot. Scrape vanilla seeds into pot and add bean. Set pot on grate over fire or on stove over medium-high heat. Cook, stirring, until mixture turns golden brown and frothy and begins to smell like caramel, 3 to 6 minutes.

3. Add fruit and stir to coat. Cover pot and cook, stirring occasionally, until fruit has released some juice and is glossy and glazed but not mushy, 2 to 4 minutes.

Make ahead: Cut fruit the morning of your outing (toss peaches with 2 tbsp. lemon juice) and chill airtight in a cooler.

PER SERVING 132 CAL., 29% (38 CAL.) FROM FAT; 1.1 G PROTEIN; 4.3 G FAT (2.5 G SAT.); 25 G CARBO (2.7 G FIBER); 11 MG SODIUM; 10 MG CHOL. GF/LC/LS/V

CAMPFIRE-GLAZED
PEACHES and FIGS

OLIVE OIL CAKE

GRILL LIKE A GAUCHO

At Belcampo Farms, a pastured-livestock ranch near California's Mt. Shasta, outdoor cooking is Uruguayan-cowboy style.

LIKE THE GAUCHOS on Belcampo's sister property in South America, Estancio Uruguay, cooks on the ranch use a magnificent custom-made grill with a heavy U-shaped firegrate, where logs burn down to embers perfect for cooking. On either side of the firegrate are slanted cooking grates hung on chains; the angle of the slant is adjustable. The embers are shoveled beneath them, and the food goes on top of the grates, with more delicate, burnable items at the high, cooler ends. Sturdier foods are roasted right in the coals.

You don't have to have a Uruguayan grill, though, to make Belcampo's delicious, rustic chicken dinner at home. (However, if you're interested in buying a Uruguayan grill, see the Resource Guide, page 244.) You can easily use your gas or charcoal grill, or an improvised firepit (see page 177) to cook chicken, sweet peppers, and a few lemons over a pan of fingerling potatoes nested in the coals below. As the chicken, peppers, and lemons sizzle on the grill, their savory juices drip into the potatoes.

When the chicken is golden and crisp, carve it and set the cutting board right on the table, with the grilled lemons alongside, for squeezing over the meat. Toast slices of good bread on the grill, pile them with peppers, and set those on another board or platter. The cast-iron pan of potatoes can go directly on the table too.

To finish a dinner as fresh and straightforward as this one, you might want just some good ripe peaches, apricots, or berries, with a little sweetened whipped cream.

Bronwen Hanna-Korpi, director of Belcampo's butcher shops (see Resource Guide, page 245), grills chicken, potatoes, and peppers on the ranch's Uruguayan-style grill.

MENU

ROASTED-PEPPER CROSTINI
(page 206)

SPATCHCOCKED CHICKEN with GRILLED LEMONS and FIRE-ROASTED POTATOES
(page 206)

RIPE SEASONAL FRUIT with WHIPPED CREAM

WINE: A well-balanced Viognier (crisp, a little minerally, and not over-oaked)

A CHICKEN DINNER TIMELINE

NIGHT BEFORE	Prep chickens.
NEXT DAY: 3 HOURS BEFORE DINNER	Light charcoal (if using wood, light a tipi-style fire about 4 hours before; see page 177 for tips. If using gas, light 2½ hours before).
2½ HOURS BEFORE	Take chickens out of fridge. Grill peppers, transfer to a heat-proof dish such as a ceramic baking dish, and cover.
1¼ HOURS BEFORE	Set pan of potatoes in coals and lay chickens on cooking grate over potatoes. (If using gas, set potatoes and chickens on cooking grate.)
30 MINUTES BEFORE	Add lemons to cooking grate.
ABOUT 15 MINUTES BEFORE	Transfer chickens and lemons to a cutting board and let rest. Remove potatoes from heat. Toast bread and top with peppers.

1. Seed and core peppers, then cut into 1½-in.-wide strips. Place in a large bowl and toss well with ⅓ cup olive oil, the salt, and pepper.

2. Heat a charcoal or gas grill, to medium (350° to 400°). Grill peppers (reserve oil in bowl) until blistered, slightly charred, and very soft, turning once or twice, 20 to 30 minutes. Return to bowl, toss in oil, and cover with foil until ready to serve.

3. Brush bread on both sides with olive oil and grill until lightly toasted, 1 to 2 minutes per side. Set toasts on a board and top with peppers. Cut into 3-in. pieces, drizzle with olive oil from bowl if you like, and serve.

PER SERVING 403 CAL., 77% (306 CAL.) FROM FAT; 7.6 G PROTEIN; 23 G FAT (3.4 G SAT.); 42 G CARBO (2.8 G FIBER); 660 MG SODIUM; 0 MG CHOL. VG

SPATCHCOCKED CHICKEN WITH GRILLED LEMONS AND FIRE-ROASTED POTATOES

SERVES 4 TO 6 ★ ABOUT 2½ HOURS, PLUS AT LEAST 4 HOURS TO SALT

"Spatchcocking" a chicken means splitting the bird down the back and flattening it out so it cooks more evenly and quickly. Small whole chickens are especially delicious grilled (they tend to be juicier) and also fit nicely on a standard charcoal grill, but you can use pieces of larger chickens too. These instructions are for charcoal and gas; if you are using wood, follow the instructions for charcoal, except light the fire 1½ to 2 hours before cooking.

4 tbsp. butter, softened
2 garlic cloves, minced
2 chickens, preferably pasture-raised (each about 3 lbs.), or 5 to 6 lbs. chicken pieces
About 2 tbsp. kosher salt, divided
About ⅓ cup olive oil, divided
About 2½ tsp. pepper, divided
3 lemons
2 lbs. fingerling potatoes, scrubbed
2 tbsp. chopped fresh rosemary

1. Prepare chickens: Mix butter and garlic in a small bowl. Rinse chickens and pat dry. Place each chicken, breast side down, on a cutting board. Using poultry shears, cut along both sides of backbone and open chicken

ROASTED-PEPPER CROSTINI

SERVES 4 TO 6 ★ ABOUT 45 MINUTES

At Belcampo Farms, the cooking grate is so big that the peppers can be grilled alongside the chicken (they throw in a few small eggplants too). Unless you have a very large grill, it works best to cook the peppers first, then cover and let them sit (and get even softer and silkier) as you grill the chickens, lemons, and potatoes. These instructions are for charcoal and gas only, since that's what most of us have at home; if you're using wood, follow the instructions for charcoal, except light the fire 1½ to 2 hours before cooking.

6 large or 8 medium peppers, preferably a mix of colors and sweet to slightly spicy varieties
⅓ cup olive oil, plus more for brushing bread
1 tsp. sea salt
½ tsp. pepper
10 to 12 slices (½-in.-thick) rustic country-style bread

like a book. Reserve backbone for stock or discard. Turn chicken breast side up and, using the heel of your hand, press firmly against breastbone until it cracks. Tuck wing tips under so they don't burn on the grill.

2. Starting at the breast end of each chicken, loosen the skin by sliding your hand carefully between skin and meat and all the way down the legs if you can. With paper towels, pat off as much moisture as you can, then spread butter under skin, starting with legs, then thighs and, last, breast. Pat bird to even out lumps and evenly distribute butter.

3. Place chickens on a large baking sheet, skin side up. Rub each chicken all over (inside and out) with 1½ tbsp. kosher salt. Cover tightly with plastic wrap and chill at least 4 hours and up to overnight.

4. Take chickens out of fridge 2½ hours before dinner. Rinse with cold running water, then dry with paper towels. Rub with 1 tbsp. olive oil and sprinkle lightly with salt and about 2 tsp. pepper. Slice lemons in half. Lightly oil cut sides and sprinkle with salt.

5. Prepare potatoes: Halve larger potatoes lengthwise; leave small ones whole. In a large bowl, toss well with ¼ cup olive oil, the rosemary, about 1½ tsp. salt, and ½ tsp. pepper.

6. Cook potatoes: *For charcoal*, pour potato mixture into a large cast-iron skillet (12 in. is ideal, but 10 in. will work too—the potatoes just may not get as crusty). Heat the grill to medium-high (about 400°). Push coals to sides of firegrate, clearing a circle, and set pan of potatoes there. Add 10 unlit briquets to lit ones, spacing evenly, and let ignite. Set cooking grate in place. *For gas*, heat grill to medium-high (400°) with a burner turned off to make an indirect heat area. Heat the cast-iron skillet over direct heat until very hot. Add potato mixture.

7. Cook chickens: Grill over direct heat, skin side down, covered, until browned and crisp, 10 to 15 minutes, rotating to brown evenly. Move chickens over potatoes (for charcoal) or over indirect heat (for gas) and cook 10 minutes more.

8. Arrange lemons cut side down over direct heat and grill until slightly charred, about 15 minutes. If the heat has dropped on charcoal grill, add 6 to 8 briquets to ring of coals. Check potatoes; they're done when fork-tender and browned, with some charred edges. If potatoes are done before chickens, wearing grilling mitts, lift cooking grate with chickens and lemons to a heatproof surface, remove potato skillet from coals, and set chickens and

SPATCHCOCKED CHICKEN with GRILLED LEMONS and FIRE-ROASTED POTATOES

lemons back over fire. On a gas grill, of course, just take the potatoes off the fire.

9. Turn chickens and grill, covered, over direct heat until undersides are browned. Then, *for charcoal*, move over potatoes. Grill until well browned and leg is very loose at the joint when wiggled (or registers 160° at thickest part), about 20 minutes total. *For gas*, move over indirect heat to reach that point.

10. Transfer chickens and lemons to a cutting board and let rest 5 to 10 minutes. Cut chickens into quarters and serve with lemons and potatoes.

PER SERVING 1,000 CAL., 64% (643 CAL.) FROM FAT; 60 G PROTEIN; 72 G FAT (21 G SAT.); 31 G CARBO (5.5 G FIBER); 1,808 MG SODIUM; 259 MG CHOL. GF

With this versatile tool, L.A. chef Ben Ford sears and roasts meat and vegetables and even toasts marshmallows.

THE FIRST TIME BEN FORD saw the massive pressed-steel basin and solid, oversize cooking grate of the Cowboy Cauldron, at a chefs' competition, he was smitten. "I wanted one really badly. I came from a craftsman family—we believed in things that are built with integrity," says Ford. (Though his dad, actor Harrison, may forever be known as Han Solo, he's also a hobby carpenter.)

Ford—owner of Ford's Filling Station restaurant in Culver City, California—snapped up two of the cauldrons, in fact. At catering events, he was soon sizzling whole fish and even a whole lamb on the mega-size version. But it was his wife, Emily, and two sons who opened his eyes to its versatility, as they roasted marshmallows over the radiant heat left after cooking dinner. "Watching them, I had this epiphany," says Ford. Today, he puts the cauldron to use in many ways beyond basic grilling (see opposite)—including as a cozy, handsome focal point for a cooking party with friends on a cool L.A. evening. That said, you can easily make his recipes (see page 210) on a regular gas or charcoal grill.

Ben Ford (in apron), wife Emily (beside him), and friends hang out as the lamb (page 210) and vegetables (page 213) grill over direct heat.

6 WAYS TO COOK IN A COWBOY CAULDRON

The Utah-made Cowboy Cauldron comes in four sizes, from the 24-in. The Dude, to the 41-in. Ranch Boss (the 30-in. Urban Cowboy is shown here; see Resource Guide, page 244). All four are portable and take just a few minutes to set up (though the largest size requires several strong people to lift it). Here are some of the ways you can cook.

1 DIRECT HEAT GRILLING. Brown and cook meat, fish, and vegetables on the cooking grate over the fire. There's plenty of room for a big paella pan or griddle too.

2. INDIRECT HEAT ROASTING. Scooch the fire onto half the firegrate and set foods you want to cook more slowly in a pan next to the fire. Replace cooking grate.

3. EMBER ROASTING. Simmer pots or cook foil packets of vegetables right in the glowing embers, once the fire has cooled a bit.

4. ROTISSERIE. With a special rotisserie accessory, you can roast a ham or other brawny pieces of meat.

5. PILGRIM-STYLE POT. Using the S-hook and forged chain accessories, hang a dutch oven full of stew over the fire.

6. MEGA-CAULDRON. Build a fire underneath the cauldron, containing it in the fire ring accessory if you don't have a firepit, then use the cauldron for a really big batch of chili or a fish fry, say.

MENU

ANDALUCIAN FRIED CHICKPEAS and SPINACH
(page 213)

ROSEMARY GRILLED LEG of LAMB
(right)

GRILLED VEGETABLE SALAD
(page 213)

S'MORE S'MORES
(page 81)

WINE: A Pinot Noir full of warm spices and pine-forest notes

ROSEMARY GRILLED
LEG of LAMB

GRILLED
VEGETABLE
SALAD
(page 213)

ROSEMARY GRILLED LEG OF LAMB

SERVES 8 TO 10 ★ 2¾ HOURS, PLUS 24 HOURS TO MARINATE AND 1¼ HOURS FOR THE FIRE

Ford's recipe is adapted from *Taming the Feast: Ben Ford's Field Manual to Adventurous Cooking* (Simon & Schuster, 2014).

1 cup olive oil
Zest of 2 lemons
½ cup lemon juice
8 large garlic cloves, sliced
4 tsp. kosher salt
1 tbsp. *each* sweet smoked Spanish paprika *(pimentón dulce)**, ground coriander, and ground cumin
1 tsp. cayenne
1 cup chopped onion
1 cup whole rosemary leaves, plus 12 (9-in.) sprigs
1 bone-in leg of lamb (about 6½ lbs.), with hip bone and upper leg bone (but not shank bone) removed*, or a 4½-lb. fully boned leg of lamb

1. Combine oil and all seasonings except for rosemary sprigs in a shallow pan. Add lamb; turn to coat inside and out. Cover; chill 24 hours, turning occasionally. Let sit at room temperature 1 hour before grilling. Brush off marinade. Tie with kitchen twine to make a compact roast.

2. Meanwhile, light a charcoal and wood fire in a Cowboy Cauldron (see "Light Your Fire" on page 213). Or heat a regular charcoal or gas grill to medium (350° to 400°) with a space left clear or a gas burner turned off for indirect heat (*for charcoal,* push coals to half of firegrate).

3. Grill lamb over direct heat, turning as needed, until browned, 10 minutes. Set lamb on a V-shaped rack in a roasting pan. Top meat with rosemary sprigs. Wearing grilling mitts, put pan in indirect heat area (for Cauldron, see page 209). Stoke a wood fire now; for charcoal, as you cook, add 6 to 8 briquets every 30 minutes. Cover charcoal or gas grill.

4. Roast lamb, rotating meat in pan every 20 to 30 minutes so each part is exposed to heat, until lamb reaches 140° in thickest part, 1½ to 2½ hours. Let lamb rest on a cutting board 15 minutes. Remove twine and carve.

*Find the paprika at well-stocked grocery stores, or see Resource Guide, page 244. Order lamb from a butcher.

PER SERVING 349 CAL., 45% (157 CAL.) FROM FAT; 44 G PROTEIN; 18 G FAT (5.1 G SAT.); 1.8 G CARBO (0.8 G FIBER); 258 MG SODIUM; 136 MG CHOL. GF/LC/LS

ROSEMARY GRILLED
LEG of LAMB

ANDALUCIAN FRIED
CHICKPEAS and SPINACH

GRILLED VEGETABLE SALAD

For an easy, crowd-pleasing accompaniment for the lamb, Ford seasons mixed **summer squashes** and **peppers** (bell peppers, mild chile peppers, and Padróns) with a little **olive oil**, **salt**, and **pepper**, then grills them until softened and streaked with grill marks. He cuts them into chunks and tosses them with **lettuces**, a little **goat cheese**, and a **white balsamic** and **olive oil** vinaigrette seasoned with **fresh basil** and **oregano**.

ANDALUCIAN FRIED CHICKPEAS AND SPINACH

SERVES 8 ★ 1 HOUR, PLUS 1¼ HOURS FOR THE FIRE

The Fords first discovered this dish in Seville on their honeymoon. "I am not saying this stuff is magic—maybe it was the flamenco music—but we did conceive a perfect little boy that evening," Ben notes. At home, he starts the dish once the lamb is roasting and serves it as an appetizer from the grill, with toasts. It's also great alongside the lamb.

½ cup olive oil, divided
2 large garlic cloves, smashed and peeled
2 cans (each 15 oz.) chickpeas (garbanzos), rinsed
    and drained
4 oz. Spanish chorizo, casing removed, diced
1 large onion, chopped
1½ cups reduced-sodium chicken broth, divided
1 lb. baby spinach
3 medium tomatoes, seeded and chopped
1½ tsp. sweet smoked Spanish paprika (*pimentón dulce*)*
1 tsp. ground cumin
About ½ tsp. *each* kosher salt and pepper
1 loaf crusty bread, sliced and toasted on the grill

1. Light a charcoal and wood fire in a Cowboy Cauldron (see "Light Your Fire" at right). Or heat a regular charcoal or gas grill to medium (350° to 450°) with a space left clear or a gas burner turned off for indirect heat. Heat ¼ cup oil in a dutch oven over direct heat. Sauté garlic in the pot until golden, 4 to 5 minutes. With a slotted spoon, transfer garlic to a small bowl.

2. Add chickpeas to pot and cook, stirring occasionally, until they begin to brown, about 8 minutes. Add chorizo and cook until lightly browned, 5 to 10 minutes more.

LIGHT YOUR FIRE

Learning to cook in a Cowboy Cauldron takes a few times, then feels intuitive. If it tips when you're moving food or fire around, set a couple of bricks inside for leveling. And you'll want to get the hang of the multi-hinged cooking grate before you fire up.

IGNITE a full charcoal chimney on firegrate, then dump out coals. Crisscross 4 split oak or fruit wood logs on top, leaving space for air.

BURN DOWN logs until they're lightly covered with ash, 40 minutes, then spread out in a single layer over half of firegrate, leaving space for air, to create direct and indirect heat cooking areas. Let burn until large flames die down, 10 minutes more. Replace cooking grate (it helps retain heat), then cook food.

STOKE THE FIRE every hour or so as you cook, adding 1 or 2 more logs to the part that's farthest from food (too close and food may scorch).

Transfer chickpeas and chorizo to a medium bowl and set aside.

3. Add 2 more tbsp. oil and the onion to pot and cook onion until translucent, 5 or 6 minutes. Stir in ½ cup broth. Add spinach, half at a time, cooking until wilted. Stir in reserved garlic, tomatoes, paprika, cumin, and ½ tsp. *each* salt and pepper. Cook uncovered, stirring often, until tomatoes soften completely, 5 to 7 minutes.

4. Stir in chickpeas and chorizo and remaining 1 cup broth. Bring to a gentle simmer. Drizzle remaining 2 tbsp. oil on top and cover pot. Lift cooking grate of Cowboy Cauldron and set pot on embers, if they're low-glowing, or next to fire, if it's hotter; or set pot over indirect heat on a regular grill. (If you're cooking this on a charcoal grill along with the Rosemary Grilled Leg of Lamb on page 210, chickpea mixture will have to go over direct heat, because the lamb will occupy indirect heat area; stir chickpeas often.) Cook until mixture thickens, 10 to 20 minutes.

5. To serve, spoon chickpea mixture onto bread.

*Find at well-stocked grocery stores, or see Resource Guide, page 244.

PER SERVING 415 CAL., 44% (184 CAL.) FROM FAT; 14 G PROTEIN; 21 G FAT (4.2 G SAT.); 45 G CARBO (4.7 G FIBER); 775 MG SODIUM; 17 MG CHOL.

BARBECUE
SANTA MARIA–STYLE

In and around Santa Maria, in central California, succulent oak-grilled meat is a way of life.

NO ONE MAKES BETTER Santa Maria barbecue than Ike Simas at the Santa Maria Elks Lodge. He and his pit crew, all in their 70s and 80s, are the keepers of the flame for this straightforward style—hugely popular in restaurants, catering halls, and home backyards all along California's Central Coast.

Meat (usually beef) is seasoned very simply and cooked over aromatic local red oak logs, on a grate that lifts and lowers. No sauce. Locals say it dates back to when California was still Mexico, and the owners of huge cattle ranches, or *ranchos,* would put on gigantic beef barbecues after the spring roundups. One approach was to skewer the meat on long poles cut from green willow and roast it over pits dug in the ground, filled with red oak coals. Tortillas, beans, and salsa were served on the side.

That's pretty much how the Elks have done it for decades—except they use 6-foot metal rods and an elevated pit, and as a starch, they serve garlic bread and macaroni. The menu stirs such pride in these parts that the Santa Maria Chamber of Commerce copyrighted it in 1978. "It's the true Santa Maria–style barbecue," says Simas. Although he says you could use a rod at home, he suggests a cooking grate—that's what most Santa Marians do, himself included.

Ike Simas, master barbecuer, with grilled top block in the barbecue room of the Santa Maria Elks Lodge.

HOW THE ELKS BBQ

1. THE WOOD. Only local red oak, also called coast live oak (*Quercus agrifolia*), is used. It's slow-burning and imparts a slightly nutty, deeply savory flavor to whatever cooks over it. The Elks keep the wood stacked to the rafters in a huge, barnlike room at the lodge.

2. THE MEAT. Tri-tip, now synonymous with Santa Maria barbecue, is a relative newcomer, first marketed by a local butcher in the late 1950s (before that, tri-tip was cut up for stews or hamburger). Back in the '30s, the barbecue cut of choice was bone-in prime rib steak. When that got too expensive, top sirloin (shown; also known as top block) took its place. The Elks still grill top block, preferring it for its rich flavor, tenderness, and juiciness. About an hour before cooking, as the logs burn down to ashy chunks, they cut the whole sirloins in half and dredge them in a mix of salt, pepper, and garlic salt.

3. THE RODS. Each hunk of top block is forced onto a 6-foot metal skewer in a tight C shape, with the fat on the outside. More pieces go on the same way, with the fat in alternating directions so it will melt evenly over the meat as it's turned, basting it.

4. THE GRILL. The skewers, or rods, are heaved onto frames that lift and lower above the burning pit. The Elks like to start out high, to avoid getting too dark a sear on the meat. They lower gradually, chasing the heat of the fire, and turn whenever the juices start to bubble to the surface. After about an hour and a half, the meat is lightly crusty—not burned—and ready to pull off and slice.

SANTA MARIA–STYLE BARBECUE AT HOME

For the backyard, home cooks use smaller grills with cooking grates that lift and lower, instead of a built-in pit with a frame for rods. In Santa Maria, they fire them up on weekends and for just about any celebration, from weddings to church socials to birthdays, all year round. (For more on the grills, see "Building Blocks of BBQ," opposite page; you can also use a gas or charcoal grill.)

ABOVE LEFT: Santa Maria resident Stephanie Correa grills flap steak, green onions, and tortillas over red oak.
ABOVE RIGHT: Top block being sliced at the Elks Lodge

SANTA MARIA–STYLE TOP BLOCK

SERVES 10 TO 12 GENEROUSLY ★ ABOUT 45 MINUTES, PLUS
1 HOUR TO SIT AND ABOUT 1½ HOURS FOR A WOOD FIRE

Top block (aka top sirloin) usually comes whole, in a Cryovac package, and weighs between 10 and 15 pounds. The Elks like to age the meat in the package for 20 to 25 days, turning it every few days, "until it's tender as can be," says Ike Simas. We found that it's great unaged too. You can try grilling the meat Elks-style on a skewer large enough to lay across your grill (see the Resource Guide, page 244), but at home, most Santa Marians cook their top block sliced thick and laid on the cooking grate.

1 top sirloin (10 to 15 lbs.)*, halved lengthwise down
   through the top (freeze half for later); or 2 tri-tips
   (5 to 6 lbs. total)
2 tbsp. *each* table salt, pepper, and garlic salt
5 to 6 logs red oak*; or, if cooking over another type of
   wood, or charcoal or gas, add 2 cups red oak chips*,
   soaked in water at least 20 minutes

1. Slice the 5- to 7-lb. piece of top sirloin lengthwise,
down through the top of the meat, into 2 or 3 pieces each
about 2 in. wide. If using tri-tips, leave whole. Trim all
but ¼ in. of fat from meat (reserve trimmings). Mix table
salt, pepper, and garlic salt together, then sprinkle pieces
generously with the mix. Let meat sit about 1 hour at
room temperature.

2. Meanwhile, *if cooking over wood*, build a tipi-style fire
(see page 177) and let burn to ashy chunks and low
flames, at least 1 hour. Spread chunks into a thick, even
bed. If you're not using red oak wood, sprinkle drained
red oak chips onto logs. *For charcoal*, heat grill to
medium-high (about 400°), with an area left clear for
indirect heat; sprinkle coals with drained chips. *For gas*,
heat a grill to medium-high (about 400°) with a burner
turned off, and put drained chips in the grill's metal
smoking box or in a small metal pan directly on a lit
burner. (See "Indirect Heat Grilling," page 88.)

3. Using tongs, oil cooking grate with a wad of oiled
paper towels and, *if using a Santa Maria grill*, crank
to about 5 in. above flames. Lay meat on grill along
with a few pieces of trimmed fat. Grill meat, turning
every 15 minutes or so and lowering screen as fire
declines, until it's a rich medium brown all over and an
instant-read thermometer registers 125° to 130° for rare,
35 minutes to 1 hour. When turning meat the first time,
top with a few pieces of now-melting fat to baste meat
as it cooks, and replace them every time meat is turned.
For charcoal or gas, cook meat with fat over indirect
heat, covered, basting with fat the same way. During last
5 minutes, move over direct heat and brown on both
sides. Transfer to a cutting board and let rest 10 minutes,
covered with foil.

4. Slice meat ½ in. thick across the grain and serve hot.

*Order top sirloin ahead of time from your butcher,
unless you live along California's Central Coast, where
it's usually in stock. For sources for top sirloin, logs, and
wood chips, see Resource Guide, page 244.

PER SERVING 255 CAL., 29% (73 CAL.) FROM FAT; 41 G PROTEIN; 8.1 G FAT
(3.1 G SAT.); 1.8 G CARBO (0.4 G FIBER); 1,248 MG SODIUM; 76 MG CHOL. GF/LC

BUILDING BLOCKS OF BBQ

All you need for good Santa Maria barbecue at
home is red oak and the right technique. For
sources, see Resource Guide, page 244.

THE GRILL Purists love
using a Santa Maria–
style backyard barbe-
cue, because it has a
sturdy bed for support-
ing a log fire and a
thick mesh cooking
grate that raises and
lowers above the heat.
This way, it's easy to
avoid burning the
meal—just lift it higher
above the flames. (See
Resource Guide for
where to order the
grills, in various sizes.)
That said, a gas or
charcoal grill will work
just fine; follow the
instructions in our
recipe for cooking over
indirect heat.

THE WOOD Red oak is
considered a seasoning
in Santa Maria barbe-
cue country, and noth-
ing else can replace its
flavor. The wood is hard
to find outside the
Central Coast, but you
can order it, depending
on how much you're
willing to pay for ship-
ping. An alternative is
to order red oak chips,
since they're lighter,
and add them to
another type of wood
fire—or to your gas or
charcoal grill—for a
comparable mellow,
oaky flavor.

IRENE'S SALSA

SERVES 10 TO 12 ★ 20 MINUTES, PLUS 1 HOUR TO CHILL

Ike Simas's late wife, Irene, made this salsa for
decades at Elks barbecues, and her recipe is still
used today.

4 cups chopped peeled ripe red tomatoes with juice
   (fresh or canned)
½ cup finely chopped canned mild green chiles
1 large white onion, finely chopped
3 tbsp. *each* apple cider vinegar and vegetable oil
1 tbsp. minced or crushed garlic
½ tsp. *each* table salt, pepper, and granulated garlic

Mix all ingredients in a large bowl. Chill at least 1 hour
to let flavors develop, and up to 2 days. Taste and adjust
seasoning.

PER TBSP. 11 CAL., 46% (4.8 CAL.) FROM FAT; 0.3 G PROTEIN; 0.5 G FAT (0 G SAT.);
1.2 G CARBO (0.2 G FIBER); 48 MG SODIUM; 0 MG CHOL. GF/LC/LS/VG

SANTA MARIA–STYLE TOP
BLOCK with CLASSIC SIDES

GARLIC BREAD

MAKES 24 TO 28 SLICES ★ 10 MINUTES

You want a squishy-soft loaf for this bread—it crisps up well on the grill and stays tender and fluffy inside. Grill it while the meat is resting.

½ cup butter
2 tsp. granulated garlic or 1 tbsp. minced garlic
1 loaf soft French bread (about 15 in. long)

1. Melt butter with garlic over low heat. Set aside until ready to toast bread.

2. Slice loaf in half lengthwise and toast, crust side down, over medium heat on a wood, charcoal, or gas grill, until crunchy, about 3 minutes. Turn and toast cut side, about 3 minutes more.

3. Brush garlic butter onto bread. Put halves together and cut into 1-in. slices. Serve immediately.

PER 2-SLICE SERVING 125 CAL., 52% (65 CAL.) FROM FAT; 2.0 G PROTEIN; 7.3 G FAT (4.2 G SAT.); 12 G CARBO (0.6 G FIBER); 200 MG SODIUM; 18 MG CHOL. LS/V

PINQUITO BEANS

7 CUPS; SERVES 10 ★ 2¼ TO 3 HOURS

Tiny, plump, light red pinquitos are grown only in the Santa Maria Valley, as far as anyone knows. They may have arrived with Mexican citrus workers in the '50s, or with the Swiss-Italians in the 1920s, or maybe with Spanish missionaries. Regardless, they're deliciously creamy beans that create their own rich sauce when cooked long and slow.

1 lb. pinquito beans* or pinto beans, sorted for debris
    and rinsed
4 strips thick-cut bacon, chopped
1 medium white onion, chopped
1 to 2 tbsp. chili powder
1 can (4 oz.) mild green chiles, such as Ortega
1 small garlic clove, minced or crushed
½ tsp. *each* table salt, pepper, and garlic salt

1. Put beans in a large pot. Add water until its level is twice as high as the beans. Bring to a boil, then cook over low heat, covered, until tender, stirring occasionally, 2 to 3 hours. Add enough hot water while cooking to keep beans covered by about ½ in. liquid (they should be a little soupy).

2. While beans are simmering, cook bacon in a medium frying pan over medium-low heat until crisp, 10 to 15 minutes. Add onion and chili powder and cook another 10 minutes. Stir in green chiles and garlic, and cook until flavors have mingled, 5 minutes more.

3. When beans are tender, gently stir in onion mixture, table salt, pepper, and garlic salt. Simmer, stirring occasionally, until liquid has thickened slightly but beans are still quite soupy, 10 to 15 minutes.

*See Resource Guide, page 244, to order pinquito beans online.

PER SERVING 277 CAL., 34% (95 CAL.) FROM FAT; 14 G PROTEIN; 11 G FAT (3.6 G SAT.); 31 G CARBO (7.7 G FIBER); 344 MG SODIUM; 21 MG CHOL. GF/LS

MACARONI SALAD

SERVES 10 TO 12 ★ 30 MINUTES, PLUS 1 HOUR TO CHILL

Bill Wilson, kitchen manager at the Santa Maria Elks Lodge, says this is a "go by your own taste" recipe, so all the amounts here are flexible. We really like it with ditalini pasta—somehow the tiny tubes trap just the right amount of dressing— but if elbow is what you have in the house, by all means use it.

Olive oil or vegetable oil
1 lb. ditalini pasta or small elbow macaroni
1 tsp. *each* salt and pepper
¾ cup mayonnaise
2 tbsp. prepared mustard, such as French's
¾ cup sweet pickle relish with juice
⅔ cup finely chopped jarred unroasted or roasted
    red peppers
⅔ cup thinly sliced canned black olives

1. Bring a large pot of salted water to a boil and add a dash of oil. Add pasta and boil until very tender, 12 to 15 minutes. Drain in a strainer and rinse with cold water until cool.

2. Mix remaining ingredients in a large bowl. Stir in cooled pasta. Taste and add more of any of the seasonings if you like. Chill until very cold, at least 1 hour.

Make ahead: Up to 2 days, covered and chilled.

PER SERVING 228 CAL., 26% (59 CAL.) FROM FAT; 5.6 G PROTEIN; 6.6 G FAT (1 G SAT.); 38 G CARBO (1.8 G FIBER); 605 MG SODIUM; 3.8 MG CHOL. LC/V

GARY'S GREEN SALAD

SERVES 10 TO 12 ★ ABOUT 15 MINUTES

Ike Simas's son, Gary Simas, is a caterer in Santa Maria. This is his go-to salad for serving a big crowd. He keeps all the vegetables prepped and in separate containers, and then tosses them with dressing right before serving.

1 medium head romaine lettuce, coarsely chopped
3 medium carrots, cut into matchsticks
⅛ red onion, thinly sliced
5-in. length of English cucumber, halved lengthwise and thinly sliced
4 Roma tomatoes, thinly sliced
Your favorite ranch dressing (see below for a recipe)
Plain or herbed croutons

Toss lettuce and vegetables with dressing. Serve topped with croutons.

PER SERVING WITH DRESSING 58 CAL., 55% (32 CAL.) FROM FAT; 0.9 G PROTEIN; 32 G FAT (5.6 G SAT.); 6.1 G CARBO (1 G FIBER); 217 MG SODIUM; 3.4 MG CHOL. LC/LS/V

BUTTERMILK HERB RANCH DRESSING

MAKES 1 CUP ★ 5 MINUTES, PLUS 1 HOUR TO CHILL

Quick and simple, this creamy, tangy dressing—a favorite from the *Sunset* archives—tastes fresher and brighter than store-bought.

½ cup *each* mayonnaise and buttermilk
1 tbsp. *each* chopped fresh chives, dill, and oregano
1 tsp. kosher salt
¼ tsp. garlic powder

Whisk all ingredients together in a medium bowl. Chill at least 1 hour to allow flavors to develop. Stir dressing well before serving.

Make ahead: Up to 1 week, covered and chilled.

PER TBSP. 53 CAL., 94% (50 CAL.) FROM FAT; 0.3 G PROTEIN; 5.5 G FAT (0.9 G SAT.); 0.6 G CARBO (0 G FIBER); 169 MG SODIUM; 4.4 MG CHOL. LS/V

ICE CREAM CUPS

MAKES 12 ★ 20 MINUTES, PLUS 1 HOUR TO CHILL

At an Elks' club buffet, dessert is often a store-bought ice cream cup; here's a quick homemade version, handy for group barbecues because it cuts down on the sticky drips that come with a sundae bar. Flavor the ice cream any way you like—by swirling in your favorite preserves, broken-up cookies or brownies, or layering it with sorbet. You'll need twelve 6-oz. small paper ice cream cups for this recipe. Ceramic ramekins will work too, but the beauty of paper is that it's safe for little children.

3 qts. vanilla ice cream, homemade or store-bought*
3 oz. dark or milk chocolate, shaved with a sharp knife
½ cup plus 2 tbsp. chopped toasted pecans or walnuts, divided
2 tbsp. good-quality store-bought chocolate sauce

1. Take ice cream out of freezer and let soften until easy to spoon, about 15 minutes.

2. Put ice cream in bowl of a stand mixer. On low speed, mix with paddle attachment until smooth (or stir in a bowl with a wooden spoon). Mix in shaved chocolate and all but about 4 tsp. chopped nuts.

3. Divide ice cream among 12 (6-oz.) paper ice cream cups, filling to the rim, and level them flush with a knife. Set cups on a rimmed baking pan and freeze for about 10 minutes to firm up ice cream. Then spoon about ½ tsp. chocolate sauce onto each cup in a cross formation and use a skewer to swirl chocolate into ice cream. Sprinkle with remaining nuts and freeze until firm, at least 1 hour.

*Some store-bought ice creams have a lot more air than others. If yours is airy, add another cup or so before mixing in the chocolate and nuts.

Make ahead: Up to 2 weeks, covered.

PER ICE CREAM CUP 623 CAL., 69% (329 CAL.) FROM FAT; 11 G PROTEIN; 42 G FAT (24 G SAT.); 50 G CARBO (0.5 G FIBER); 145 MG SODIUM; 240 MG CHOL. V

ICE
CREAM
CUPS

TWO PIZZA OVENS: READY-MADE AND DIY

Whether you buy an oven or build it yourself, you can count on it for relaxed dinners outside that your family and friends will never forget.

ROASTING FOOD IN AN OUTDOOR OVEN is one of humanity's oldest forms of cooking. Maybe that's why using a pizza oven feels so natural. It takes only a couple of tries to get the hang of how it works, and you'll quickly see how forgiving it is. Temperatures can fluctuate by 100° or more and your food will still turn out fine; the high temperatures and radiant heat from the dome and the floor seem to extract maximum flavor from anything you cook.

You can certainly use a pizza oven for pizzas only, but its full value lies in its ability to retain heat for many hours, long after the fire has crumbled into ash. That makes it possible to cook a whole series of foods from a single oven-firing (see page 224).

Apart from the fun of the cooking, a pizza oven has an almost gravitational appeal at parties. It's an object of fascination even for non-cooks—a ready-made icebreaker. Install one and start using it, and your social life is bound to buzz.

We cooked a three-course menu from this ready-made Forno Bravo Primavera60 pizza oven—and also from an oven we built ourselves (see page 232). Recipes begin on page 226.

At *Sunset*, we have two entry-level pizza ovens: one ready-made and one we built ourselves (instructions are on page 232). We chose them based on affordability, ease of use, and size: Each is about 5 feet high and 3 to 4 feet wide, suitable for a small backyard.

Our ready-made Primavera60 oven, from Northern California–based Forno Bravo, is one of the company's best-selling models, and reasonably priced compared with other professionally built ovens (see Resource Guide, page 244, for more information). The dome and hearth are comprised of high-tech insulating and refractory materials—meaning they can retain and withstand high heat extremely well. The morning after a cooking session, the oven temperature is typically still around 200°. We also like the Primavera's jaunty pale yellow stucco dome and graceful iron stand, and have found it to be a beautiful, functional focal point in our garden. However, it's delivered in a crate in two pieces (the company does not install), and requires at least four very strong people to lift the 450-pound dome onto the stand. But once it's set up, you're good to go.

Our homemade adobe oven, which we built in a single day with the help of a half-dozen friends, was a pleasure from start to finish. Constructing an oven this way—from mud and sand, then firing it until it hardens like brick—is an ancient technique used around the world, including in the Southwest, by Native Americans. The process, although detailed, wasn't complicated, even for those of us who can barely tell a hammer from a crowbar. Working together made it seem more like play, and we were thrilled by the oven that emerged: a little rustic, being made mostly of soil dug a few feet away, yet extremely handsome. The basic model has an uninsulated dome, but is capable of cooking our menu on page 226—and much more. (You can add insulation to the dome if you like, so it retains heat longer.) And building it cost only a few hundred dollars—a fraction of the price of the ready-made oven.

Whichever oven you choose, if you're cooking several courses, give the menu a test run before inviting guests over so you can get a feeling for how to manage the fire and maintain the cooking temperatures. On the next pages, we outline the tools and techniques you'll need to know.

PIZZA OVEN ESSENTIALS

These guidelines apply to both the ready-made and DIY ovens. Before you can start cooking in either, you need to cure it—and have a few key tools ready.

FIRST, CURE THE OVEN

Your first step, after the oven has been freshly installed or built, is to "cure" it. This means gradually warming it to drive out excess moisture and reduce the risk of cracking. For the ready-made oven, this involves burning a fire for 6 hours a day for 5 days, each fire hotter than the last. For the DIY oven, 1 or 2 days should be enough—there should be no dark line around the base of the dome indicating moisture.

DAY ONE: Heat to 300°, measured on the far inside wall of the dome with an infrared thermometer (see "Tools," opposite). Arrange 3 sticks in a triangle, ends overlapping, over 2 paraffin fire-starter cubes; for the Forno Bravo oven, keep door partly closed to maintain heat, and add more kindling as necessary to maintain temperature.

DAY TWO: 350° (use 4 sticks kindling in a tic-tac-toe pattern).

DAY THREE: 400° (use 5 sticks).

DAY FOUR: 450° (use 6 sticks).

DAY FIVE: 500° (use 3 sticks kindling and one small log).

When the oven has been out of use for several months or when the weather has been rainy, it's a good idea to repeat the Day One drying before cooking.

NOW YOU'RE READY TO COOK

Unlike a regular oven, a pizza oven must be heated to its maximum at the start of cooking in order to radiate heat properly over the span of a cooking session. The initial white-hot heat is perfect for pizzas, which cook in 2 minutes or less.

Afterward, as the oven slowly cools, use the infrared thermometer (see "Tools," opposite) to measure the temperature on the oven floor; when you have the degrees you need for the next food, slide in your dish. It's that simple. If the temperature is falling too quickly, add a few pieces of kindling; if it's not dropping quickly enough, remove some of the coals.

Make sure your food is at room temperature before you put it in the oven; cold food will suck the heat out of the floor, especially in the adobe oven.

For some of our favorite books on cooking in a pizza oven, see Resource Guide, page 245.

FIRE IT UP

Kiko Denzer, Oregon-based author of *Build Your Own Earth Oven* (Hand Print Press, 2007), taught us to make a top-down cooking fire for a pizza oven. An open, airy construction and falling embers from an upper layer make for a clean, hot burn.

With the door off, set 2 or 3 small (wrist-thick) logs in the center of the oven, parallel to each other and with their ends facing the opening. Arrange a layer of about 3 small logs on top of and perpendicular to the logs; then add a layer of kindling perpendicular to the layer below, so you have a kind of stacked tic-tac-toe; be sure to leave plenty of air space. Top with crumpled newspaper or small twigs. (Or slide a couple of paraffin fire-starter cubes in between the bottom logs.) Light the newspaper or paraffin. Once the fire is well lit, add 2 or 3 fresh wrist-thick or smaller logs (and more, if you need them), stacking them on top of the fire, again tic-tac-toe—style (use long tongs or a fireplace poker to help you arrange

LEVEL 1: PIZZA

LEVEL 2: ROASTING

LEVEL 3: BAKING

them). Make sure the fire is in the center of the oven, so it heats dome and floor evenly. And be sure the door is off whenever you have live coals or flame in the oven. Shutting it could cause a fireball when you open it again.

Heat Level 1: Pizza

Using a top-down fire, heat the oven until the entire dome turns from sooty black to white (anywhere from 700° to 800°; the main thing to watch for is the change in color, which means the oven has absorbed enough heat to carry you through cooking). This will take anywhere from 1 to 1½ hours. As soon as it's hot enough, push the fire to one side and sweep the cleared space free of coals with a metal brush (see "Tools," at right). Add a few pieces of kindling or a small log to the fire to get the flames curling across the ceiling into the middle of the dome. Bake your pizzas in the cleared space with the oven door open, adding more fuel every 20 minutes or so to keep the flames rolling.

Heat Level 2: Roasting

Let the flames die, leaving hot coals, and allow the oven temperature to drop until the floor is between 600° and 650°. With the door off, roast vegetables or meat, turning the pans every few minutes for even cooking.

Heat Level 3: Baking

Let the oven's floor temperature drop to what's called for in your recipe (generally 350° to 450°; meanwhile, if the oven has a wood door, soak it in a pan or tub of water 1 hour before using). Sweep out all the coals, set the food in the area where the temperature is right, and set the door in place (or slightly ajar if the oven is a bit hotter than you want). Check food every few minutes; if it's not cooking quickly enough or if the heat is dropping too fast, shut the door fully.

TOOLS

Measure your oven opening before buying any tools and cookware to make sure they'll fit. See Resource Guide, page 244, for sources.

★ Heatproof worktable

★ Long matches or butane fire lighter

★ Infrared thermometer for reading temperature of oven floor and dome (aim the laser at the dome's far walls or the floor—not flames or coals)

★ Grilling gloves

★ Long, sturdy grilling tongs

★ Small round metal peel for placing pizzas and turning them as they cook

★ Long-handled, large metal grilling spatula to help place and turn pizzas

★ Metal brush for sweeping ashes

★ Rag for wiping excess ash from peel

★ Lightweight metal ash shovel

★ Lidded metal can for hot coals and ashes

FIREWOOD

Every firing takes 15 to 20 pieces of kindling (each about 1 in. diameter) and up to 16 small or split hardwood logs (for a small oven, they should be no thicker than 2 inches, and no longer than about 1½ feet). For firewood types, see page 178. You'll also need newspaper and twigs, or paraffin fire-starter cubes.

COOKWARE

Any of these will work, as long as they fit in the oven: a cast-iron dutch oven or skillet, heavy stainless steel pans, heavy metal baking sheets, paella pan, and terra-cotta (clay) baking dishes. If clay dishes are unglazed, soak them before each use in room-temperature water for at least 3 hours, then let dry. When filled and ready to go in the oven, let them sit in the opening of the oven for several minutes to acclimate to the heat before sliding all the way in.

PIZZA PARTY TIMELINE

1 DAY TO 4 HOURS AHEAD	Make dough for pizza, rub for steaks, butter for corn, and topping for crisp.
3 HOURS AHEAD	Make pizza topping. Prep steak, green bean, and corn recipes. Prep rest of dessert.
1½ TO 2 HOURS AHEAD	Start fire in oven (see "Fire It Up," page 224).
1 HOUR AHEAD	If using DIY oven with wooden door, soak door: Submerge it in a large container of water, weighted with a brick. Rotate it if needed so the whole door gets soaked.
PARTY TIME	Form, top, and cook pizzas. The pizza is a cook-and-eat first course, best served right near the oven. Then, if using Forno Bravo oven, remove about half of coals to reduce oven temperature more quickly for roasting.
	Roast green beans (10 minutes), followed by steaks (15 minutes), followed by corn (10 minutes). Serve together as the main course.
	While everyone eats the main course, bake crisp (30 minutes). Let cool at least 10 minutes before serving.

POTATO, ROSEMARY, AND GOUDA PIZZAS

MAKES 5 OR 6 SMALL PIZZAS ★ 20 MINUTES TO PREP, PLUS TIME FOR DOUGH, IF MAKING; 20 MINUTES TO COOK

The combination of tender, wafer-thin potatoes and nutty melted gouda cheese is irresistible. It is helpful to use a hand-held slicer to thinly slice potatoes.

½ lb. medium Yukon Gold potatoes
¼ cup finely chopped white onion
About 2 tbsp. olive oil
Half-recipe Pizza Dough for the Grill, prepared through step 3 (page 109); half-recipe Michael Chiarello's Pizza Dough (page 180); or 1 lb. store-bought pizza dough
Flour
1½ cups coarsely shredded gouda cheese
1 tbsp. chopped fresh rosemary leaves
Sea salt (optional)

1. Peel potatoes and thinly slice. Boil potatoes in plenty of salted water, stirring to separate, until barely tender, 3 to 4 minutes. Drain, rinse with cold water, and drain again. Pat dry with paper towels and toss with onion and 2 tbsp. oil.

2. Heat pizza oven to Pizza temperature (see page 225).

3. Turn dough out onto a floured work surface and cut into 5 portions (each about 3 oz.; for pizzas that are thinner and crisper but a bit trickier to handle, cut dough into 6 portions). Using well-floured hands, form each portion into a tight ball by stretching and tucking ends under. Put on an oiled baking sheet and rub tops with oil.

4. Generously dust a small pizza peel with flour. On a floured work surface, roll, stretch, or pat a dough ball into a 6-in. round and place on peel. Arrange no more than a double layer of potato-onion mixture on top. Quickly sprinkle with cheese and rosemary. Slide pizza onto oven floor and cook, rotating with peel or long-handled spatula as needed for even cooking, until crust is well-browned and cheese is bubbling, 2 to 4 minutes total. Sprinkle with salt if you like. Make remaining pizzas the same way.

Make ahead: Through step 1, up to 3 hours, at room temperature. Dough balls, up to 1 day, chilled and covered with plastic wrap (remove from refrigerator 45 minutes before using).

PER ½-PIZZA SERVING 179 CAL., 63% (65 CAL.) FROM FAT; 6.9 G PROTEIN; 7.3 G FAT (3.1 G SAT.); 22 G CARBO (0.9 G FIBER); 391 MG SODIUM; 16 MG CHOL. V

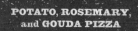
POTATO, ROSEMARY, and GOUDA PIZZA

ROASTED GREEN BEANS with
SHALLOTS and TOMATOES

CHILE-RUBBED
HANGER STEAKS

CORN with CILANTRO
QUESO FRESCO BUTTER
(see page 230)

ROASTED GREEN BEANS WITH SHALLOTS AND TOMATOES

SERVES 4 TO 6 ★ 25 MINUTES TO PREP; 10 TO 15 MINUTES TO ROAST

Parboiling the beans allows them to brown in practically no time, and also keeps them tender. Mixing in fresh, ripe cherry tomatoes just before serving adds bright flavor and color.

1¼ lbs. green beans, stem ends trimmed
8 shallots, separated into cloves and larger cloves halved lengthwise
About 1½ tbsp. olive oil, divided
Several sprigs *each* thyme and oregano
Kosher salt and pepper
About 1 cup cherry tomatoes, cut in half

1. Blanch beans in boiling water until tender-crisp, 2 to 3 minutes. Drain and rinse with cold water. Transfer to a bowl.

2. Put shallots in a 10-in. cast-iron or heavy stainless steel skillet, drizzle with about 2 tsp. oil, and toss to coat.

3. When pizza oven floor's heat has fallen to Roasting temperature (see page 225; 600° to 650°), slide skillet into oven and roast, stirring often, until shallots start to brown, 2 to 4 minutes.

4. Slide pan from oven and add beans and herbs. Season with salt and pepper and drizzle in remaining oil. With tongs, toss to coat. Slide back into oven.

5. Roast beans, stirring once, until tender and starting to brown, about 7 minutes. Remove and stir in tomatoes. Transfer to serving platter and wipe out skillet to use for corn (page 230). Serve warm or at room temperature.

Make ahead: Through step 2, up to 3 hours, at room temperature.

PER SERVING 114 CAL., 29% (33 CAL.) FROM FAT; 5.3 G PROTEIN; 3.7 G FAT (0.6 G SAT.); 16 G CARBO (5.4 G FIBER); 3.8 MG SODIUM; 0 MG CHOL. GF/LC/LS/VG

CHILE-RUBBED HANGER STEAKS

SERVES 4 TO 6 ★ 15 MINUTES TO ROAST, PLUS AT LEAST 1 HOUR TO MARINATE

This is such a simple recipe, but the flavors are big and bold. Serve on a platter with the roasted green beans (at left) if you like.

2 hanger steaks (about 1½ lbs. total) or New York strip steaks
1½ tbsp. vegetable or olive oil
Cumin Chile Rub (page 112)

1. Coat steaks with oil, then season all over with rub (use all or most of the rub; steaks should be thickly coated). Let stand 1 hour at room temperature.

2. When pizza oven floor's heat has fallen to Roasting temperature (see page 225; 600° to 650°), set a 10-in. cast-iron or heavy stainless steel skillet in oven to heat a few minutes. Add steaks and roast, rotating pan and turning steaks once, until an instant-read thermometer registers 135° for medium-rare, 10 to 12 minutes. Let rest 10 minutes; then slice and serve.

Make ahead: Through step 1, 1 hour at room temperature (4 hours chilled; bring to room temperature before cooking).

PER SERVING 252 CAL., 44% (110 CAL.) FROM FAT, 33 G PROTEIN; 12 G FAT (3.7 G SAT.); 0.7 G CARBO (0.5 G FIBER); 267 MG SODIUM; 87 MG CHOL. GF/LC/LS

CORN WITH CILANTRO *QUESO FRESCO* BUTTER

SERVES 4 TO 6 ★ 10 MINUTES TO ROAST, PLUS 1 HOUR TO SOAK

Blended with soft, fresh Mexican cheese, the butter is wonderful melted onto smoky oven-roasted corn. The recipe for the butter comes from Mark Fischer of Town and other restaurants in and around Carbondale, Colorado. It's great on warm bread too. (See photo on page 228.)

3 ears corn on the cob, shucked and cut into thirds
¼ cup kosher salt
1 tbsp. olive oil
¼ cup *queso fresco* (Mexican-style fresh cheese)*
   or asiago cheese
2 tbsp. *each* softened butter and mayonnaise
½ tsp. lime zest
1 tsp. lime juice
⅓ cup coarsely chopped cilantro

1. Put corn in a large bowl with the salt and enough water to cover. Soak about 1 hour. Drain and put in a bowl. Drizzle with oil.

2. With pizza oven floor still at Roasting temperature (600° to 650°), toss 2 to 3 pieces kindling on fire (to create flame for browning corn) and slide in an empty 10-in. cast-iron or heavy stainless steel skillet (the same one used for beans). Heat 2 minutes, then add corn and return to oven. Roast until browned, turning once with tongs, 5 to 10 minutes.

3. Meanwhile, whirl queso fresco, butter, mayonnaise, zest, and juice in a food processor until fairly smooth. Add cilantro and pulse to blend. Place in a small bowl.

4. Remove corn from heat and spoon on half of butter mixture, letting it melt all over the kernels and onto the skillet. Serve with remaining butter in a bowl.

*Find queso fresco at well-stocked grocery stores and Latino markets.

Make ahead: Through step 1, up to 3 hours at room temperature.

PER SERVING, USING HALF OF BUTTER MIXTURE 144 CAL., 48% (69 CAL.) FROM FAT; 4 G PROTEIN; 7.7 G FAT (3.5 G SAT.); 18 G CARBO (1.9 G FIBER); 459 MG SODIUM; 15 MG CHOL. GF/LC/V

RASPBERRY RHUBARB CRISP

SERVES 6 TO 8 ★ 15 MINUTES TO PREP; 25 MINUTES TO BAKE

Carolyn Beth Weil, author of Williams-Sonoma *Pie & Tart* (Simon & Schuster, 2003), created this recipe for *Sunset* years ago. You can also bake the crisp ahead of time, in a regular oven at 350°, for about 45 minutes. If you're baking in the DIY oven, using a soaked wooden door, drain the door just before baking.

1 cup regular rolled oats
½ cup *each* flour, finely chopped walnuts, and packed light
   brown sugar
½ tsp. *each* cinnamon and ground ginger
⅛ tsp. salt
½ cup cold butter, cut into chunks
1 cup granulated sugar
2 tbsp. cornstarch
1 qt. raspberries (18 oz.)
3 cups sliced rhubarb (cut ½ in. thick; about 12 oz.)
Vanilla ice cream

1. Combine oats, flour, walnuts, brown sugar, cinnamon, ginger, and salt in a large bowl. With your fingers, rub butter into oat mixture until blended and coarse lumps form. Chill until used.

2. Combine granulated sugar and cornstarch in another large bowl. Put raspberries and rhubarb in a third bowl.

3. When pizza oven floor has fallen to high Baking temperature (about 450°), use metal brush to sweep out all coals into a metal can. Quickly combine raspberries and rhubarb with cornstarch mixture. Pour into a shallow 2- to 3-qt. terra-cotta or cast-iron baking dish and sprinkle evenly with topping.

4. Bake crisp with oven door barely ajar (if it's at 450°), or fully closed, if temperature dips below that. Rotate dish 180° a few times, and bake until topping is golden brown and fruit is bubbling, about 25 minutes (check frequently, and tent with foil if the top is getting too dark). Serve warm or at room temperature, with ice cream.

Make ahead: For topping, up to 1 day, chilled airtight. Mixed fruit, up to 4 hours at room temperature (and make sure it is at room temperature before baking). Cornstarch mix, up to 4 hours at room temperature.

PER SERVING 417 CAL., 37% (155 CAL.) FROM FAT; 5.2 G PROTEIN; 17 G FAT (7.7 G SAT.); 64 G CARBO (6.7 G FIBER); 127 MG SODIUM; 31 MG CHOL. LS/V

RASPBERRY RHUBARB CRISP

A DIY PIZZA OVEN

While there are lots of good reasons to build your own adobe oven, or earth oven—the pleasure of pulling crackly crusted pizza from the wood-fired hearth, the fun of creating a party-perfect gathering place, the savings compared with buying a ready-made oven—there's one reason that Kiko Denzer, an earth-oven expert based in Oregon, hears the most: the satisfaction of creating something beautiful and useful. "When you make it with your own hands, from the dirt under your feet," Denzer says, "you can see and feel *everything* come together—food, fire, family, and all the gifts of life and nature."

With the popularity of *Sunset's* previous backyard-oven projects in mind, we asked Denzer, author of *Build Your Own Earth Oven*, to help us design an oven for the next generation. We were looking to strike a balance between local, natural materials and readily available ones from garden supply and home improvement stores. We wanted to save on the cost of a ready-made oven (about $400 for materials for this oven, versus $2,100 and up). And we wanted an oven that people with little experience but plenty of energy and willing friends could create.

Denzer's design is handsome and well-planned, yet it's a true beginner's oven that requires no special skills. With about six friends you can build the basic model, an uninsulated oven, in a day, once you've assembled the materials and tested your building mix (see "Start with a Muffin Oven," page 234). You can fire the oven, try it out, and leave it rustic, with no countertop or brick face (see photo, page 240).

If you decide to go further, the oven is easily upgradable. On page 241, we show you how to beautify it with a natural concrete stain, add a simple counter, and put a layer of insulation underneath so the oven requires less fuel and retains heat longer. (Adding the decorative brick face is part of putting in the insulation.) For maximum fuel efficiency, you can go on to insulate the oven dome as well, following the directions in Denzer's book (see Resource Guide, page 244; we highly recommend the book as background reading). You'll also need to protect the oven with a tarp or roof during rainy weather.

Before you begin, though, we can offer two pieces of advice, learned the hard way: Test your materials. Start small. By first testing your soil (see "Get Ready," on opposite page) and making a tiny "practice" oven just big enough for baking a muffin—projects that take half a day at most—you'll develop the skills, confidence, and enthusiasm for a full-scale oven.

GET READY

1 MONTH AHEAD

1 LEARN THE RULES. Check with your city's building department to see if you need a permit, and find out about any regulations concerning property-line setbacks. Some cities consider such ovens a type of barbecue and don't require a permit. Check with your fire department about its rules too, and find out whether your state or county has laws governing wood-burning fires.

2 FIND SOIL WITH A HIGH CLAY CONTENT. The ideal building soil may exist right in your yard. To test clay content, dig up a shovelful of subsoil from below grass and topsoil (subsoil is typically firmer and a shade lighter). Mix enough dirt and water in your hand to make a smooth, golf ball–size lump (it's important to work it until smooth). Roll it into a snake about ⅜ in. wide, then drape it over your palm with at least 2 in. dangling off (**A**). If the snake doesn't crack, your clay content is high enough.

You'll need about six sifted 5-gal. buckets of the soil. If you don't have the right soil, or don't have enough of it, try looking for free fill dirt online. Another option is to buy fireclay (also called mortar clay) from a home improvement store; it's pure clay, and you can add it to your own soil to increase its clay content, or use it straight. Repeat the snake test until you have what you need.

3 DIG AND SIFT YOUR SOIL. Break up clumps, then shake subsoil through a screen in a compost sifter over a wheelbarrow until you have enough (**B**). (Make your own sifter or buy one; see Resource Guide, page 244.) If soil is damp, spread it out on a tarp until dry before using.

4 PREPARE A LEVEL, FIREPROOF SPOT. The building site should be at least 6 ft. square and well away from overhanging trees or structures (check local fire regulations). We used decomposed granite packed hard with a tamper. A concrete or brick patio or hard, cleared dirt also works well. Check that the area is level using a large carpenter's level set on a long, straight board.

5 GATHER MATERIALS. Have all your ingredients ready before you start (see page 235).

6 LINE UP VOLUNTEERS. We found that 6 to 8 was ideal.

7 BUILD A MUFFIN OVEN. At least 1 to 2 weeks ahead of the build date for the full-size oven, build the muffin oven (see page 234) so you'll have time to assess how it turned out.

START WITH A MUFFIN OVEN

TIME: 1 HOUR, PLUS TIME FOR FIRING

Building this 10-in.-high oven takes little time but teaches you the skills for building the full-scale version. Most important, you'll determine the right proportions of soil, sand, and water to create a building mix for a strong and crack-resistant dome. Each soil is different, so you must test your mix to know when it's right. Note that we use a 5-gal. bucket as a measuring cup, so "2 buckets soil" means to fill the bucket twice.

1 CUT CEMENT BOARD (see materials opposite). Set it on a flat surface. Using a straightedge, score board with edge of a cold chisel at least 1/16 in. deep to make a 13-in. square. Snap board along lines. If you're doing the insulation upgrade on page 242, save the rest of the cement board.

2 MAKE BUILDING MIX. Lay a tarp on the ground. Make a pile of 2¼ buckets of sand. Onto that, pour ¾ bucket of soil (it's the "fat," like butter in pie dough). With your feet, mix the two together. Gradually and thoroughly work in just enough water until the mix feels like modeling clay, twisting and sliding it back and forth with your feet (**A**), and occasionally turning the mix over by lifting a corner of the tarp toward you while standing in the center. Keep it on the dry side so you can complete the mini oven in 1 day.

3 DO THE DROP TEST. To test your soil-sand building mix, shape some into a ball. Slap it back and forth in your hands 50 to 100 times until it's very smooth. Now drop it (on dirt, not concrete). If it holds together, flattens only slightly, and has just small cracks, the mix is good to go (**B**). Too much sand, and the ball will crumble. Too much clay, and it will flatten into a pancake with lots of cracks. If needed, blend in more sand or clay, then drop a ball again, until you have the right mix. If in doubt, add more clay. *Note your*

final proportions (you'll need them to make the full-size oven on page 236; ours was nearly equal parts sand and soil, but 3 to 1 sand to soil is more typical). Pack mix into several buckets.

4 MAKE A BASE AND A MINI HEARTH. Set a concrete block on its side (photo shows 2 decorative pavers, but we went to 1 block for stability) and stack 2 pavers on top. Set cement board on pavers. Arrange 2 firebricks side by side on cement board and a third brick across the back (**C**).

5 MAKE A SAND FORM. Using your feet on the tarp, mix ½ bucket sand with just enough water to be packable. On the firebricks, leaving 2 in. clear in front for hearth, mound and tamp the sand layer by layer with your hands (**C**) to build an egg-shaped mound about 9 in. high, and slightly taller in the back than in the front. (This shape encourages good airflow.)

6 ADD BUILDING MIX. Build an even shell of building mix around the sand, packing it a handful at a time in a band 1½ to 2 in. wide (two to three fingers' width; **D**). As you work higher, angle the band's layers into the center. Push each handful of mix into the mix below it (rather than into the sand), until you've covered the sand completely.

7 COMPACT THE DOME. Using 2-by-4s, firmly tap the dome all over until it's firm and smooth (**E**). This also evens out moisture.

8 CUT THE DOORWAY. Using a table knife, cut an opening through the building mix that's two-thirds the height of the dome and as wide as the firebricks. Score first, then angle the cut downward (**F**). The doorway should cut neatly (if needed, let oven dry until fingertip pressure leaves only a small dent). Lift door shape out.

9 SCOOP OUT THE SAND. If the top of the dome feels firm when pressed, the sand is ready to be removed. (If it still feels wet, let the oven dry for a few days first.) Using a soupspoon, scoop out the sand (**G**).

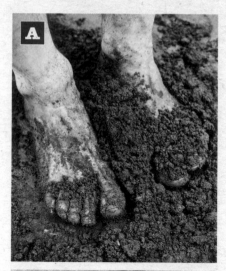

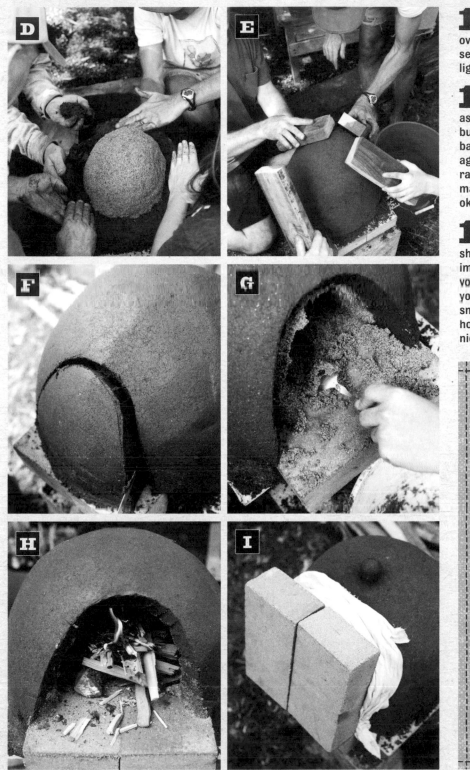

10 LIGHT A SMALL FIRE. Crisscross kindling inside the oven, ignite, and bake the oven dry over several hours (**H**; it will become a shade lighter), adding more fuel as needed.

11 BAKE A MUFFIN. Build another fire and let it burn to ashy chunks. Lift chunks to a heatproof bucket. Make a foil cup, fill it with muffin batter, and set in oven. Lean 2 firebricks against opening. Seal edges with a wet rag (**I**). Bake an hour or so. (The oven may not hold heat very well, but that's okay—it's just practice!)

12 EVALUATE THE OVEN. Once it's cool, the surface should look and feel hard and relatively impervious to scratching. If it crumbles, you need more clay. If it cracks severely, you need more sand. It should also be smoothly egg-shaped. Now you'll know how to adjust your building mix or techniques for the full-scale oven.

MATERIALS AND TOOLS

(see page 245 for sources)

- 1 sheet cement board (¼-in. by 3- by 5-ft.)
- Straightedge
- ¾- by 7-in. cold chisel
- Heavy-duty tarp
- 5-gal. plastic bucket (your "measuring cup")
- About 3 buckets (180 lbs.) all-purpose sand or play sand
- About 2 buckets dry, sifted clay soil (see steps 2 & 3 in "Get Ready," page 233)
- 1 concrete block (8- by 8- by 16 in.)
- 2 concrete pavers (7 in. sq.)
- 5 standard firebricks (2¼- by 4½- by 9 in.)
- Several 2-by-4 scraps
- Table knife and soup-spoon
- Kindling and fire tools (see page 225)
- Foil and muffin batter (optional)

BUILD A BASIC OVEN

TIME: 5 TO 8 HOURS, PLUS SEVERAL HOURS EACH DAY OVER A COUPLE OF DAYS TO CURE
COST: ABOUT $400, ASSUMING YOU ALREADY OWN TOOLS

Now that you've gotten the hang of the muffin oven (page 234), you're ready to use the same building mix and principles to create a full-size, basic oven.

This oven will cook small pizzas, a batch of bread, and other fairly quick-cooking foods. It takes about 1 hour to fire and is designed for occasional (rather than daily) use. If you'd like to bake more often or for longer stretches

of time, you'll want to insulate the base (page 242), and if you're using it as often as every week, insulate the dome as well.

If you're definitely planning to insulate the base (it's easy), it's simplest to do it during the main building process rather than once the oven is complete; see step 3 for details.

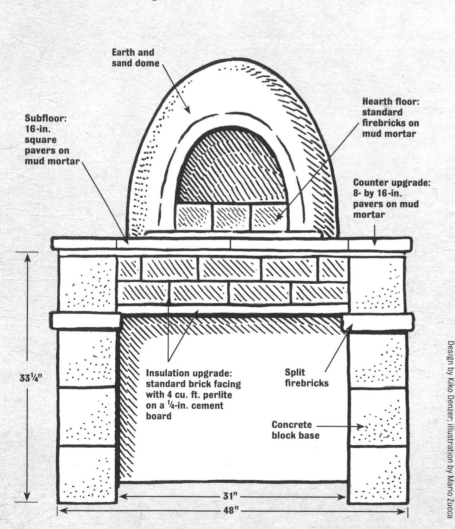

- **Earth and sand dome**
- **Subfloor: 16-in. square pavers on mud mortar**
- **Hearth floor: standard firebricks on mud mortar**
- **Counter upgrade: 8- by 16-in. pavers on mud mortar**
- **Insulation upgrade: standard brick facing with 4 cu. ft. perlite on a ¼-in. cement board**
- **Split firebricks**
- **Concrete block base**

33¼"
31"
48"

Design by Kiko Denzer; illustration by Mario Zucca

MATERIALS AND TOOLS
(see page 245 for sources)

- Six 5-gal. plastic buckets (your "measuring cups")
- About 500 lbs. all-purpose sand or play sand(exact amount depends on the ratio of your mix)
- 5 buckets (25 gal.) dry, sifted clay soil (see page 233; exact amount depends on your mix)
- Two 8- by 10-ft. heavy-duty tarps
- Wheelbarrow
- 26 concrete blocks (8- by 8- by 16-in.)
- Measuring tape
- 4 half-size concrete blocks (8- by 8- by 8-in.)
- 24 split firebricks* (1⅛- by 4½- by 9-in.)
- 10 steel C-channel bars (aka channel irons;
- ⅛- by 2- by 36-in.)
- Four 16-in. sq. gray concrete pavers (1½ in. thick)
- 13 standard firebricks (2¼- by 4½- by 9-in.)
- Several 2-by-4 scraps
- Newspaper
- Slender 16-in. stick or dowel
- Table knife and metal serving spoon
- Handsaw
- One 6-ft. redwood 2-by-4**, or four 2-by-4 scraps (three 15 in., one 12 in.)
- 2 wooden garden stakes (1½- by 12-in.)
- Electric drill and drill bit to fit screws (below)
- Eight 1¾-in. #8 exterior-grade ceramic-coated wood screws
- Firewood and fire tools (see page 225)

*Split firebricks are used for the insulation upgrade (page 242), but must be inserted when the basic oven is built. We recommend adding them now to give you the option to upgrade. Plus, they're decorative and inexpensive.

**You will have leftover wood.

1 MAKE YOUR BUILDING MIX. Near the building site, create 5 buckets' worth of building mix on a tarp (**A**), using the same method and final proportions you used in your muffin oven (steps 2 and 3, page 234), and keeping it on the dry side. Keep mix covered with another tarp or in buckets when it's not in use.

2 MEANWHILE, BUILD THE OVEN BASE. Lay down 7 full-size concrete blocks, hollow sides up, in a squared-off U shape to create the first layer. Measure the building site and the oven base as you go to be sure sides are parallel (**B**). The U should be 3 blocks (48 in.) wide at the back and each arm should be 2 blocks long; the center opening should be 31 in. square. Slide blocks against each other—making them "kiss"—as you set them in place, to ensure a tight fit.

Add a second layer, using a half-size concrete block at the end of each arm and 2 full blocks behind each half-block to overlap those beneath. Lay 2 full-size blocks at the back.

For the third layer, repeat pattern of the first. On top of layer 3, add a layer of split firebricks, arranging them so one short side is flush with the exterior of the base and the other short side extends into the interior (**C**). The front two split bricks should also extend about 1 in. out from front of base. These will hold the cement board for the optional insulation on page 242—and in front of the board will be the bricks that give the oven its finished look.

For the fourth layer of blocks, repeat the pattern of the second.

3 LAY SUPPORTS FOR THE OVEN SUBFLOOR. Nest 5 pairs of C-channel bars, each with one cupped side up and the other down, and a long edge overlapping. Evenly space the 5 sets across the opening between the arms of the base, positioning the front set ½ in. inside the edge. (Photo C shows only 3 single bars, but after it was taken, we went to 5 sets of bars for additional strength; see illustration on next page.)

Optional: Do the insulation upgrade now. Follow directions on page 242 for Upgrade 2 to position the cement board and seal the front of the base. Then you can simply pour in the perlite, rather than chipping out a hole for it to go into.

4 LAY THE OVEN SUB-FLOOR. Position 4 concrete pavers on top of the C-channel bars so their edges are flush with the inside edges of concrete blocks and flush with the front of the oven (**C**).

5 MAKE MUD MORTAR FOR THE HEARTH. On the tarp, combine ¼ bucket building mix with ¼ bucket sand and enough water (about ½ bucket) for a peanut butter consistency (**D**); mix mortar with your feet as you did for the building mix (step 1).

continued

6 LAY THE HEARTH. Arrange 13 firebricks over subfloor as shown in the illustration at right to get a feel for the space they'll take up. Remove them, then smear the subfloor with an even ½ in. of mortar, using a scrap of 2-by-4. Pull the edge of the 2-by-4 through the mortar to create parallel grooves (**A**). Lay firebricks in mortar, centering brick no. 1 at front of subfloor (see illustration). Lay bricks in order shown at right. After the first brick, "kiss" the next brick's side against its neighbor, sliding into place. Repeat with remaining bricks (**B**). When all bricks are in place, tap them with edge of the 2-by-4 (**C**) so hearth is level and bricks are seated in mortar. Scoop away any excess wet mortar. Lay a double layer of wet newspaper over bricks.

7 MAKE THE SAND FORM. Using your feet on the tarp, mix 200 lbs. of sand with just enough water so it's packable, like what you'd use for a sand castle. On the firebricks, leaving 4 in. clear for front of hearth, mound and tamp the sand layer by layer with your hands (**D**) to build an egg-shaped mound as wide as the bricks. Build up layers, keeping sides vertical at first to make the biggest possible space in your oven. Insert a slender 16-in. stick into sand about two-thirds of the way back and make form 16 in. high, sloping down toward the front, with the crest where the stick is; when sand reaches top of the stick, you're done. Smooth the sides with scrap 2-by-4s (**E**), checking that shape is even from side to side and front to back. Lay a double layer of damp newspaper over sand; paper should be flat and not drape onto bricks.

8 ADD A LAYER OF BUILD-ING MIX. Starting on the oven subfloor (the pavers beneath the fire-bricks), build an even shell of building mix around the sand form, packing a large handful at a time with one hand and holding the other hand against the form to keep the mix in place. Shape a horizontal band 1½ to 2 in. wide (two to three fingers' width; **F**). As you work higher, angle the band's layers into the

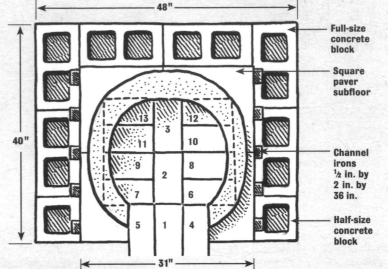

48"

40"

31"

Full-size concrete block

Square paver subfloor

Channel irons ½ in. by 2 in. by 36 in.

Half-size concrete block

Design by Kiko Denzer; illustration by Mario Zucca

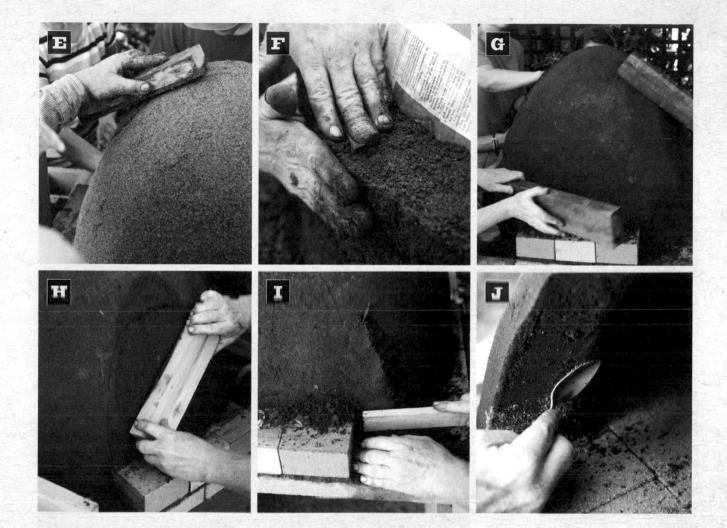

center, as though they're the segments of an orange laid on its side. Push each handful of mix down into the mix below it, rather than into the sand, until you've covered the sand completely.

9 COMPACT THE DOME.
Using the sides of scrap 2-by-4s, firmly tap the dome all over until it's firm and smooth (**G**). Doing this also evens out moisture.

10 SHAPE THE OPENING.
With a table knife, mark the high point of your door frame, 11 in. up from hearth. Score an arc from there to edge of hearth on both sides. Scrape arc with the side of a 2-by-4 (**H**). Build up outer edges of the arc with building mix so the door frame will be flat (**I**).

11 CUT THE DOORWAY.
Using a table knife, cut through score marks, angling down into the center as though you're cutting the lid of a jack-o'-lantern (see photo F, page 235).

If you kept the mix on the dry side, the doorway should cut neatly (if it doesn't, let oven dry until fingertip pressure leaves only a small dent). Lift the door shape off. Check the height of the inside of the cut. It should be 10 in.; trim if you need to.

12 SCOOP OUT THE SAND.
If the top of the dome feels firm when pressed, the inner sand form is ready to be removed. (If it still feels wet, let the oven dry a couple of days, then continue.) Using your hands and a large metal serving spoon, remove sand and the stick until you reach the newspaper layers, then pull them out as well (see photo G, page 235). Smooth and round out edges of the door opening by tapping them with a soupspoon (**J**).

Use some of the sand to fill the hollow centers of the top layer of concrete blocks in the oven base (**K**, next page); pack it as you go, then tamp down with the end of a 2-by-4.

continued

13 BUILD A LEAN-TO OVEN DOOR. Using a handsaw, cut redwood 2-by-4 into lengths big enough to cover the door area crosswise (you'll likely need 3 pieces about 15 in. long and another about 12 in. long). Lay them flush on a flat surface with the shortest board at the top.

Lay 2 garden stakes, slightly apart, over 2-by-4s. Drill 4 evenly spaced pilot holes through each stake into the boards for 1¾-in. wood screws. Drill screws through stakes into boards (**L**).

14 CURE THE OVEN. Follow the directions on page 224.

15 FIRE IT UP AND COOK. See page 224 for the basics of lighting and tending a cooking fire in your oven. Note that masonry naturally expands and contracts when you heat it up. Over time, you'll likely get some small surface cracks in the oven. This is normal, and won't affect durability or heat retention.

WHETHER YOU OPT FOR THE BASIC MODEL OR THE UPGRADES, YOU'LL NEED TO COVER THE OVEN WITH A TARP OR ROOF IN RAINY WEATHER. A WET OVEN WON'T COOK.

The basic oven, with some of the materials for the upgrades.

ADD SOME UPGRADES

TIME: ABOUT 3 HOURS FOR ALL THREE

You can beautify your oven with a natural concrete stain, put in a layer of insulation underneath so it's more fuel-efficient, and add a concrete countertop—all for about $75. All three upgrades are easy enough that you could do them on your oven-building day. Saving them for later simplifies the building day, but the insulation process will take longer, as you'll be working around the oven dome.

Whether you insulate before building the dome or after the fact, it must be done before adding the countertop.

If you use the oven constantly, you may want to consider insulating the dome as well for even greater heat retention; Kiko Denzer's *Build Your Own Earth Oven* contains an excellent guide to this optional step.

Upgrade 1: Concrete Stain

1 MAKE THE STAIN. Mix 1 cup ground coffee and 1 qt. boiling water in a large stainless steel bowl. Let stand at least 5 minutes. Stir in 1 qt. cool water. Wearing gloves, add 1½ cups iron sulfate and stir 2 to 3 minutes with a paint stirrer. (You're extracting color, but the stain won't show its final color until the next day.) Pour mixture through a strainer lined with a doubled sheet of cheesecloth into a clean container (**A**). When it's cool, pour into yogurt containers. Use this, then make a second batch if needed.

2 STAIN THE CONCRETE. Set newspaper all around oven base to protect anything you don't want stained. If you're going to stain the cement top caps for a countertop (see page 243), set them also on sheets of newspaper. Wearing gloves and using paintbrushes, apply stain until the concrete is saturated (**B**). (We left the base's top layer of blocks unstained, for contrast.) The concrete won't finish changing color until the next day.

Upgrade 2: Insulation for the Base

1 PREP MATERIALS. Set cement board on a flat surface. Using a straightedge, score cement board with edge of a cold chisel at least 1/16 in. deep to make a 31-in. square. Snap cement board along lines.

Cut angle irons with hacksaw to 31 in. Set 1 brick on a flat bed of sand; score crosswise down the center with cold chisel. Tap chisel with hammer along score line to cut brick in half (**A**).

Make mud mortar: On a tarp, combine building mix with sand (same proportions and techniques as for the hearth mortar, step 5 of the basic oven method, page 237), adding enough water for a peanut butter consistency.

2 SET CEMENT BOARD IN PLACE. Slide it onto the split-firebrick "shelf" beneath oven (**B**).

3 SEAL FRONT OF OVEN. Beneath oven, set angle irons with ends resting on split firebricks (and just in front of cement board) to make a shelf that's wide enough for bricks to sit upright on a long side. Check fit: Slide 2 layers of bricks (4 along bottom, and on top, 3 full-size and 2 cut half-bricks— one at either end) into shelf, then remove. If there's room for mud mortar, thinly smear ends of 4 bricks with it (if it's too tight, omit mortar) and slide bricks into place on bottom of shelf. Reach around over top of bricks and lay some mortar between bricks and cement board to close gap. Add bricks for top layer, mortaring if possible.

Smear mortar into joints between the bricks, using a finger. With a wet paintbrush, brush off any mud on front of bricks (**C**).

4 ADD INSULATION. If insulating after step 3 of the building process (page 237), fill cavity with perlite before proceeding with the build. If oven is already built, chip out a tennis ball–size hole in a cement block on each side of oven by tapping a cold chisel with a hammer. Wearing masks, gradually pour perlite into openings, working it into cavity with bamboo pole (**D**).

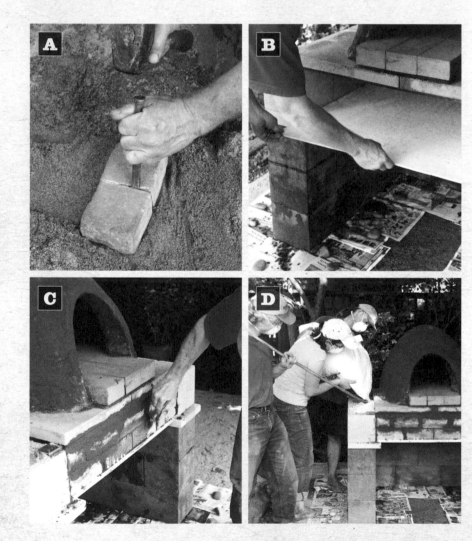

MATERIALS AND TOOLS

(see page 245 for sources)

- 1 sheet cement board (1/4-in. by 3- by 5-ft.)
- Long straight-edge
- 3/4- by 7-in. cold chisel
- 2 steel angle irons (each 1/8- by 2- by 36-in.)
- Hacksaw
- 1/3 bucket all-purpose or play sand; use a full bucket if you're also making the counters
- 10 regular bricks (you'll use only 8; extras allow for breakage)
- Hammer
- Heavy-duty tarp
- 1/3 bucket building mix (see page 234); use a full bucket if you're also making the counters
- 1-in.-wide paintbrush
- 4 cu. ft. perlite or vermiculite
- Dust masks
- 1 bamboo pole or other stick (about 6 ft. long)

Upgrade 3: Concrete Countertop

1 PREP MATERIALS. Stain concrete top caps if you haven't already (see page 241). Make mortar if you didn't already make it for the insulation (at left), using ½ bucket building mix, ½ bucket sand, and enough water for a peanut butter consistency.

2 SET COUNTERTOP. On top of a concrete block on oven base, make a rough ridge of mortar around perimeter and across center (**A**). Keep mortar away from channel bars. Push a top cap into mortar and jiggle it to fix in place. Repeat to set remaining caps, putting a little mortar between caps as well as under them (**B**). Tap countertop level with end of a 2-by-4 scrap or the handle tip of a mallet. Wipe off excess mortar with a damp rag.

3 LIGHT FIRST CURING FIRE. For instructions, see page 224. Now, stand back and admire your handiwork!

MATERIALS AND TOOLS
(see page 245 for sources)

- 7 concrete top caps (2- by 8- by 16-in.)
- ½ bucket building mix (see page 234)
- ½ bucket all-purpose or play sand
- Small 2-by-4 scrap; or use a mallet
- Smooth rag

Kiko Denzer, our guide and oven designer, at the end of our one-day build.

RESOURCE GUIDE

←———— ★ ————→

Here's where to find the gear, ingredients, books, and supplies
for the recipes and projects in this book.

CAMPFIRES

GEAR

amazon.com
GSI Outdoors JavaGrind hand-crank
coffee grinder

excaliburdehydrator.com
Excalibur food dehydrator

lodgemfg.com
Cast-iron skillets and camp dutch
ovens

organize.com
Picnic and storage baskets (with
handles) by Iris

rei.com
Backpacking stoves, such as Jetboil
Flash Cooking System and Whisperlite
Universal. *Camp stoves*, such as
Primus FireHole 100. *Headlamps*.
Kitchen gear, such as Sea to Summit
collapsible bowls and sinks, REI
Campware cutting board (rolls up),
Snow Peak Titanium French Press,
and GSI Outdoors Espresso Maker.

INGREDIENTS

amazon.com
Panang curry paste, such as Mae Ploy

highplainsbison.com
Bison dogs

rei.com
Freeze-dried food mixes

worldspice.com
Zaatar seasoning blend (search alpha-
betically under Spice Blends)

BOOKS

Pacific Feast (Skipstone, 2010) by
Jennifer Hahn, and its accompanying
pocket guide, *Pacific Coast Foraging
Guide*.

The Wild Table (Viking Studio, 2010)
by Connie Green and Sarah Scott.

HOME FIRES

GEAR

amazon.com
Charcoal Companion Cabernet
Wine–Soaked Oakwood Chips

bbqgalore.com
Assorted wood chips and chunks
for smoking

homedepot.com
Fire & Flavor Cedar Grilling Planks

solarovens.org, sunoven.com
Solar ovens

spanishtable.com
Paella pans

INGREDIENTS

asianfoodgrocer.com
Furikake (Japanese rice seasoning)

silvasausage.com
Linguiça (spicy Portuguese sausage)

spanishtable.com
Spanish chorizo and paprika and
Valencia rice

umami.com/shop
Umami Dust and Umami Master
Sauce

INSPIRED FIRES

For pizza ovens, see separate listing
at right.

GEAR

cowboycauldron.com
Cowboy Cauldron firepit grills

firewood.com
Kindling and firewood

homedepot.com, lowes.com
Paraffin fire-starter cubes

lacajachina.com
Caja China roasting box, brining injector, and magnetic digital thermometer

norcalovenworks.com
Uruguayan grills

santamariagrills.com
Santa Maria–style backyard barbecues
and red oak firewood

stansport.com
Stansport heavy-duty camp grill,
a portable grate with legs

superskewer.com
The skewer is large enough to lay
across your grill, and keeps meat from
rotating.

susieqbrand.com
Red oak wood chips

williams-sonoma.com
10-in.-diameter, 2-in.-deep cake pan

INGREDIENTS

Arroyo Grande Meat Company
Top-block sirloin for in-store pickup
only. 120 E. Branch St., Arroyo Grande,
CA; *agmeatcompany.com*.

belcampomeatco.com
Butcher shops and online store for Belcampo's pasture-raised meat

napastyle.com
Silafunghi hot chili sauce (Calabrian chile paste)

ranchogordo.com, susieqbrand.com
Pinquito beans

PIZZA OVENS

GEAR
firewood.com
Firewood and kindling

fornobravo.com
Long-handled lightweight metal shovel, metal pizza peel, and metal brush; Primavera60 and other pizza oven models.

homedepot.com
Metal can with lid for hot coals or ash

qcsupply.com
Infrared laser thermometer

BOOKS
The Art of Wood-Fired Cooking
(Gibbs Smith, 2010) by Andrea Mugnaini.

Build Your Own Earth Oven (Hand Print Press, 2007) by Kiko Denzer. See also *handprintpress.com* for Denzer's video on the top-down fire, as well as other resources.

Wood-Fired Cooking (Ten Speed Press, 2009) by Mary Karlin.

SUPPLIES FOR DIY ADOBE OVEN
Go to a hardware store or home improvement store for items such as tarps and saws that aren't listed here.

Garden and Landscaping Supply Stores
Iron sulfate (ferrous sulfate). In California's Bay Area, we like Summer Winds Nursery *(summerwindsca.com)*. Perlite is sold in bulk, often at a lower price than at home improvement

PIZZA OVEN TOOLS

stores. In California's Bay Area, we like Lyngso Garden Materials *(lyngsogarden.com)*.

homedepot.com, lowes.com
All-purpose sand (one brand is Quikrete) or play sand, cement board, cold chisel, concrete blocks, concrete top caps, perlite (as well as vermiculite), and steel angle irons.
Go to *homedepot.com* for C-channel bars (also called channel irons) and fireclay (mortar clay). One brand of fireclay is H.C. Muddox (see *hcmuddox.com* for other retailers). Go to *lowes.com* for 16-in. concrete pavers.

Stone, Brick, and Building Materials Supplier
Full-size firebricks, split (half-size) firebricks, and regular bricks: A home improvement store may sell these, but you'll have the most choices in colors at a specialty store. In Northern California, we like Peninsula Building Materials Co. *(pbm1923.com)*.

sunset.com
Instructions for making your own compost sifter. Or buy a compost sifter at garden supply stores or from Peaceful Valley *(groworganic.com)*.

A GUIDE TO OUR NUTRITION FOOTNOTES

←———★———→

Part of good cooking involves knowing how to make your food suit your tastes—and your health.

Every *Sunset* recipe comes with an analysis of its main energy-yielding components, based on USDA guidelines: fat, protein, and carbohydrates, plus a tally of its sodium, saturated fat, and cholesterol content. And when appropriate, each recipe also has abbreviations indicating whether it meets criteria for special diets.

Generally, the analysis is for a single serving; if a range is given, the analysis is for the larger number of servings. Also, if an ingredient is listed with a substitution, only the ingredient listed first is analyzed. Optional ingredients, and those for which no stated amount is given, aren't included in the calculations.

Here's how to decode our nutritional footnotes:

CAL (CALORIES). How many you need to maintain your current weight depends on your height, on how active you are, and on how your body burns energy. As a benchmark for the calories an average person requires per day, the USDA suggests 2,000.

CAL. FROM FAT. The current advice from the USDA's Dietary Guidelines for Americans *(health.gov/dietary guidelines)* is that 20% to 35% of your total daily calories come from fat. However, numbers can be misleading: Take, for instance, a green salad tossed with vinaigrette. Because the main ingredients are so low-calorie, most of the calories come from the vinaigrette, and the percentage of fat can make the salad seem like a high-fat food.

PROTEIN. The USDA recommendation is for 46 grams per day for adult women and 56 grams per day for adult men, based on a 2,000-calorie diet.

FAT. While fat can and should be part of a healthful diet, the type of fat makes a difference. Monounsaturated and polyunsaturated—which come primarily from fish, nuts, seeds, and vegetable oils—promote heart health. Saturated fats, which come mainly from animal sources, and especially trans fats, mostly coming from the hydrogenation of oils, are linked to heart disease. For now, the official recommendation is that no more than one-third of total calories should come from fat (less than 10 percent of calories should come from saturated fats, with trans fats as low as possible).

CARBO (CARBOHYDRATES). These provide the main energy source for our bodies and are the only source of fiber, which helps digestion and protects against heart disease, obesity, and diabetes. Whole-grain sources of carbohydrates have much higher levels of fiber and nutrients than refined sources. The USDA suggests that carbs should make up 45 to 65 percent of total daily calories, with 25 grams of fiber in a 2,000-calorie diet.

SODIUM. A major mineral, it is essential to nerve and muscle function. Salt is the main form of sodium in our diets, and too much of it can contribute to high blood pressure. The recommended daily maximum for sodium is 2,300 mg (about 1 teaspoon of table salt), but for adults over 51, all African Americans, and anyone with diabetes, hypertension, or chronic kidney disease, the recommendation is 1,500 mg.

CHOL. Cholesterol is a fatty substance found in all animal products. The relationship between dietary cholesterol (from the foods we eat) and cholesterol made by our bodies is influenced by our genes and not totally understood. The current guideline is to consume no more than 300 mg. a day.

GF (GLUTEN-FREE). No wheat, rye, barley, or oats. Check any processed food ingredients you use to verify they're gluten-free.

LC (LOW-CALORIE). Less than 500 calories for a main dish, 250 for a side dish, 150 for an appetizer, and 350 for dessert.

LS (LOW-SODIUM). Less than 500 mg for a main dish, and 350 for a side dish, appetizer, or dessert.

V (VEGETARIAN). Contains no meat products.

VG (VEGAN). Contains no animal products (including eggs and dairy).

MEASUREMENT EQUIVALENTS

Refer to the following charts for metric conversions as well as common cooking equivalents. All equivalents are approximate.

COOKING/OVEN TEMPERATURES

	Fahrenheit	Celsius	Gas Mark
Freeze Water	32°F	0°C	
Room Temp.	68°F	20°C	
Boil Water	212°F	100°C	
Bake	325°F	160°C	3
	350°F	180°C	4
	375°F	190°C	5
	400°F	200°C	6
	425°F	220°C	7
	450°F	230°C	8
Broil			Grill

DRY INGREDIENTS BY WEIGHT

1 oz.	=	1/16 lb.	=	30 g.
4 oz.	=	1/4 lb.	=	120 g.
8 oz.	=	1/2 lb.	=	240 g.
12 oz.	=	3/4 lb.	=	360 g.
16 oz.	=	1 lb.	=	480 g.

(To convert ounces to grams, multiply the number of ounces by 30.)

LENGTH

1 in.	=					2.5 cm.
6 in.	=	1/2 ft.	=		=	15 cm.
12 in.	=	1 ft.	=		=	30 cm.
36 in.	=	3 ft.	=	1 yd.	=	90 cm.
40 in.	=					100 cm.	= 1 m.

(To convert inches to centimeters, multiply the number of inches by 2.5.)

LIQUID INGREDIENTS BY VOLUME

1/4 tsp.	=					1 ml.
1/2 tsp.	=					2 ml.
1 tsp.	=					5 ml.
3 tsp.	=	1 tbsp.	=	1/2 fl. oz.	=	15 ml.
2 tbsp.	=	1/8 cup	=	1 fl. oz.	=	30 ml.
4 tbsp.	=	1/4 cup	=	2 fl. oz.	=	60 ml.
5 1/3 tbsp.	=	1/3 cup	=	3 fl. oz.	=	80 ml.
8 tbsp.	=	1/2 cup	=	4 fl. oz.	=	120 ml.
10 2/3 tbsp.	=	2/3 cup	=	5 fl. oz.	=	160 ml.
12 tbsp.	=	3/4 cup	=	6 fl. oz.	=	180 ml.
16 tbsp.	=	1 cup	=	8 fl. oz	=	240 ml.
1 pt.	=	2 cups	=	16 fl. oz.	=	480 ml.
1 qt.	=	4 cups	=	32 fl. oz.	=	960 ml.
				33 fl. oz.	=	1,000 ml.	= 1 l.

EQUIVALENTS FOR DIFFERENT TYPES OF INGREDIENTS

Standard Cup	Fine Powder (e.g., flour)	Grain (e.g., rice)	Granular (e.g., sugar)	Liquid Solids (e.g., butter)	Liquid (e.g., milk)
1	140 g.	150 g.	190 g.	200 g.	240 ml.
3/4	105 g.	113 g.	143 g.	150 g.	180 ml.
2/3	93 g.	100 g.	125 g.	133 g.	160 ml.
1/2	70 g.	75 g.	95 g.	100 g.	120 ml.
1/3	47 g.	50 g.	63 g.	67 g.	80 ml.
1/4	35 g.	38 g.	48 g.	50 g.	60 ml.
1/8	18 g.	19 g.	24 g.	25 g.	30 ml.

INDEX

Sunset

ISBN-10: 0-376-02807-6
ISBN-13: 978-0-376-02807-5
Library of Congress Control Number: 2013939860
First printing 2014.
Printed in the United States of America.

OXMOOR HOUSE
VP, Brand Publishing: Laura Sappington
Editorial Director: Leah McLaughlin
Creative Director: Felicity Keane
Managing Editor: Elizabeth Tyler Austin
Assistant Managing Editor: Jeanne de Lathouder

TIME HOME ENTERTAINMENT INC.
Publisher: Jim Childs
VP, Brand & Digital Strategy: Steven Sandonato
Executive Director, Marketing Services: Carol Pittard
Executive Director, Retail & Special Sales: Tom Mifsud
Director, Bookazine Development & Marketing: Laura Adam
Executive Publishing Director: Joy Butts
Publishing Director: Megan Pearlman
Finance Director: Glenn Buonocore
Associate General Counsel: Helen Wan

SUNSET PUBLISHING
Editor-in-Chief: Peggy Northrop
Publisher: Brian Gruseke
VP, Marketing & Brand Development: Shannon Thompson
Creative Director: Maili Holiman
Photography Director: Yvonne Stender
Food Editor: Margo True

THE GREAT OUTDOORS COOKBOOK
Editors: Elaine Johnson, Margo True
Managing Editor: Karen Templer
Production Manager: Linda M. Bouchard
Art Director: Catherine Jacobes
Copy Editor: Tam Putnam
Senior Imaging Specialist: Kimberley Navabpour
Photo Editor: Susan B. Smith
Project Editor: Lacie Pinyan
Proofreader: Eve F. Lynch
Indexer: Ken DellaPenta

SPECIAL THANKS

Recipe editor Amy Machnak; test kitchen managers Stephanie Spencer and Paula Freschet; former food editor Jerry Anne DiVecchio; wine editor Sara Schneider; and food writers Linda Lau Anusasananan, Jessica Battilana, April Cooper, Charity Ferreira, Julia Lee, Adeena Sussman, Amy Traverso, Kate Washington, and Molly Watson; plus the *Sunset* recipe retesters—Kevyn Allard, Kay Bates, Angela Brassinga, Marianne Cullinane, Dorothy Decker, Sarah Epstein, Lenore Grant, Doni Jackson, Melissa Kaiser, Marlene Kawahata, Eve F. Lynch, Rebecca Parker, Bunnie Russell, Laura Berner Shafsky, Jill Soltau, Vicki Sousa, Linda Tebben, and Sue Turner

A big thank-you as well to Forno Bravo pizza ovens and to Pat Hennigan at Stevens Creek Quarry, and to our pizza oven volunteers (on both ovens): Frederick Basgal, Rosalyn Carson, Marian Cobb, Kiko Denzer, Claire Elliot, Audra Farrell, Phil Fox, Art Friedman, Bill Frink, Gina Goff, Aislyn Greene, Keegan Groot, David Hoag, Deborah Hoag, Paul Hobson, Liz Jensen, Thomas Keller, Tina Keller, Doug Kent, Kevin Lynch, Harriot Manley, Jasper McEvoy, Patrick McEvoy, Rowan McEvoy, Loren Mooney, Corinna Mori, Matthew Mori, Rob Mori, Fred Oliver, Lizanne Oliver, Walter Roach, Sara Schneider, Audrey Schneider-Hawes, Margaret Sloan, Molly Vanderlip, Scott Vanderlip, Ann Waldhauer, and Maryanne Welton

We would also like to thank Erika Ehmsen, Scott Gibson, José Guzman, Danielle Johnson, Stephanie Johnson, Michelle Lau, Jim McCann, Megan McCrea, Marie Pence, Alan Phinney, and E. Spencer Toy.

FRONT COVER

Main image: Mt. Rainier, Washington. *Bottom row left:* Coppa, Ricotta, and Arugula Pizza (recipe, page 110); *bottom row middle:* Soy-*Furikake* Corn (recipe, page 163); *bottom row right:* Grilled Spareribs with Fennel Seeds and Herbs (recipe, page 122).

PHOTOGRAPHY CREDITS

Iain Bagwell: 116, 120, 132; **Iain Bagwell/Getty Images:** 24; **Leigh Beisch:** 142 (all), 143, 151; **Annabelle Breakey/Getty Images:** 56, 99, 131; **Annabelle Breakey:** 93, 144, 126; **Jonathan Buckley/Getty Images:** 43 #1; **Brown Cannon III:** 8, 85L, 175L, 175TR, 204–205, 206, 207; **Jennifer Cheung:** 102–103; **Kathy Collins/Getty Images:** 43 #2; **Philip Condit II/Getty Images:** 43 #3; **Alex Farnum:** front cover BR, 115, 123; **David Fenton:** 13, 232, 233 (both), 234 (all), 235 (all), 237 (all), 238 (all), 239 (all), 240TL, 240TR, 241 (both), 242 (all), 243 (all); **Leo Gong:** 165; **Thayer Allyson Gowdy:** 63, 72, 156; **Jupiterimages/Getty Images:** 33; **Thomas Keller:** 240B; **Erin Kunkel:** front cover BL, front cover BM, 19B, 35, 39, 40, 44, 47, 52, 60, 64, 67, 70, 77, 78, 80, 85MR, 85BR, 86, 90, 95, 96, 100, 104, 107, 108, 111, 118, 119, 135, 138, 141, 149, 152, 155, 158, 161, 162, 169, 173, 221, back cover top; **Dave Lauridsen:** 178, 214, 215 (all), 216 (both), 218; **Nancy Nehring/Getty Images:** 43 #6; **Glenn Oakley:** 68–69; **Ed Reschke/Getty Images:** 43 #4; **Lisa Romerein/Getty Images:** 4–5 (all), 85TR, 91, 128, 166, 170; **Dave Schiefelbein:** front cover top; **Thomas J. Story:** 1, 2–3, 15 (all), 17, 19T, 21, 22, 25, 26, 28, 29 (all), 31, 32, 48, 51, 55, 59, 73, 74, 83, 109, 146, 147R, 176, 177 (all), 179, 180, 181, 182, 184, 185, 186, 187, 191T #1, 191T #3, 191M (all), 191B, 192, 193, back cover bottom; **E. Spencer Toy:** 7, 10 (all), 11 (all), 12T, 12M, 16, 89, 113, 189, 191T #2; **Mark Turner:** 43 #5; **Coral von Zumwalt:** 175MR, 175BR, 196–197 (all), 199, 200, 201, 203, 208–209, 210, 211, 212; **Gary Weathers/Getty Images:** 42; **Rachel Weill:** 125, 136, 137, 188–189, 195, 222, 223 (both), 224, 225 (all), 227, 228, 231, 245; **Woods Wheatcroft/Getty Images:** 255

ILLUSTRATION CREDITS

Lucy Engelman: 209 (all); **Mario Zucca:** 18, 87, 88 (both), 121 (both), 147, 236, 238